T0271210

UNDERSTANDING THE PRIVATE–PUBLIC DIVIDE

Markets are taken as the norm in economics and in much of political and media discourse. But if markets are superior why does the public sector remain so large? Avner Offer provides a distinctive new account of the effective temporal limits on private, public, and social activity. *Understanding the Private–Public Divide* accounts for the division of labour between business and the public sector, how it changes over time, where the boundaries ought to run, and the harm that follows if they are violated. He explains how finance forces markets to focus on short-term objectives and why business requires special privileges in return for long-term commitment. He shows how a private sector policy bias leads to inequality, insecurity, and corruption. Integrity used to be the norm and it can be achieved again. Only governments can manage uncertainty in the long-term interests of society, as shown by the challenge of climate change.

AVNER OFFER is Chichele Professor Emeritus of Economic History at Oxford University, Fellow of All Souls College and the British Academy. His books include *The Challenge of Affluence: Self-Control and Well-Being in the United States and Britain Since 1950* (2006) and the co-authored *The Nobel Factor: The Prize in Economics, Social Democracy, and the Market Turn* (2016).

UNDERSTANDING THE PRIVATE–PUBLIC DIVIDE

Markets, Governments, and Time Horizons

AVNER OFFER

University of Oxford

CAMBRIDGE
UNIVERSITY PRESS

CAMBRIDGE
UNIVERSITY PRESS

University Printing House, Cambridge CB2 8BS, United Kingdom

One Liberty Plaza, 20th Floor, New York, NY 10006, USA

477 Williamstown Road, Port Melbourne, VIC 3207, Australia

314–321, 3rd Floor, Plot 3, Splendor Forum, Jasola District Centre,
New Delhi – 110025, India

103 Penang Road, #05–06/07, Visioncrest Commercial, Singapore 238467

Cambridge University Press is part of the University of Cambridge.

It furthers the University's mission by disseminating knowledge in the pursuit of
education, learning, and research at the highest international levels of excellence.

www.cambridge.org
Information on this title: www.cambridge.org/9781108496209
DOI: 10.1017/9781108866415

© Avner Offer 2022

First published 2022

A catalogue record for this publication is available from the British Library.

Library of Congress Cataloging-in-Publication Data
NAMES: Offer, Avner, author.
TITLE: Understanding the private-public divide : markets, governments, and time horizons / Avner Offer, University of Oxford.
DESCRIPTION: Cambridge, United Kingdom ; New York, NY : Cambridge University Press, 2022. | Includes bibliographical references and index.
IDENTIFIERS: LCCN 2021051479 (print) | LCCN 2021051480 (ebook) | ISBN 9781108496209 (hardback) | ISBN 9781108791663 (paperback) | ISBN 9781108866415 (ebook)
SUBJECTS: LCSH: Economics. | Welfare economics. | Free enterprise. | Public administration. | Public-private sector cooperation.
CLASSIFICATION: LCC HB71 .O33 2022 (print) | LCC HB71 (ebook) | DDC 330.01–dc23/eng/20211020
LC record available at https://lccn.loc.gov/2021051479
LC ebook record available at https://lccn.loc.gov/2021051480

ISBN 978-1-108-49620-9 Hardback
ISBN 978-1-108-79166-3 Paperback

For Leah, again

Contents

Figures

Tables

Preface

Governments loom large in market societies because business is impatient and the state endures. The Thatcher–Reagan regimes of the 1980s were enthused by ideology, economic theory, and the thrill of getting their way. They asserted self-interest, competition, and animal spirits against a tired social democracy. Voters elected neo-liberal parties concurrently into power and opposition, but continued to count on governments for their long-term welfare.

What follows is not about how markets and governments differ, but about why it is government which looks after the long run. The private–public divide runs across the future, not the present. It is a time horizon that lies a few years hence. Running up to that boundary is the playground of market competition. Beyond it is terrain which business prefers not to enter on its own. The time horizon is both prescriptive and real: it suggests where the private–public divide ought to be and predicts where it actually settles. It provides an unfamiliar perspective on markets, government, and democracy that applies the experience of the past to the problems of the present. Battersea bridge on the Thames in London (shown on the cover) exemplifies this story. A wooden toll bridge was built in 1771 by a nobleman, John, Earl Spencer, when he acquired the rights to operate the ferry there. After a century of precarious existence, the bridge was taken into public ownership in 1879. A steel and stone replacement opened six years later and continues to stand there for the sort of thing that governments exist to do.

These ideas were first presented at the Ellen MacArthur Lectures in Cambridge in 2018. Many thanks to my hosts there, Amy Erickson, Sarah Horrell, Leigh Shaw-Taylor and Simon Szreter, for their warm hospitality. Colleagues, friends, students, and research assistants helped along the way, among them Masud Ally, Martin Chick, Richard Davenport-Hines, Rui Esteves, Massimo Florio, Nimrod Hass, Christopher Hood, William Janeway, Vijay Joshi, Steve Keen, Urvi Khaitan, Henry Leveson-Gower, Roger Lewis, Alexander MacDonald, Shinobu Majima, Meredith Paker, Shaun Reidy, Antoninus Samy, Raphael Schapiro, Moritz Schularick, Damien Shannon, and those who attended my presentations and spoke there. Early support from the British Academy project on the future of the corporation and its leader Colin Mayer is gratefully acknowledged. All Souls College at Oxford, my academic home, continues to provide estimable company, a study to work in, and financial support. It will soon be 600 years old and its future knows no bounds.

Much of the source material came off the internet and the references are sufficient to trace it back there. There is a copy available of almost every text cited: if in doubt, please ask. A few short passages are taken unattributed from my previous writings. More substantial ones in Chapter 1 come from a discussion paper on 'Patient and impatient capital: Time horizons as market boundaries' (2019).[1]

Most of this book was written under self-isolation during the Covid-19 pandemic, in surroundings of comfort and companionship at home. It is dedicated to Leah, my partner of many decades. I am mindful of my good fortune.

---

[1] Offer, 'Patient and impatient capital'; some also appear in Lewis and Offer, 'Railways as patient capital'.

Abbreviations

APPG	All Party Parliamentary Group on Responsible Tax
CEO	chief executive officer
DICE	William Nordhaus's Dynamic integrated climate-economy model (see RICE)
FBI	Federal Bureau of Investigation
FHA	Federal Housing Administration
FSA	Financial Services Authority
GB	Great Britain
GDP	gross domestic product
HC	House of Commons
IAM	integrated climate assessment model
ILO	International Labour Office
IMF	International Monetary Fund
IPCC	Intergovernmental Panel on Climate Change
IRR	internal rate of return
MIRAS	mortgage interest relief at source
NAO	National Audit Office
NBER	National Bureau of Economic Research
NEST	National Employment Savings Trust
NGO	non-governmental organisation
NHS	National Health Service
NPV	net present value
ONS	Office of National Statistics
PAYGO	pay-as-you-go
PFI	private finance initiative
PPP	public–private partnerships

PUK	Partnerships UK
RICE	William Nordhaus's Regional Integrated Climate-Economics (see DICE)
S&L	savings and loans associations in the USA
SPV	special purpose vehicle

Introduction

We dwell in an eternal present, which is forever receding into memory and history. Think of it as a cruise ship. On board it is always now, but the ship is steaming ahead,

> Away from a youth beyond retrieve,
> Towards an end with no reprieve.

In economics likewise, the present is all there is. Past costs are sunk and can be ignored. The future is only what we make of it today. When people are poor they see little beyond now. As they prosper they care more for the future. Dynastic kings and nobles look beyond their own lifetimes. For everyone else modern economic growth created futures by making them better off. 'The luxuries of one age become the necessities of the next.'[1] Government has expanded to take care of those futures. In 1883 the German economist Adolf Wagner wrote that the growth of government was driven 'by the desire for development of a progressive people'. Governments began to appropriate a growing share of economic output. Between 1913 and 1980 the economies of Europe and the United States grew more than fourfold. During the same period governments grew much faster, from allocating about a tenth of gross domestic product (GDP) up to between 35 and 50 per cent in most advanced countries.

Despite the current hegemony of market doctrines, the public sector does not contract. In addition to government, a further 5 to 15 per cent of GDP is provided privately not for profit. Households

---

[1] Robson, 'Public utility services', 300.

engage in unmeasured non-market production of children and home comforts. Overall, less than half of economic welfare is provided for profit. Of that a great deal would not be available without government support. Forty years after Thatcher and Reagan set out to work for market ascendancy, only a small fraction of economic welfare is provided under conditions of genuine market competition. The 'Scully curve' traces the relation between public sector size and economic growth. It is an inverted U-curve. For nineteen developed countries between 1974 and 1995 the 'sweet spot' of maximum growth was a public sector share of 40 per cent.[2] It was lower in previous periods when the public sector had not yet grown so large. In the last three decades the anti-government Republican party has captured almost half of American states, but they have not managed to wind down the size and scope of government. Where they tried seriously, as in Kansas, they failed.[3] Government does not remain so large because of vested interests, obstruction, or ideology, though all of these play a part. The argument here is that limits of efficient market provision arise from economic fundamentals and more specifically from finance.

Private investment needs to pay off in a short period of time. How short depends on the interest rate: the higher the rate, the shorter the wait. Long-term activities are difficult to undertake for profit. Every economy has a prevailing commercial interest rate at any given time. This figure defines a unique break-even period for private investment. Ventures that pay off in less time are suitable for competitive markets. Many vital activities are not, if they ever pay off at all in a financial sense, for example, health, education, science, art, universities; nuclear power; defence and war; new railway projects like the UK Crossrail and HS2; motorways (freeways, highways); urban and national parks; museums, libraries, symphony orchestras, and opera; space exploration; mitigating climate change. Such activities, with long durations and fixed capital locked in, cannot be undertaken for profit by business alone. To carry them out, commercial credit constraints need to be overridden. They can be managed directly by government, not-for-profits, or philanthropy. Or

---

[2] Di Matteo and Summerfield, 'The shifting Scully curve', fig. 4, 4269.
[3] Grossmann, *Red blue states*.

government can empower a private-sector agent by assuring them a market rate of return or, in our terms, a 'franchise'.

What is this interest rate, and why pay interest at all? There is a long-standing intuition that interest is unethical. One should lend 'hoping for nothing thereby' (Luke 6:35). Ancient Greece and Rome prohibited credit intermittently. Islam does not tolerate interest, it was condemned in Buddhism and Hinduism, while the Catholic church discouraged it for centuries. In medieval Europe, the Jews took up moneylending because it was forbidden to Christians, and they continue to be reviled for it today. In old English law interest was termed usury and only became legal in 1545, with an upper limit. In early modern Europe usury laws often capped interest rates at a fairly low level. In England the cap of 8 per cent established in 1624 went down to 5 per cent in 1713.[4] Adam Smith, an advocate of 'natural liberty', accepted that rate as 'perhaps as proper as any'.[5] Such caps persist in many states of the USA and were only abolished there for government-backed mortgages in 1980.

There was a good economic reason: early modern economies had low rates of growth, typically below 1 per cent a year. That was also the aggregate annual rate of return to the efforts of labour and capital. If the rate of interest is more than the real return on investment, then credit requires a net transfer from borrowers to lenders, and in the longer term will impoverish rather than enrich. Another view is that usury laws are a form of social insurance to facilitate redistribution in conditions of periodic dearth.[6] When growth is low, credit is only productive if it enables large local opportunities, for example a profitable merchant shipping venture. Such opportunities opened up in eighteenth-century Britain with the commercial and industrial revolutions. In 1854, all laws against usury were finally repealed.[7] Responding to these revolutions, Karl Marx depicted profit and interest as a form of exploitation, i.e. (in legal terms) unjust enrichment. What he challenged was the legitimacy of property rights, which allow owners to take the economic rent, i.e. all value over and

---

[4] Koyama, 'Evading the "taint of usury"'; Knights, 'Old corruption', 5.
[5] Smith, *Wealth of nations*, Bk. II, ch. 4, 357.
[6] Glaeser and Scheinkman, 'Neither a borrower nor a lender'.
[7] Williams, *Law of real property*, 416.

above economic cost. This critique was telling. To challenge it required a new conception of economics.

The classical economists argued that economic value arose from production. For Smith, Ricardo, and J. S. Mill the rents of land were a burden on society which provided no incentive for production, although they acted impersonally to allocate land to its best use. Marx (who built on their legacy) went further, insisting that labour was the origin of all value. Any surplus taken over and above the existence and reproduction costs of labour was exploitation when appropriated as interest, profit, and rent. The economic argument was also a moral one. In the words of a French socialist, Proudhon, property was theft. Classical economics was a standing reproach to the economic order and its foundation in property rights.[8]

In the 1870s a new generation of political economists rejected this classical teaching entirely and replaced it with a completely different 'neoclassical' economics. Instead of production, what gave things value was their subjective desirability. Value arose from the ability of people to pay for what they wanted. Not the cost of acquiring land, the toil of labour, the cunning of management, and the application of capital, but the preferences of those with means to gratify their desires. This innovation was anticipated by the German civil servant Hermann Heinrich Gossen in 1854, who was completely overlooked. By 1870 the time was ripe for independent versions by three academics, Léon Walras in Switzerland, William Stanley Jevons in England, and Carl Menger in Austria, and the new doctrine of marginal economics gradually took over the discipline.

For Menger and his acolytes the interest rate was at the heart of a new school of 'Austrian economics' which still persists.[9] In Austrian teaching, interest arises from the 'period of production', the delay between investment and payoff, for example from plough to harvest. Now is better than later and interest measures the mental preference for the present over the future. It pays the owner of capital for waiting, for abstaining from consumption, for being patient. In the aggregate, it measures the intensity of preference for immediate consumption in society as a whole, or rather what has to be sacrificed

---

[8] Gaffney and Harrison, 'Neo-classical economics'.
[9] Caldwell, *Hayek's challenge*, pt. 1; Wasserman, *Marginal revolutionaries*.

now (the 'opportunity cost') by saving or investment. Austrian economists considered interest not as a social construct but as part of the nature of things. And if interest is natural, so is the prevailing distribution of income and wealth. Against this view it might be said that capitalists sacrifice little or no satisfaction in order to lend – they mostly earn more than they consume. And money is borrowed for consumption as well as for production, by governments and speculators as well as businessmen and entrepreneurs. For the Austrians, however, this account of interest provided a plausible alternative to Karl Marx's theory of exploitation, and dignified property with a productive social function.

In Austrian teaching, economy and society were driven exclusively by the choices of people acting for themselves ('methodological individualism'). People's mental worlds were radically subjective, with their own distinctive, unobservable, and innate perceptions. They interacted with each other by buying and selling. The value of things was conveyed by market prices. The higgling of the markets settled down to an equilibrium, a 'spontaneous order', which did not have to be planned or imposed. Everyone acting in their own interest ensured the well-being of all without striving to do so. Entrepreneurs had a particularly acute understanding of opportunities and prices and provided alternative heroes as agents of progress to the radical agitator. The entrepreneur borrowed money and invested it, discovered new opportunities to enrich society while enriching (or sometimes impoverishing) himself.[10] Knowledge was always incomplete, and businessmen drove technological progress and price discovery when they competed in markets. The distribution of income and wealth arose from a natural order with no role for government. Taxation violated legitimate property rights. This sweeping rejection of government can be taken as the most important attribute of the Austrian tradition from its inception to the present.[11]

The common thread in more than a hundred years of Austrian economics is the upholding of privilege. Between the 1930s and the 1970s the Austrians were sidelined in economics first by the influence of Keynes and then by the Arrow–Samuelson 'neoclassical synthesis', which sought to reconcile Keynes with the original neoclassical

---

[10] Schumpeter, *Theory of economic development.* [11] Mirowski, 'Naturalizing the market'.

economics. For Keynesians, an efficient economic equilibrium could not be taken for granted – it required government intervention to counteract the boom and bust of the business cycle. But the Austrians came back in the 1970s, with the first harbinger being the Nobel Prize in economics that Hayek received in 1974. Throughout the dark years of social democracy the flame had been kept alive by Hayek and Milton Friedman's Mont Pèlerin society, and in the 1980s it blazed out as the policy doctrine of neoliberalism. This was not a libertarian small state doctrine. In neoliberalism the state has a critical role, of ring-fencing and safeguarding private enterprise against the predations of the democracy. There is an irony here, which is consistent with the theme of this book: capitalism is a long-term project and neoliberalism concedes that (like any long-term project) it requires the protection (and hence implicit subsidy) of the state.[12] Neoliberals were not averse to coercion in defence of 'freedom', the latter conceived narrowly as the freedom of business from social obligation. 'I would prefer temporarily to sacrifice … democracy' said Friedrich von Hayek in an interview in Pinochet's Chile in 1981, 'before having to do without freedom.'[13] More precisely, the freedom in question was freedom from taxation. Between the 1970s and the 1990s, the neoclassical theory of optimal taxation challenged the high-tax regimes of social democracy, and helped to justify reduction in marginal tax rates, which fell by about half in developed countries.[14]

The defence of privilege implied the protection of private enterprise. An aspect of the rise of neoliberalism was a strong presumption that private was more efficient. Theoretical justification came out of neoclassical economic doctrines of static efficiency. Driven by incentives for individuals, a competitive market economy would settle at an equilibrium at which no hands were idle and no goods were left on the shelf. No matter that no such economy has ever existed, nor that another analytical result, the theory of the second best, shows that this ideal state cannot be attained incrementally.[15]

[12] Mirowski, 'Postface: defining neoliberalism'.
[13] Caldwell and Montes, 'Hayek and his visits to Chile', 47.
[14] Mankiw et al., 'Optimal taxation in theory and practice'.
[15] Lipsey and Lancaster, 'General theory of second-best'.

For the last four decades, ever since the Thatcher–Reagan market turn, the policy presumption both in Britain and internationally has been that private enterprise is superior. The UK privatisation programme proceeded from that premise.[16] Internationally as well, the World Bank and International Monetary Fund (IMF) conditionality policies incorporated requirements for public enterprises to be privatised. Likewise the European Union. The arguments invoked superior economic incentives to private ownership, but economic theory is actually ambiguous. Economic incentives lead to superior social outcomes only under conditions of perfect competition which do not exist in any real world. This model has no role for ownership.[17] So the advocates of privatisation invoke experience instead to support the policy.

The weight of empirical evidence now strongly supports those who believe that private ownership is inherently more efficient than state ownership . . . this is true even for natural monopoly.[18]

The actual experience is mixed. Outcomes have been more successful in manufacturing, commerce and finance, and where the criterion of success is financial.[19] The empirical evidence is indeed that privatised companies earn more profit, but that is not compelling: the point of public enterprise is to serve the public, not to turn a profit. Since privatised companies are typically monopolies, all this tells us is that they are allowed to keep more for managers and shareholders at the expense of consumers and workers. In the case of infrastructures and utilities there are few positive outcomes to report.[20] There is selection bias: profitable companies are privatised first.[21] And if experience is invoked, in Eastern Europe mass privatisation failed on many fronts, and played a role in the bad economic experience of transition.[22] Overall, at the end of the 1990s privatisation worked poorly for utilities worldwide and better for non-utilities. This is consistent with our argument, which regards competitive markets as suitable for short-term product cycles.[23]

[16] Florio, *Great divestiture*; Parker, *Official history.*
[17] Offer and Söderberg, *Nobel factor*, ch. 1; Roland, 'Private and public ownership'.
[18] Megginson, *Financial economics of privatisation*, 66.
[19] Millward, 'Privatisation', 138; review of Roland, *Privatisation.* [20] Millward, ibid., 139.
[21] Roland, *Privatisation*, 3. [22] Hamm et al., 'Mass privatisation'.
[23] World Bank, 'Economic growth in the 1990s', ch. 6.

There is no prior presumption in theory that private enterprise will be more efficient. The arguments are complex, and point both ways. Theory also says nothing about how the gains will be distributed, even assuming greater efficiency.[24] A large literature now shows that private enterprise has not been more efficient technologically or economically than comparable firms in the public sector.[25] Note that private enterprise is not generally less efficient either (the privatised railways in Britain are an exception to this).[26] That suggests that efficiency is not determined by the incentives of ownership, but by technical staff, middle management, and other workers, who face similar incentives in both types of enterprise.

Consumer price comparisons may not be sufficient either. The main consideration is the wider effect (what economists call externalities): at the extreme, for nuclear power or global warming, the total impact on global society. A joint-stock company might deliver water at the same or lower price, at the same or higher quality. But if its bankers, managers, and shareholders are very highly paid, the overall effect on society could still be negative in comparison with public management, due to the social pathologies associated with rising inequality. There are also ethical externalities: whatever the efficiency advantages of private water supply, healthcare, or education, it is wrong that people should be kept without. Finally, there are financial externalities: if a service is deemed to be vital, it will not be allowed to fail and the potential cost of bail out needs to be taken into account.

In Europe the UK led the way in privatising a range of network utilities, culminating with the railways in the 1990s. The public good justification was to align private incentives with public benefits.[27] Privatisation was accompanied by a large one-off increase in income

---

[24] Vickers and Yarrow, 'Economic perspectives'; Stiglitz, 'Foreword'; Roland, 'Private and public ownership'.

[25] Barlow, 'Europe sees mixed results'; Bogart and Chaudhary, 'Off the rails'; Florio, *Great divestiture*; idem, *Network industries*; Foreman-Peck and Millward, *Public and private ownership*, 218–19; Glaeser, 'Introduction'; IMF, 'Public-private partnerships'; Iordanoglou, *Public enterprise revisited;* Jomo, 'Critical review'; Kondor, 'Relative efficiency of enterprises'; Kwoka, 'Comparative advantage of public ownership'; McCartney and Stittle, 'A very costly industry'; Millward, 'Political economy', 170–173; idem, *Private and public*, ch. 14; Monbiot, *Captive state*; Stiglitz, 'Foreword'; Vickers and Yarrow, 'Economic perspectives', 113.

[26] McCartney and Stittle, 'A very costly industry'.   [27] Florio, *Great divestiture*.

and wealth inequality. In the absence of clear public benefits this may well be seen as the real objective of these reforms, which were also aligned with Conservative party ideology. Hardly anyone tries to explain why there is such large public sector. From the 1980s onwards market doctrines have dominated. There is much agonising about corporate short-termism,[28] but in economics and in much of mainstream politics and media discourse, markets have been taken as the norm. In contrast, what follows is a new approach to the public sector. It identifies the limits of effective private, public, and social activity. It is 'positive': it accounts for the division of labour between business and public sector activities that is actually observed, and how it changes over time. It is also 'normative': it says where boundaries ought to be placed, and what happens if they are not. The argument is simple, perhaps deceptively so – it is not entirely intuitive and is easy to misunderstand. It has a surprisingly large application.

Chapter 1 starts by showing how credit time horizons place limits on what business can do, and what these limits are, as exemplified by private–public partnerships. In Chapter 2, credit time horizons are also ethical boundaries: the state often delegates power to private agents. This gives rise to several kinds of corruption. Autocrats and democracies have learned how to keep administration honest by means of impartial bureaucracies. Chapter 3 shows how the neoliberal market turn has subverted this achievement and restored politics back to eighteenth-century-style 'Old Corruption'. Chapter 4 points out that the rearing of children is rarely undertaken outside the family, although outsourcing is possible, e.g. in plantation slavery and in social institutions as widely divergent as utopian communities, boarding schools, and orphanages. Nevertheless, both child-rearing and education are generally not undertaken for profit. Schools and universities remain almost entirely not-for-profit. The personal life cycle passes through long periods of dependency. Indigence is avoided by means of social insurance underwritten by pay-as-you-go taxation. Chapter 5 shows that despite encroaching privatisation, there is no other way of supporting old age for

---

[28] Kaplan, 'Are U.S. companies too short-term oriented?'; Martin, 'Yes, short-termism'; Mayer, *Firm commitment*, 211–212.

everyone. In Chapter 6, owner-occupied family housing is seen, not least by its advocates, as a bastion of individualism. In historical fact, the emergence of mass housing has required social and government sanction, and continues to do so today. That most households are paying to buy their dwellings or already own them outright underpins democratic consent for neoliberal policies. It is an irony that popular support for private property depends on government activism. In Chapter 7, the time-horizon perspective helps to clarify the largest challenge of all, climate change and global warming. To summarise the argument: government and other collective social action exists to undertake vital activities which the private sector cannot do on its own. A society relying on markets alone, if that were ever possible, would be a poor, dishonest and miserable place.

The public–private divide is not primarily a matter of ideology or even self-interest. It arises from economic fundamentals. Hence it is likely to take a similar form in different settings. Take it as a hypothesis. Much of the evidence comes from the UK, studied here in detail, supported by North American and international comparison. It is not intended to provide finality. More than a century of history is rich in 'natural experiments', many of them responses to the same challenges. Long-term commitment is difficult to undertake for profit, and more of it is needed as societies become affluent. The aggressive market advocacy of the 1980s onwards was unable to undo this and has caused more harm the more successful it was.

CHAPTER I

Patient Capital

The future will be present one day and needs to be cared for. How much and how far is affected by uncertainty, which expands as the future deepens. Market advocates have dominated policy since the 1980s and if markets will provide, why is the long term a problem? The argument here is that the prevailing market interest (or discount) rate sets a limit on future provision and that this time horizon is typically short. Within this horizon, private enterprise does and should provide. Beyond it, private enterprise alone is not enough.

That is why the public sector has not contracted. Public spending typically allocates 35 to 50 per cent and more of GDP in most advanced countries. Levels are generally flat and, despite a decade of austerity policies, were rising after 2008 as a proportion of government expenditures.[1] In the academic discipline of economics, support for public provision is thin. The persistence and size of the public sector remain largely unremarked. But the free-standing markets assumed as the norm in economic theory produce much less than half of total economic welfare. Public sector persistence suggests that something more powerful than ideology is at work.

I.I THE ARGUMENT

In my *Challenge of affluence* (2006), personal well-being was shown to depend on achieving a good balance between immediate gratification and delayed reward. Here a similar approach is extended to the public sector. The formal decision procedures of cost-benefit discounting aspire to do the same. They are subtle, endlessly ingenious, and

---

[1] OECD, 'General government spending'; Kersetenetzky and Guedes, 'Great recession'.

ultimately inconclusive.[2] They are normative, i.e. designed to achieve the most efficient or equitable outcome. Mathematical models of discounting provide a semblance of precision at a cost of arbitrary premises, unrealistic abstraction, and indeterminate results. In contrast, history is positive: it tells us what has actually been tried out, how, and with what results. Our model here is simple. Its validity is confirmed by financial practice and historical experience. As in economics more generally, this is not a law but a tendency, and exceptions are also revealing.[3]

Free markets have short time horizons. But why? The interest rate provides a benchmark for expected returns, and the same interest rate defines the maximum time horizon within which to break even on an investment. At any time the economy has a prevailing interest rate. We take this rate as exogenous, given to firms by policy or the market, i.e. not a 'natural' variable arising from economic equilibrium (which is a theoretical construct and difficult to identify). This actual interest rate (adjusted upwards or downwards for the risk of any particular activity) draws a line across the future. The prevailing interest rate represents the current cost of capital. A commercial undertaking must recover its initial outlay in less time. If a project can only break even beyond this boundary, it cannot be undertaken by business alone. Likewise undertakings that are locked into long-lived structures or machinery. They need external help through co-ownership, subsidy, management, regulation, a concession, or a licence. For European railways in the nineteenth century, 'Private capital to ensure their extension at such a pace as was needed was not available ... The Governments were therefore compelled perforce to render a large measure of direct assistance'.[4] The Croton Aqueduct in New York was built over a seven-year period starting in 1835, and took thirty years until annual revenues exceeded expenses.[5]

Bank loans specify a precise schedule for repayment, but many indispensable activities have indeterminate or distant break-even horizons. A public body (including monarchy, nobility, the locality, and the church in the past; in modern times, government, not-for-profits,

[2] Gollier, *Pricing the planet's future*; Lind et al., *Discounting for time and risk*; Millner and Heal, 'Choosing the future'; see Chapter 7.
[3] Hausman, *Inexact and separate science.* [4] Pim, *Railways and the state*, 134.
[5] Glaeser, 'Public ownership', 29.

and philanthropists) can commit to long-term projects even if success is uncertain. It spreads the risk among the whole of society.[6] Families can do this too. In contrast, in market societies, undertakings that pay off inside the credit time horizon are typically undertaken by business. This suggests a division of labour: market competition for short-term provision; government, not-for-profits, and the family for long or uncertain durations. This boundary predicts where the limit is likely to run and sets down where it ought to be. When violated in either direction, poor outcomes are likely, inefficiency, corruption, or failure

Economic undertakings have an intrinsic duration: winter wheat is planted in the autumn and the harvest returns a surplus in seven or eight months; it can easily be funded with bank credit. In contrast, a stand of hardwoods (black cherry or maple) cannot be funded from scratch with bank loans: 'during the first 50 years, the tree is worth, at best about a dollar or two for pulpwood'.[7] Waiting this long is well beyond business time horizons. Virgin forest can be cut down but new growth requires subsidies or tax relief. In the 1970s it was estimated that the average economic life of capital equipment was fifteen years.[8] In telecommunications, landline systems were innovated privately but became regulated monopolies or state enterprises. The lines and exchanges would last for decades, the handsets for ten years. In contrast, mobile phone technology changes about once a decade and handsets last for two years. The presumption is for private ownership and it is difficult to find a state-owned mobile phone company outside China, North Korea, and Cuba.

1.2 THE HIGHER THE RATE, THE SHORTER THE WAIT

The higher the market interest rate (or the private discount rate), the less time is available to break even. That is all that the argument requires, but it can be made a little more precise. The time boundary between private and public enterprise is easy to draw. It is the 'pay-back period', the time required for interest on a loan to add up to the original advance, under the prevailing interest rate. For the lender, this is the time their money is locked in and at risk. For the borrower

---

[6] Arrow and Lind, 'Uncertainty'. [7] Jacobson, 'Forest finance 8', 7.
[8] Lind, *Discounting for time and risk*, 85.

it defines how long it takes for cash flow to add up to the principal: 'counting the number of years it takes before the cumulative cash flow equals the initial investment'.[9] A project which takes longer than the payback period to break even cannot pay its capital cost and cannot be undertaken for profit. An investor can get more by lending at the prevailing interest rate. If a project takes longer to break even, or the capital is locked in for longer, then business cannot do it alone. It requires some protection from risk until the project pays off.

The number of years to payback can be calculated using the following short-cut: take 100 and divide it by the interest rate. That is the number of years to the time horizon. For example, if the interest rate is 10 per cent, the time horizon is at 100/10, i.e. it is ten years in the future. If the interest rate is 5 per cent, the payback period is twenty years. When interest rates are lower, the number of years is greater, and vice versa. For example, with interest at 10 per cent, a venture that can repay its initial investment in less than ten years should normally benefit from private enterprise. If it requires more time, business cannot do it alone, and likewise at other interest rates. The next section works out the argument in more detail, and can be skipped by readers in a hurry. It can be taken up again in section 4.

1.3 CREDIT TIME HORIZONS IN MORE DETAIL

The credit time horizon is defined here as the time it takes a lender to break even on a loan out of successive equal payments of interest (i.e. without repayment of principal). This is the 'payback period' method of investment appraisal. Investment manuals do not recommend it because it ignores the time value of money (a dollar tomorrow is worth less than one today) and any cash flows beyond break-even. But it is one of three main methods in common use for project appraisal.[10] A USA survey in the 1990s found that 57 per cent of 392 chief financial officers always used the payback period method to evaluate

---

[9] Brealey et al., *Corporate finance*, 133.

[10] Treynor and Black, 'Corporate investment decisions', 314; Blatt, *Dynamic economic systems*, ch. 13; Thibierge and Beresford, *Practical guide*, 74–83.

investment.[11] The venerable measure of 'Years Purchase', often used to value real estate, is the same as payback: it is obtained by dividing the market value by the annual rent, i.e. the number of annual payments that add up to the market price.[12] Interest-only credit (without repayment of principal) is a simplification but is not unusual. A machine delivers a flow of output and only scrap value at the end. For more than two centuries the British government borrowed against perpetual bonds ('consols') with no maturity, and public debt today is rolled over, not reduced. Before the First World War, most housing was financed with interest-only open-ended mortgages, and the main form of business credit was the overdraft which was serviced with interest but not repaid.[13]

The payback method is not endorsed as practical tool, but as a rough-and-ready diagnostic used here to specify an outer bound for bank credit to break even. To make a profit, a business has to recover its investment in less time. Business cash flow needs to be more than the cost of finance, so their rate of return is higher, which implies (on the payback method) a shorter time to break even. With capital repayment, the time to break even is shorter still. In practice, business sets out hurdle rates for expected profits that are considerably higher than prevailing interest rates.[14] Three different studies suggest rates of return around 15 per cent (payback 6.6 years).[15]

It is necessary to show how the payback period defines the outer boundary time limit on private enterprise. The canonical method of project appraisal is net present value (NPV). This is the cumulative value today of all future cash flows produced by an investment, discounted by the rate of interest, less the initial investment.[16] For investment to go ahead the NPV needs to be positive. The discount rate applied represents the satisfaction lost now by postponing it to the future (the 'opportunity cost'), including the risk of failing to

[11] Graham and Harvey, 'Theory and practice', 196–200.
[12] Smith, *Wealth of nations*, e.g. Bk. II, ch. iv, 359; Marshall, *Principles of economics*, 593; Tarbuck, *Handbook of house property*, 125.
[13] For mortgages, see Chapter 6, (6.3).
[14] Dixit and Pindyck, *Investment under uncertainty*, 6–7, citing Summers, 'Investment incentives', 300.
[15] Gollier, *Pricing the planet's future*, 27; Stockfisch, 'Measuring', Table 7–3, 268.
[16] Thibierge and Beresford, *Practical guide*, 76–77.

achieve it. In the mechanics of discounting, the present value of each future revenue instalment is calculated as the previous year's discounted revenue reduced by the given discount rate. For example, for a loan today of £100 at 10 per cent interest, the £10 interest paid at the end of the first year is worth £9 today; the £10 paid in the second year is worth £8.1 today, £7.29 in the third year etc.: always 10 per cent less than the previous year. The more distant a future payoff of given size, the less it is worth today. These payoffs are cumulated to arrive at NPV.

A project is worth undertaking if the NPV is equal to or more than the initial investment, i.e. if the ratio of NPV to initial investment is 0 or greater. To go back to our example (the rate is set for ease of calculation, the interest rate can be anything), for a loan of £100 at 10 per cent interest the payback period is ten years, but all the discounted interest instalments for evermore never add up to £100. NPV is less than 0 and the loan never pays off. The other canonical method is the internal rate of return (IRR) which is the rate of return required for break-even, i.e. for the NPV to equal 0. In our loan example, when NPV is calibrated to break even (NPV=0) in ten years, the same as the payback period, the IRR is 16 per cent (Figure 1.1). NPV and IRR are therefore related. For the same break-even period IRR is always higher than the payback interest rate on the money borrowed or invested so the payback period of the IRR is always shorter.[17] This is what we set out to demonstrate: the business hurdle rate needs to be higher than the payback rate of return. In the American survey already mentioned, NPV and IRR were always used by three-quarters of the 392 chief financial officers.[18]

NPV and IRR privilege the present over the future, expectations over outcomes. But to refrain from discounting can also be reasonable.[19] Discounting is the tyranny of the present. It is no less rational to maximise welfare at any other point in time.[20] Payback is also simple to apply and to understand.[21] Its nominal revenues are not discounted. If there are future liabilities, business people are properly

[17] The bank can lend at the payback rate because it pays less for the money than it charges.
[18] Graham and Harvey, 'Theory and practice', 196–200.
[19] Price, *Time, discounting and value*, chs. 19–20, and Chapter 7.
[20] Millner and Heal, 'Choosing the future', 19; Offer, *Challenge of affluence*, 46–52.
[21] Graham and Harvey, 'Theory and practice', 200.

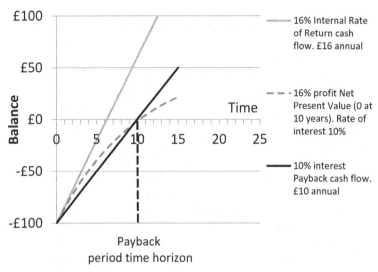

Figure 1.1 £100 loan, 10 per cent interest: break-evens of Internal Rate of Return, Net Present Value, and Payback Period.

concerned about nominal cash flow, not about its speculative value today. NPV measures opportunity ('ex ante'), payback the exposure to failure ('ex post'). During the payback period both lender and borrower are exposed to loss. Downside risk is a worry and the payback method may reflect loss aversion.[22] Hence, while NPV and IRR may be compelling for business, they are not for individuals or society.

For the public sector the established method of investment appraisal is cost-benefit analysis (sometimes 'benefit-cost' in the USA). It is an attempt to quantify all the benefits and costs, including indirect and non-monetary ones. The existence of this separate appraisal method acknowledges that the public sector is different. There is, however, a view that public sector investment should only be undertaken if it satisfies market criteria, i.e. produces rates of return that are equal or higher than the market 'hurdle rate'. That position was taken by the United States and British Treasuries in the run up to privatisation in the 1970s and 1980s, with some allowance for the different circumstances of the public sector, e.g. sometimes the absence of

---

[22] Blatt, *Dynamic economic systems*, ch. 13.

a financial return, no taxation and cheaper funding. A market hurdle rate represented a bias against public spending.[23] The market rate applied (itself a composite) is not reliable, because the assets it is based on mature at different times (i.e. repay the principal after different delays).[24] A business rate of return for the public sector is inconsistent with our own view that it exists to undertake what business is unable to do. A business rate of return target implies that the public sector is redundant, a prospect aspired to by libertarians and market fundamentalists but belied by reality even in its North American heartland. Cost-benefit analysis today attempts to take account of what makes the public sector different and most experts accept that the appropriate discount rates should be lower than those of the market.[25] But there is no single accepted benchmark rate of return. The British Treasury and the USA Environmental Protection Agency apply a 'social rate of time preference' that is lower than market rates of return (discussed in Chapter 7, 7.3), while government investment in the USA still uses a market comparison. Other countries vary.[26]

1.4 UNCERTAINTY

Formal project appraisal assumes fixed cash flows, and such expectations are also written into credit contracts. But uncertainty increases over time and undermines these agreements. Figure 1.2 shows how uncertainty over the future rate of inflation fans out into the future.

Long-term projects set off cascades of risk and uncertainty which arise at several junctures.[27] Any list would include specification and design, construction (on time and budget), quality on completion and in use, operating cost, sustained future demand and revenue, interest rate/inflation, financial risk (provision and price), default of contractors, residual value, competing technologies, obsolescence,

---

[23] Chick, *Electricity and Energy*, 94–103; Lind, *Discounting for time and risk*, 5–6, 55–59; Spackman, 'Discount rates', 1–3.

[24] Millner and Heal, 'Choosing the future', 12.

[25] Baumol, 'Social rate of discount'; Millner and Heal, 'Choosing the future', 65; Spackman, 'Time discounting'.

[26] European Commission, *Guide to cost-benefit analysis*, 299–303.

[27] Grimsey and Lewis, *Public private partnerships*, 172.

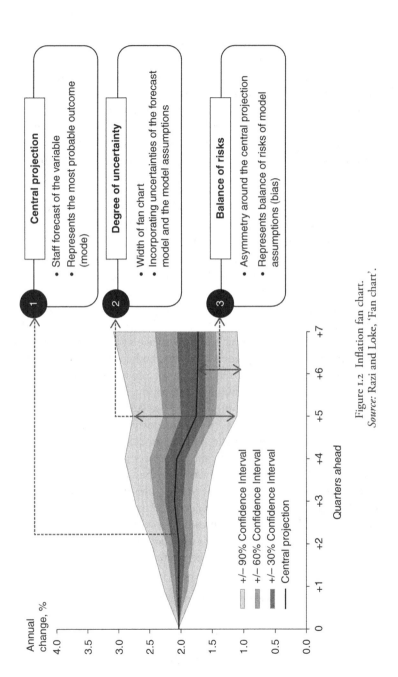

Figure 1.2 Inflation fan chart.
Source: Razi and Loke, 'Fan chart'.

regulation and politics, environmental change, civic disturbance, war, and unknown unknowns.

Large projects are rarely completed on time and budget. 'The iron law of megaprojects' is 'over budget, over time, under benefits, over and over again'.[28] The exceptions are said to be outliers, one to eight projects per thousand. This causes heart-searching among clients and academics. One common explanation is genuine or feigned over-optimism on the part of promoters, clients, and contractors. Another is that bidders make unrealistically low estimates while overstating the benefits.[29]

The iron law may yet arise, however, because the wrong bench-mark is used. This benchmark is also metallic, the 'iron triangle' of cost, time, and quality locked in at the outset. The initial design is given an authority which it cannot bear. Long-term projects are too complicated to specify completely in advance and it is therefore wrong to regard early estimates as binding.[30] Both law and economics understand that contracts are incomplete and cannot anticipate every contingency.[31]

The full benefits of a project and how to achieve them cannot be known fully in advance. Promoters, clients and contractors learn as the project moves ahead and specifications are revised. 'Learning by doing' is a source of productivity improvement.[32] Technologies improve incrementally. In complicated ones such as aircraft, com-puters, and smartphones, it has proven impossible to jump directly from initial breakthrough to the current models. A big long-term project is a 'Great Leap Forward', and not everything will go to plan. Bad faith may be involved, but even with the best intentions mis-specifications and overruns are inevitable. The question is how to deal with them. Compliance with defective plans is the wrong bench-mark. Indeed, it is completion on time and within budget that may be suspect. 'Did they do it right?' is not the same as 'did they get it right?' A project may be completed at projected cost, time, and

---

[28] Flyvbjerg, 'Introduction', *Handbook of megaproject management,* 12.
[29] Flyvbjerg et al., 'Underestimating costs in public works'.
[30] Atkinson, 'Project management'.
[31] Hart, *Firms, contracts, and financial structure*; idem, 'Incomplete contracts and public ownership'.
[32] Arrow, 'Economic implications of learning by doing'.

quality, and still be unfit for purpose. The Sydney Opera House is iconic but it cost fourteen times the initial estimate, and the original architect had to be removed.

For lenders, their own rigidity is a source of risk. When payments are missed projects can go into terminal failure.[33] Whatever the outcome, it is difficult to know whether bad faith is not implicated. Long-term projects inevitably give rise to an asymmetry in which the contractors know more than the client. This 'agency problem' presents opportunities for cheating. A desirable but difficult solution is credible trust.[34] Another is to take the project in-house.

1.5 BEYOND THE PAYBACK LIMIT: FRANCHISE AND FINANCIAL MANIA

Two devices make it possible for business to operate beyond the payback limit. One is a government or social franchise. The second is financial manias. The payback horizon can be overridden using the device of the 'franchise', defined here as a revenue flow with some protection from competition, pricing power, long duration, and low variance. Such revenue flows are available to 'natural monopoly' network utilities, electricity, gas, water and landline telephones, or strong commercial brands supported by advertising. Governments support the franchise with limited liability, rights of way, tax concessions, natural resource grants, patents and copyrights, outright subsidies, guarantees and bailouts, regulated marketplaces, contract enforcement, and a legal personality for corporations. Hence a great deal of business enterprise has little to do with free markets and is carried out at the pleasure of the state.[35] In a franchise, government confers some powers on a corporation or other private entity. This gives rise to mutual dependency: government comes to depend on business to provide a service, while the corporation relies on government for secure income streams. The ultimate franchise is the state itself: it controls a territory and owns a tax base. Not even the state is entirely secure: it is open to challenge from the outside and can be

---

[33] Flyvbjerg, 'Introduction'. [34] Weihe, 'Towards a process perspective', 516–519.
[35] Ciepley, 'Beyond public and private'; Eeckhout, *Profit paradox*; Philippon, *Great reversal*.

captured from within. Privatisation can be seen as such a quest, to capture tax revenues for a private franchise.

The crucial benefit of franchise is the access it provides to cheaper finance, and hence to longer break-evens. With benefit of a franchise, it is possible to issue bonds at much lower cost and longer maturities than equity or bank loans. The interest cost, unlike the return on equities, is tax deductible (another government subsidy). Long-term finance is locked in, while the investor (unlike a bank) can exit at any point by selling the bonds. With cheap finance, business can undertake projects extending for longer than bank or equity finance would allow. When that is not enough, government steps in to carry out the projects itself. Government can borrow for even less, and, if necessary, can forgo a financial return entirely or take a loss (as in the case of military expenditure).

Commercial banking, whose lending rate defines the payback boundary, is itself a franchise, underpinned by central banking, with clearing, licensing, regulation, and lender of last resort functions. In 2014, 61 per cent of the liabilities of the American financial system were covered by explicit or implicit protection from loss by the federal government.[36] Between 2008 and 2014, the fifty largest US companies 'received approximately $27 in federal government loans, loan guarantees and bailouts for every $1 they paid in federal taxes'.[37] In 2012–13, the UK government spent £1.4 on subsidies, direct grants and tax breaks to big business for every pound it received in corporation tax.

During the first globalisation before the First World War, between 1880 and 1913, almost all the massive British, French, and German foreign investment was guaranteed by governments or government entities.[38] Private enterprise depends on public goods: the legal system, money, transport and communication infrastructure and bandwidth, the skills and abilities imparted by households and public education, not to mention regulation, administration, and national defence.

The franchise system affects finance, network infrastructures, mass housing, defence and war, internal security and the legal system,

---

[36] Marshall et al., 'Bailout barometer'. [37] Oxfam America, 'Broken at the top', 6.
[38] Bent and Esteves, 'Government-supported industries', table 3.

social insurance, social and cultural infrastructure, environmental protection, even the household and the family. In recent years there is a surge in social enterprise which seeks a profit in providing public and social goods.[39] Our payback model suggests that this is made possible because low interest rates since 2008 have pushed out payback boundaries. At 2 per cent, the payback limit is fifty years. But social enterprise is vulnerable to rising interest rates. A similar movement of 'five-percent philanthropy' for working-class housing in late-Victorian Britain came to grief on this issue.[40] The sway of franchise runs counter to the assumption in economics that business is superior due to market competition: private enterprise can only flourish long term under protection. Within the payback boundary competition works, beyond it a franchise is needed.

Every once in a very long while some breakthrough, real or imagined, offers investors a prospect of enrichment, of super-profits way beyond the humble returns of prevailing interest rates. Such prospective windfalls attach themselves to unlikely objects, tulips in seventeenth-century Netherlands, or the unspecified enterprises of the South Sea company in Britain shortly afterwards.[41] In the latter case, as in many others, the windfall was underwritten by a state franchise. In Britain in the 1830s and 1840s, newly developed railways promised a vastly superior productivity over existing networks of roads, canals, and stage coaches. The windfalls would go to those who moved early, as borne out by an investment stampede in 1835. A new investment mania began in 1844 and lasted until 1847. Such opportunities induce a temporary blindness: cash-flow calculations are set aside as investors become speculators. Banks, however, did not invest. Within a few short years liquidity overwhelmed real opportunities and gave rise to over-investment, over-construction, and to large losses, and many companies collapsed. Only early movers realised windfalls. The mania was all the more remarkable given the enactment of the Railway Act of 1844 which allowed for the expropriation of any railway whose dividends exceeded 10 per cent (with compensation only for profits below that ceiling). For the rest, it was either wipe-out or the unexciting steady returns of a blue-chip

---

[39] Nicholls et al., *Social Finance.*   [40] Morris, 'Market solutions for social problems'.
[41] Kindleberger and Aliber, *Manias, panics and crashes*; Quinn and Turner, *Boom and bust.*

investment. After the dust had settled, however, society was equipped with a dense railway system, indeed so over-equipped to the extent that even a normal profit was difficult to make.[42] Railway construction was piecemeal and bottom-up. Promoters had local horizons and MPs with local priorities defeated government intentions to lay out a more integrated public system.[43] Some 20,000 miles of line were built when 13,000 would have sufficed. 'Railways could have been nationalized in 1844 (or later) without adverse effects.'[44]

During mania episodes prudence is suspended and speculators fly blind in the hope of landing in Eldorado. Innovation is driven not by market returns but by the prospect of outsize windfalls. 'The central dynamic is that the price of the financial asset is separated from any concern with the underlying cash flows.'[45] If society is fortunate and speculators are disappointed, investors find themselves in possession of long-term low-return assets. Such positive legacies of financial manias are even less frequent than the episodes themselves. For a productive legacy, apart from English railways, two others that come to mind are the electric tramway (and underground metro) revolution of the 1900s, and the telecom bubble of the late 1990s, which left a similar legacy of (in this case) long-distance fibre-optic telecommunication backbone lines, after some of the main enterprises failed.[46] Another example might be the Channel Tunnel, a technological success but a financial failure. Episodes of mania are sometimes rife with corruption: promoters mislead investors with outsize promises, set up and skim excessive start-up costs, and sometimes end up in prison. The effect is the same: investment is driven by delusion, not by a realistic calculation of market returns.

A natural experiment is provided by the development of railways and energy utilities in Europe and the settler societies overseas. Piped water, canals, and railways were undertaken for profit initially. Eighteenth-century British toll roads (turnpikes) were built not-

[42] Arnold and McCartney, 'Rates of return'; Casson, *World's first railway*; Lewin, *Railway mania*; Mitchell et al., 'How good was the profitability?'; Odlyzko, 'Collective hallucinations'.
[43] Lewin, *Railway mania*; Casson, *World's first railway*; dissenting, Odlyzko, 'Early British railway system'.
[44] Casson, *World's first railway*, 2, 26.
[45] Janeway, *Doing capitalism*, 2; Perez, *Technological revolutions*, pt II.
[46] McKay, *Trolleys and tramways*; Malik, *Broadbandits*.

for-profit and the Post Office was a public service. Roads, pavements, street lighting, and sewers were laid out sometimes by developers but mostly by self-governing towns. In more recent times the highway system has always been provided by government. By the end of the nineteenth century, a good deal of the new network utilities had shifted into in public hands after government conflicts with their private owners, while the others made use of a public subsidy or at least a public right of way.[47] Battersea bridge, pictured on the cover, followed this course as well.

The railway systems of continental Europe, when they were not built by governments directly, all required subsidies and guarantees. Likewise colonial railways in nineteenth-century Australasia, India, and South Africa, as well as those in the 'informal empire' in Latin America. North American railways received massive grants of public land which usually came with a monopoly right of way. In railways globally public ownership was increasingly preferred and was not inimical to efficiency.[48]

Of all countries, Britain alone ran a truly private company railway system. That single exception occurred due to investor miscalculation in the special circumstances of the railway mania. In Britain, investor mania overpowered uncertainty and made government intervention unnecessary. Initial finance was mostly by means of equity, made possible by the privilege of limited liability conferred on the railways before it was made available to other business. Every line had to be authorised by an act of Parliament and empowered for compulsory purchase of its rights of way, and all of them continued to be regulated thereafter. Everywhere else uncertainty required government investment, subsidy, or guarantee, i.e. some kind of franchise or outright government ownership. The security of the franchise (or government ownership) then made it possible to rely on bond finance, which tapped public savings directly, and with much longer maturities and lower cost than bank credit. In the British case, once the basic network was in place with its quasi-monopolies, the product was no longer the

---

[47] Millward, *Private and public enterprise*, 22.
[48] Bignon, 'Big push or big grab?'; Bogart, 'Engines of development'; idem, 'Nationalizations'; idem, 'A global perspective'; Chaudhary and Bogart, 'Public-private partnerships and efficiency'; Bogart and Chaudhary, 'Off the rails'.

long-lived permanent way and rolling stock, but a perishable commodity, journeys made and concluded in the course of hours, which
could be financed if necessary by ordinary commercial credit. Bond
finance could be secured by a network that already existed, with
a record of operation and profits.

British railways were taken over by the state during the First World
War, were knocked together into four companies in 1923, and nationalised in 1945. London underground railways, which began as
private ventures in the 1860s, were subsidised and municipalised,
and were finally amalgamated with surface transport as a public
system in 1933.[49] In the 1990s, free-market convictions motivated
a return to private ownership, but despite the government's best
efforts this remains incomplete and is being rolled back.[50] The
track is in public ownership again, and investment in rolling stock
is only partly private. The East Coast railway, one of the main long-
distance passenger arteries, has now reverted three times into public
ownership due to private failure, and other private lines (in the
London Underground and the Channel Tunnel) have collapsed.
New lines (Crossrail, HS2) are being constructed by government.
In June 2018, 'every single homegrown train operator is damaged
goods'.[51] Of the privatised British passenger franchises, 74 per cent
were owned by foreign government railway companies in 2014.
A rigorous recent survey concludes that 'even after conservative
assumptions, rail privatisation has resulted in considerable additional
costs: it was a major public policy error'.[52]

In the United States intercity passenger railways had to be nationalised in 1971 and continue to be run as a public service. The freight
railways there are currently in private ownership and operate successfully. These companies inherited the sunk costs of a large passenger
and freight system, much of which had gone out of business and was
salvaged by government. For eight years the largest system (Conrail)
was run successfully by government before it was sold off. Much of
the business is with captive clients, carrying bulk commodities on

[49] Barker and Robbins, *History of London transport*.
[50] Lewis and Offer, 'Railways as patient capital'; McCartney and Stittle, 'A very costly industry'.
[51] Lea, 'Bumps and dents in all the operators'.
[52] McCartney and Stittle, 'A very costly industry', 1.

long-term contracts and over long distances, as well as containers.[53] This gives them pricing power, and they carry very little debt. In Japan the main railways were nationalised in 1906 and privatised in 1987. Privatisation there has succeeded due to special local conditions: high urban densities and levels of passenger rail use, very low interest rates, and (it might be added) a corporate culture of patient capital.[54]

Most forms of transport rely on the public sector. In motor cars the product cycle is short, several years for most models, but their use depends on the public infrastructure of roads.[55] For air transport, on the face of it a competitive industry, the product cycle (flights) is measured in hours. Government underwrites the lion's share of commercial aircraft development costs and builds the airports (Figure 1.3).[56] Likewise, ocean shipping moors in ports constructed

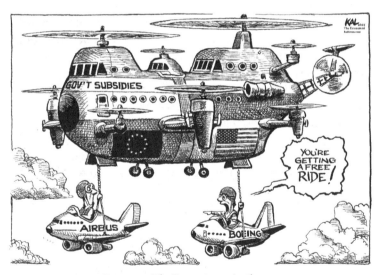

Figure 1.3 *The Economist*, 13 April 2019.
Copyright: Kevin KAL Kallaugher, *The Economist*, Kaltoons.com

---

[53] Stover, *American railroads*, chs. 9–10.
[54] Fukui and Oda, 'Who should take responsibility'; Shoji, 'Lessons from Japanese experiences'.
[55] Offer, *Challenge of affluence*, chs. 9–10. [56] Mowery and Rosenberg, *Technology*, ch. 7.

by governments. It escapes government tutelage by plying a public
right of way (policed, however, by sovereign navies), and flying flags
of convenience.

Privately held companies (like philanthropists) are not beholden
to market time horizons. Capital can wait, but only for large windfall
returns. Private equity investment takes an asset (usually an existing
one) off the bourse and into private ownership. Notionally this might
seem like 'patient capital' seeking long-term returns. But private
equity is a quest for large windfall profits: 'After the investment,
the general partners would hold the entity for five years or so' before
selling it on. This implies a rate of return well in excess of market
interest rates. There was no 'abstinence' involved. The windfall was
anticipated by hefty management fees as well as a 20 per cent share of
the ultimate profit.[57] It can be a form of looting, an opportunity to
strip existing enterprises by loading them with debt and extracting
heavy dividends.[58] Venture capital can also wait but depends on
innovation. The purpose is not to nurture long-term vital low-return
activities, but to gamble on windfalls arising from technological
breakthroughs. Dealing with the unknown, there is no basis for
calculation: 'absence of market discipline is the essence of the
process'.[59] The expected return (usually obtained by floating the
investment on the stock exchange) is meant to be well in excess of
ordinary business returns. The first great wave of venture capitalism
in the United States strove to marketise innovation from the Cold
War. Development was undertaken by private firms under government contracts, which financed from one-half and up to two-thirds
of research and development in the USA during the Cold War
years.[60]

1.6 PUBLIC–PRIVATE PARTNERSHIPS

Public–private partnerships (PPP) were designed to leapfrog the
credit time horizon. Introduced in the 1980s, they spread throughout
the world, especially in middle-income developing countries and in

[57] Ivashina and Lerner, *Patient capital*, x. [58] E.g. Eley, 'Debenhams liquidation'.
[59] Janeway, *Doing capitalism*, 2.
[60] Janeway, *Doing capitalism*, ch. 10; Mowery and Rosenberg, *Technology*, ch. 6.

English-speaking ones. They deliver the services of public infrastructure like roads, schools, and hospitals by means of private investment, secured by government revenue guarantees.[61] Three decades later their flaws are evident and PPPs are in retreat. Their trajectory shows how violating credit time horizons can be fraught with trouble.

Public–private contracts diffused to developing countries at the behest of the World Bank as part of the 'Washington Consensus' in which the international monetary and credit agencies imposed market-friendly reforms as a condition of access to credit. The IMF and the World Bank provided loans, guarantees, and intermediate access to much larger private loans.[62] The PPP contractual framework provided a secure outlet for the funds of large banks and financial institutions in the United States, Britain, Europe, India, and Japan; they also provided a lucrative role for international consultants, suppliers, and contractors.[63]

The Washington Consensus is now discredited, and the experience of PPP is mixed. This is reflected in the trajectory of these ventures. Their implementation internationally peaked in 2013 at about $220 billion of investment a year in less-developed countries. Since then PPP investment has gone into steep decline (Figure 1.4). The payments, however, will continue far into the future. The attractions of PPP for lenders remain large, and financial institutions, the G20, and the UK government (until recently) were still trying to pump it back into life.[64]

1.7 THE PRIVATE FINANCE INITIATIVE IN THE UK

The British version, the private finance initiative (PFI), was introduced in 1992 by a Conservative government to attract commercial credit into infrastructure investment, at business rates of return with

---

[61] Hodge et al., *International handbook*.
[62] Noubma-Um, 'Empirical evidence', 472–3; World Bank, 'Sources of financing'; Offer and Söderberg, *Nobel factor*, 233–246.
[63] Bayliss and Van Waeyenberge, 'Unpacking the public private partnership revival'; Finnerty, *Project financing*, ch. 5; World Bank, 'Sources of financing'; World Bank, 'Private participation in infrastructure'.
[64] Bayliss and Van Waeyenberge, ibid.; Dujovne, 'G20 economies must push'; Plimmer and Parker, 'Theresa May sticks'.

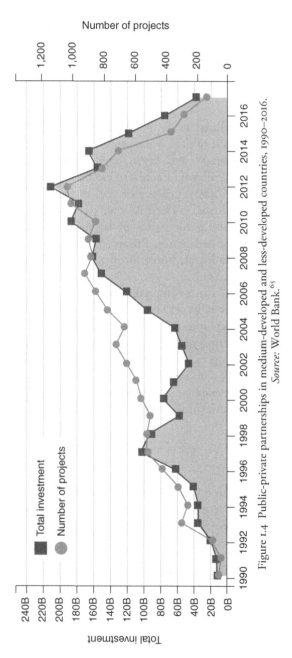

Figure 1.4 Public-private partnerships in medium-developed and less-developed countries, 1990–2016.
Source: World Bank.[65]

[65] ppi.worldbank.org/visualization/ppi.html#sector=&status=&ppi=&investment=&region=&ida=&income=&ppp=&md
b=&year=&excel=false&map=&header=true

a government guarantee.[66] Under PFI, a commercial venture became a fixed-income financial asset with the security of public debt, but at commercial interest rates typically two to three times as high.[67] In these British PPPs, a public agency commissioned a project from a corporate consortium, usually a 'special purpose vehicle' (SPV) created for the purpose. Special purpose vehicles were formed for the benefit of the lenders, i.e. to make the projects 'bankable',[68] and were designed to protect parent companies from project liabilities. The SPV raised the money, erected the structures, and delivered the service. The public authority paid regular fees which combined loan service, capital repayment, and service charges. Typically, about one-half of the payment is to service and pay back the initial finance.[69] Payment continued for the economic life of the project, e.g. twenty-five to thirty years for schools and hospitals, regardless of suitability or need. Partnerships were contractually insulated from changes in the government budget, and payments were linked to the retail price index.

Coming into power in 1997 after a long period in opposition, the New Labour party embraced sound money policies in a quest for acceptance by finance. It promised to comply with the Maastricht Treaty limit of borrowing no more than 3 per cent of GDP a year and its own self-imposed public debt ceiling of 40 per cent of GDP. PFI appeared in the national accounts as expenditure, not borrowing, an accounting ruse that made investment possible without incurring public debt. Although never admitted, that is still widely understood to have been its prime motivation.[70]

For Labour in opposition this prospect was enticing as early as 1991, but not a word of it has appeared in subsequent justifications.[71] Instead, the argument was that PPP was efficient.[72] Every PPP

---

[66] Great Britain (GB) House of Commons (HC) Treasury Committee, 'Private finance initiative', 3; GB National Audit Office (NAO), 'Choice of finance', 41–50, esp. 47–50.

[67] Finnerty, *Project financing*, ch. 2; Hare, 'PPP and PFI', 100.

[68] Bayliss and Van Waeyenberge, 'Unpacking the public private partnership revival', 580; Finnerty, *Project financing*, ch. 2.

[69] GB NAO, Comptroller and Auditor General, 'PFI and PF2', 26.

[70] Atkins et al., 'Public versus private', 15–16; Foot, 'P.F. Eye', 11; GB HC, Committee of Public Accounts, 'Public finance initiatives', 3; Hellowell, 'UK's private finance initiative'; Nelson and Hoskin, 'The great debt deceit'.

[71] Brown et al., 'Financing infrastructure', 13–14.

[72] GB HC, Committee of Public Accounts, 'PFI in housing and hospitals', 8–16; GB HM Treasury, 'Public private partnerships', 16–17; idem, 'PFI', 1–2.

project was meant to be tested by means of 'value for money' comparisons with a public sector alternative. Commercial finance costs at least twice as much as public borrowing. The comparison had to show, therefore, that private efficiency was more than twice as high as that of the public sector.[73]

Advocates of market efficiency in finance (the 'efficient market hypothesis') argue that when the same technology is used, government projects are no less risky than corporate ones, and that commercial interest rates are therefore appropriate.[74] Superior efficiency was meant to be achieved by means of 'risk transfer', i.e. the greater capacity of the private sector to absorb risk would more than offset the higher cost of finance. Government documents insisted that PFI was more efficient, and even quantified the savings achieved over public sector comparators.[75]

These savings were soon shown to be bogus. Government has much greater capacity to absorb risk than any private entity.[76] 'The only publications which are broadly positive about PFI tend to be those that have been compiled by official bodies as part of their statutory remit.'[77] Value for money tests were biased in favour of PFI.[78] Even using the Treasury's own method the purported advantage was razor-thin, while alternative measures showed it to be strongly negative.[79]

Biases took a variety of forms. Foremost among them was the costing of risk transfers. At the outset the cost and completion record of PFIs was better than the public sector comparators, but the public sector caught up, and in later reviews any advantage was small (non-PFI in

[73] Brown et al., 'Financing infrastructure', 14; Edwards, 'The private finance initiative (PFI) and value for money?', 11–20; Hare, 'PPP and PFI', 98–106.

[74] Spackman, 'Time discounting', 472, 477, 505.

[75] GB HM Treasury, 'Public private partnerships', 17–18. [76] Arrow and Lind, 'Uncertainty'.

[77] Wall and Connolly, 'Private finance initiative', 712.

[78] Atkins et al., 'Public versus private'; Boardman and Hellowell, 'Comparative analysis'; Edwards et al., 'Evaluating the operation of PFI'; Gaffney et al., 'NHS capital expenditure'; idem, 'PFI in the NHS'; Heald, 'Value for money tests'; GB NAO, Comptroller and Auditor General, 'Lessons from PFI'; idem, 'Review of the VfM assessment'; idem, 'PFI and PF2'; GB HC Treasury Committee, 'Private finance initiative'; Pollock et al., 'Private finance and "value for money" in NHS hospitals'; Pollock et al., 'Private finance initiative'; Siemiatycki and Farooqi, 'Value for money and risk'.

[79] GB NAO, Comptroller and Auditor General, 'Review of the VfM assessment process', fig. 4, 19; fig. 6, 25.

brackets): in a survey in 2008, 69 (65) per cent of PFI projects had delivered on time and 65 (54) per cent within budget.[80] It had to be shown that the difference had any practical significance. Even if it did, as we have argued in Chapter 1 (1.4), that is not necessarily a virtue. PFI may have contained its costs better because its budgets already embodied a premium for cost overruns: they tended to be about a quarter more expensive than public sector equivalents, and costs often escalated between the announcement and signing of contracts, when the test benchmark was set.[81] For PFI, the clock started ticking only after a long process of negotiation and planning, making completion look more timely than it was.[82] A marginal advantage in completion time is hardly a justification for thirty-year contracts: that could be achieved by contracts for construction alone. With all the contracting required, high legal, consultant and accountancy fees were incurred by both sides. These were estimated at 3.5 per cent for the public sector client, 3.8 per cent for the winning bid and about 5 per cent for the failed ones, for a total of 12.3 per cent.[83] The discount rate for the public sector comparators was fixed in 2003; after the financial crisis of 2008 this was twice as high as the rate at which government was currently borrowing, but the comparator remained unchanged, adding another bias against the public sector.[84] In response to such criticism the Treasury withdrew its value for money guidance in 2012.

Initially the Treasury promised careful retrospective evaluations of the projects,[85] but none was ever undertaken: there is no official analysis available to show whether PFI has delivered value for money, and none is currently envisaged.[86] This is also the case more generally for PPP.[87] Particulars of PFI projects were placed beyond scrutiny by 'commercial confidentiality'.[88] If PPPs could be

[80] GB NAO, Comptroller and Auditor General, 'Performance of PFI construction', 7–8.
[81] Boardman et al., 'Theory and evidence', 17. [82] Ibid., ii.
[83] Dudkin and Välilä, 'Transaction costs', 14.
[84] GB NAO, Comptroller and Auditor General, 'PFI and PF2', 20.
[85] GB HM Treasury, 'Public private partnerships', 32.
[86] GB HC, Committee of Public Accounts, 'Public finance initiatives', 5; GB NAO, Comptroller and Auditor General, 'PFI and PF2', 19–20.
[87] Hodge, 'Reviewing public–private partnerships', 94–105.
[88] Jubilee Debt Campaign, 'UK's PPP disaster', 5; Siemiatycki and Farooqi, 'Value for money and risk', 288.

shown as superior, we can be sure it would have been done. External evaluations of individual projects showed poor value for money.[89]

Insurance pools share individual risk with many others, the larger the number the lower the premium. Hence the public sector, whose resources encompass the whole of the tax base, can insure more cheaply than a private entity.[90] Public sector comparators were typically imputed a premium for 'optimism bias' and 'risk transfer'; but if the public sector has to pay a premium to the SPV in order to avoid the risk, there is no risk transfer

Uncertainty cannot be dissipated by mere contract. The government was exposed to supplier default, while remaining locked into the projects. If an SPV failed, the parent company could walk away, but not the government.[91] In several instances contractors failed and did just that. The Channel Tunnel company was set up as a free-standing private enterprise project with no subsidy, but when it failed the government took it over.[92] The £3bn Channel Tunnel rail link PPP required successive government rescues.[93] The £15.7bn thirty-year Metronet Underground maintenance contract and the parallel Tube Lines PPP reverted to public management.[94] Several hospital and IT projects faltered.[95] In the aftermath of the financial crisis, when lending dried up, the government stepped in with funding.[96] Carillion, the second largest government contractor, collapsed in January 2018 with more than £2bn of unfinished projects.[97]

Over and above the cost of credit, PFI projects incurred costs additional to those of public sector projects. PFI took out expensive insurance while the public sector self-insured. Contractors held costly cash balances and paid extra fees to consultants and

[89] e.g., Edwards et al., 'Evaluating the operation of PFI'. [90] Arrow and Lind, 'Uncertainty'.
[91] Edwards et al., 'Evaluating the operation of PFI', 97; Zhang, 'Financial viability analysis', 657.
[92] Finnerty, *Project financing*, ch. 20.
[93] Wikipedia, 'International Finance Corporation'; Wikipedia, 'High Speed 1'; Wikipedia, 'Partnerships UK'.
[94] BBC, 'Tube maintenance back "in house"'; *Economist*, 'Mind the money gap'; *Private Eye*, 'Tubular balls-up'; Wright, 'Private buyers sought for Metronet'.
[95] Carvel, 'Flagship PFI hospital'; Carr-Brown and Gould, 'Series of blunders'; Edwards, 'The private finance initiative'; Robinson, *Unconventional minister*, 104–106; Timmins, 'NHS trust buys back PFI Hospital'; Timmins, 'PFI projects switched to tax havens, report claims'; Wikipedia, 'Hinchinbrooke Hospital'.
[96] Barker and Timmins, 'Taxpayers' cash'. [97] Plimmer et al., 'Cable warns'.

lenders.[98] The taxes incurred by SPVs were given as a reason why the public sector (which pays no taxes) had lower costs.[99] One enticement of PFI was corporation tax due to be paid.[100] But much of the profit found its way to tax havens.[101] Offshore funds owned about half of the equity, typically paying less than 1 per cent in tax. The most risky stage was the initial one of design and construction. Once it was over, assets were often refinanced more cheaply or sold on at a large profit. Public sector efforts to share the gains had only limited success.[102]

PFI turned out to be expensive. By 2013, nine out of ten government departments would have bought out their PFIs if they could. They were still paying high pre-2008 interest rates.[103] Local authorities, with no independent sources of finance, were told that if they wanted to build it was PFI or nothing. It was 'the only game in town'. Likewise for the NHS.[104] But no additional funding was provided for the extra cost, so services were cut instead. NHS hospitals constructed under PFI typically had fewer beds than the ones they replaced.[105]

For those who promoted them, the main difficulty was packaging these projects in 'bankable' form. So, despite the purported advantages of PFI, it only twice exceeded 10 per cent of annual government capital expenditure. Figure 1.5 shows how the trajectory of PFI has gone into steep decline. In Britain, PFI has run its course.[106]

[98] GB NAO, Comptroller and Auditor General, 'PFI and PF2', 16.

[99] Baumol, 'Social rate of discount'.

[100] GB HC, Committee of Public Accounts, 'Public finance initiatives', 6.

[101] GB NAO, Comptroller and Auditor General, 'PFI and PF2', 20; Jubilee Debt Campaign, 'UK's PPPs disaster', 4; Timmins, 'NHS trust buys back PFI hospital'; idem, 'PFI projects switched to tax havens'; Whitfield, 'PPP profiteering'.

[102] GB HC, Committee of Public Accounts, 'Update on PFI debt refinancing'; Whitfield, 'PPP wealth machine'; Jubilee Debt Campaign, 'UK's PPPs disaster', 4.

[103] GB NAO, Comptroller and Auditor General, 'PFI and PF2', 32.

[104] 1999 quote from GB HC, Committee of Public Accounts, 'PFI in housing and hospitals', 7; Edwards et al., 'Evaluating the operation of PFI'; GB HC, Treasury Committee, 'Private finance initiative', 33; Grimsey and Lewis, *Public private partnerships*, 362; Hare, 'PPP and PFI', 109–110; Timmins, 'NHS trust buys back PFI hospital'; idem, 'PFI projects switched to tax havens'.

[105] Edwards et al., 'Evaluating the operation of PFI', 152.

[106] GB HC, Committee of Public Accounts, 'Public finance initiatives', 7.

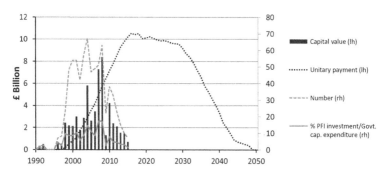

Figure 1.5 PFI investments in the UK
Source: UK Treasury.
Note: Unitary payment is the ongoing combined debt and service charge. Typically,
about half is debt service.

1.8 FOR WHOSE BENEFIT?

PFI failed. Despite a renewed commitment by Conservative governments and attempts to fix its defects, the number of new projects
declined almost to nothing. 'These schemes are now widely discredited' wrote the *Financial Times* in 2017.[107] The new left-wing
leadership of the Labour Party threatened to cancel many of the
existing contracts.[108] PFI was finally laid to rest on 29 October 2018.
But most of the liabilities lie in the future and will continue to be paid
until the middle of the current century (Figure 1.5).

Removing debt from the public balance sheet was a deception with
no benefits. It was a 'fiscal illusion', no more than an accounting
device. There was no saving, just the opposite. An excessive cost was
imposed on future taxpayers in return for a semblance of prudence
and self-control.[109] Local authorities continue to pay for unwanted
buildings and for sub-standard ones.[110] Some £47 million will

---

[107] *Financial Times*, 'UK's ailing infrastructure'.
[108] Packard and Plimmer, 'Labour Party threatens'.
[109] GB HC, Committee of Public Accounts, 'Public finance initiatives', 3, 15–16; GB NAO,
   Comptroller and Auditor General, 'PFI and PF2', 12; Irwin, 'Accounting devices and fiscal
   illusions'.
[110] GB NAO, Comptroller and Auditor General, 'PFI and PF2', 17; Jubilee Debt Campaign,
   'UK's PPPs disaster', 5–7.

eventually be paid for a school in Liverpool which has stood empty since 2014.[111]

Why was PFI sustained for so long? Initially even Conservatives, the party of business, had been sceptical. The concept was rejected by the Treasury and by the Conservative minister for Social Services Keith Joseph as early as the 1970s.[112] The former Conservative Chancellor of the Exchequer Nigel Lawson told the House of Lords in 2018:

My Treasury officials [in the 1980s] were keen on it but I refused to have anything to do with it. Subsequently, my successors – particularly, but not exclusively, Mr Gordon Brown – were enthusiastically in favour of it. Its purpose, in the eyes of the Treasury officials who tried to persuade me to take it up, was that it enabled you, at least in the short term, to dress up considerable amounts of public expenditure and put them off the public sector balance sheet. That is not a good reason for adopting something which, in my judgment, does not give good value for money for the taxpayer, and it introduces a degree of moral hazard, which we see very much in the Carillion affair . . . We have now had enough evidence that it is not good value for money and therefore not sensible from the point of view of the taxpayer.[113]

PFI inspired magical thinking. 'Mr Blair and Mr Brown talk as if the PFI was free cash, a capitalist cargo cult from their friends in the city', wrote Simon Jenkins (a leading journalist) in *The Times*.[114] The test, wrote Brown while still in opposition, was not whether PPP was value for money, 'The real comparison should be between the cost of private finance and the cost (economic and social) of not undertaking the project at all'.[115] That is the only underlined sentence in a 22-page document. The shackles were self-imposed. As Chancellor, Brown would only borrow up to 40 per cent of GDP but Maastricht allowed him 60. And no European Union country was ever punished for exceeding a 3 per cent deficit.

One might accept the off-budget reasoning at face value, but it was never made openly: there was no face to value. If undertaken in good

[111] GB HC, Committee of Public Accounts, 'Public finance initiatives', 6.
[112] Levitt, 'Rightwinger who saw risks'.
[113] Lord Lawson, House of Lords Debates, 15 Jan. 2018, 5.06pm.
[114] Jenkins, 'No man is an island'.
[115] Brown et al., 'Financing infrastructure', 14.

faith, then it was done without due diligence. Some explanation is called for, but none ever came, not in any sources I have seen. PFI is mentioned only once in passing in the Treasury's high-class apologia for New Labour,[116] and merely as an efficiency measure. Despite persistent denials, the Treasury continued to prefer PFI because it did not show up as public debt.[117]

Who benefits? Howard Davies is a British policy economist who has also worked as a financier and a senior public official. He has been the Chairman of the financial regulator, the Financial Services Authority (FSA), of the Audit Commission, Director of the London School of Economics, and, since 2015, Chairman of the Royal Bank of Scotland. In 2018, in front of more than two million television viewers, he stated that 'PFI has been a fraud on the people because essentially the government is always the cheapest borrower'.[118]

The benefits went largely to the banks who obtained a revenue flow at commercial rates of interest, underwritten by the full faith and credit of the state. Risks were shifted to contractors, operators, and public sector clients.[119] Private finance cost at least twice as much as public borrowing. Precisely how much is difficult to know because the contracts are not in the public domain. But finance benefited by more than just the difference in interest rates. In the UK, about 90 per cent of PFI projects were financed by debt. Profits on the equity share were higher, typically in double figures and up to 15 per cent. When they were sold on, projects provided windfall returns. A study of 118 sales revealed an average return to investors of 28.7 per cent.[120]

The markup on PFI loans was likely to be large. It is increasingly understood that commercial lenders can create money out of nothing if the borrower is credible.[121] No borrower is more credible than the state. Syndicating the loans helped reduce liquidity risk. For the

[116] Brown et al., *Reforming Britain's economic and financial policy.*
[117] GB HC, Committee of Public Accounts, 'Public finance initiatives', 16.
[118] BBC Question Time, 'Chairman of RBS, Howard Davies', 18 January.
[119] Lea, 'Carillion rivals warn MPs'.
[120] GB HC, Committee of Public Accounts, 'Private finance initiatives', 11.
[121] Deutsche Bundesbank, 'The role of banks'; McLeay et al., 'Money creation'.

lenders, PFI was a licence to print money: debt could be issued with high leverage and at little cost.

PFI responded to the financial sector's quest for yield. During the 1980s many restrictions on lending were lifted. The consequence was a surge of credit into real estate, bonds, and shares. Credit drove up asset prices but also acted to reduce their yields.[122] Where did the funding come from? The ten-fold expansion of bank assets during these years cannot have come out of household and corporate savings. The various schools of Modern Monetary Theory argue that credit is generated endogenously in response to demand from credible borrowers: not that deposits generate loans, but that loans create deposits.[123] The PPP system provided money market returns with government guarantees. Recently it was reported that, 'PPP policy is now driven far more by the availability of global finance than by the previously perceived potential for efficiency gains through privatisation'.[124]

Corruption requires at least two parties. The instigator of fraud was the New Labour government which came to office in 1997. The party curried favour with business with its code word of 'modernisation'. The term conveyed a disavowal of historical working-class affinities, a quest for middle-class voters, and for acceptance by finance and business.[125] In mitigation, New Labour believed that finance had the power to derail its government. It was also influenced by North American market fundamentalism, the conviction that government was powerless to control corporations or defy them.[126]

PFI was launched by the Conservatives in 1992 but made little progress because the Treasury insisted on better value than public sector investment ('the universal test'). Labour spoke against PFI in Parliament, but the party leaders already endorsed it in opposition.[127] Once in power in 1997 they wasted no time in ramping it up. Geoffrey Robinson, a shadowy businessman and Labour MP, came into government as Paymaster General with

---

[122] Offer, 'Narrow banking', 167–170.   [123] Offer, 'The market turn', 1057–1062.
[124] Bayliss and Van Waeyenberge, 'Unpacking the public private partnership', 581.
[125] Rawnsley, *Servants of the people*, 298–302; Finlayson, *New Labour*, ch. 6, esp. 97.
[126] Ramsay, *Rise of New Labour*, 70–82.
[127] Brown et al., 'Financing infrastructure investment'.

a mission to seduce lenders into PFI.[128] He appointed City bankers to serve on a Treasury task force and recruited one of them to lead it. The task was to relax PFI contractual terms. The Treasury's 'value for money' tests straddled the line between advocacy and corruption. In 2000 the task force was privatised as Partnerships UK (PUK), with a majority stake sold off to a consortium of banks, and staffed by corporate lawyers, bankers, and consultants in a manifest conflict of interest.[129] Steve Robson, the Treasury's privatisation advocate, was knighted, retired, and took up several directorships, including one at the Royal Bank of Scotland. At PUK, however, he remained the 'Treasury nominee', although the bank he worked for was doing business with the scheme. PFI scholar Jean Shaoul wrote that 'we have a government that acts in the interests of a financial oligarchy'.[130]

'Nothing in modern politics is more curious', wrote Simon Jenkins in 2002, 'than Labour's adoption of the most radical privatisation in Europe . . . Mr Blair has been sold on there being only one salvation for public services. It lies in the complete reversal of Labour dogma, in subjugating the public service ethos to the "daring" incentive of private profit. The future lies in bankers and lawyers, not public officials and do-gooders.'[131] For Labour politicians (like social democratic ones everywhere at the time) there was a heady sense of sin, of connection with the high and mighty, of an entitlement confirmed by the voters' mandate. New Labour fell for grand follies, for the 'four sublimes': the techno-challenge of grand projects, the rapture of political monuments, the financial windfalls for all concerned, and the awe of iconic achievements.[132] In a Faustian bargain, the progressive leadership surrounded itself with people from finance.[133]

Petty corruption is breaking the rules. Grand corruption is writing them (see Chapter 2). Making it legal confers impunity. 'Modernisation' was a code word for supping at the table of mammon. The failure was fiduciary: sacrificing the public good for an

[128] Bower, *The Paymaster*.
[129] Ibid., ch. 8, esp. 141–143; Foot, 'P.F. Eye'; Wikipedia, 'Partnerships UK'.
[130] Owen and Brady, 'Like paying for schools'. [131] Jenkins, 'No man is an island'.
[132] Flyvbjerg, 'Introduction', 6.
[133] GB HC, Public Administration Select Committee, 'Goats and Tsars'.

expediency that was never declared or admitted, and which is hard to pin down; not breaking the rules but re-writing them for sectional and even personal advantage.[134] From its very inception, PFI was widely and vigorously criticised, not least by public agencies. It exemplified the New Labour culture of dissimulation, of pervasive bad faith which has poisoned trust in government more widely.[135] Finance returned the favour: since the 1990s, outsourcing and privatisation opened a revolving door between government and business. Corporate employees were seconded to government to write contracts with their own sectors. Ministers and officials moved into firms and industries that they had regulated only a short time before.[136] The three leaders of the New Labour revolution, Blair, Mandelson, and Brown, won lucrative sinecures with financial companies and consultancies.[137] Such reciprocity makes a mockery of rationality in policy and of 'value for money' rhetoric. Fluid, uncertain projects depend on good faith for success. They are also prone to its opposite, bad faith and corruption.[138]

1.9 CONCLUSION

Friedrich von Hayek argued famously that socialism was impossible because it required omniscience on the part of the central planner. In contrast, in market systems spontaneous order emerges out of local knowledge.[139] But for long-term provision the higgling of the market is not sufficient. The opposite is the case. Those who insist on certainty are commercial bankers, not central planners. The task of social planning is to manage uncertainty. It needs to apply expert judgement to the pitfalls and opportunities of long-term projects, and to implement them with integrity and competence. Failure in one project is offset by success in another. The obsession of public

[134] Rothstein and Varraich, *Making sense of corruption*, 26.
[135] Rawnsley, *Servants of the people*; Oborne, *Rise of political lying*; idem, *Triumph of the political class*.
[136] Barret, 'Fixing the revolving door'; Brooks and Hughes, 'Public servants, private paydays'; GB HC, Public Administration Select Committee, 'Goats and Tsars'; Transparency International, 'Cabs for hire?'; Wilks, 'Revolving door'.
[137] Brooks and Hughes, 'Public servants, private paydays', 22.
[138] OECD, 'Public-private partnerships', 121–124, and Chapter 3.
[139] Hayek, 'Use of knowledge in society'.

authorities with clearing the ground for business has created perverse incentives. The storied risk-takers of business are only risking their own and borrowed money. For society, the risk-taker is government. Private enterprise works best in the short term, public management for the long. The alternative is asking for trouble: mismanagement and corruption are inherently related to time horizons, as shown amply in the case of PFI.

CHAPTER 2

Corruption and Integrity

The long term cannot be managed by business on its own. When it is, the result is often inefficiency, corruption, or failure. In contrast, government is open ended: it endures for long periods and undertakes long-term projects. Its officials are meant to serve, not to compete. Bureaucracy is not immune to failure, but there is no alternative to what it can do.

Corruption used to be associated with developing countries and is currently on the rise elsewhere. Before 1980 a competent civil service gave the countries of north-western Europe a century's respite. How this immunity was achieved can be studied and perhaps emulated. Integrity and expertise are connected by a common respect for the truth. Reliable, honest administration is implemented by qualified staff appointed by competition and promoted on merit. Corruption can be defined by its opposite, impartiality, the requirement to treat everyone with equal respect. Impartiality is an ethical norm. Pervasive corruption degrades the quality of life.[1] Its incidence in English-speaking societies is rising and affects their effectiveness and purpose.

2.1 THREE TYPES OF CORRUPTION: PETTY, GRAND, AND CRONY

For the corrupt, self-interest comes before duty. It is easy for them to live with: a clandestine lapse that harms nobody in particular: 'The

---

[1] Holmberg et al., 'Quality of government'; Rothstein, *Quality of government*; Rothstein, 'What is the opposite of corruption?'

party leaders may be getting more than they should out of the city, but that doesn't hurt me.'[2]

'Petty corruption' is payment for favours (bribery, 'quid pro quo', 'something for something', 'pay for play'). It is furtive, illegal, and widespread.[3] It breaks the law. In contrast, 'grand corruption' is protected by law. Those who control government can use it to their advantage.[4] The best way to rob a bank is to own one. This is commonplace even in supposedly well-governed societies.[5] For example, in 2013 Andrew Cuomo, Governor of New York, set up a commission to investigate corruption in state politics. When it impinged on his own transgressions he closed it down.[6] In 2015 the Governor of Wisconsin signed an act to limit political corruption inquiries.[7] In 2017 the South Dakota governor and legislators moved to annul an ethics measure passed by referendum.[8]

Judicial independence can also enable grand corruption. In *Citizens United vs. Federal Election Committee* (2010) the United States Supreme Court removed the limits on political donations as constituting free speech. Large sums flowed from business donors to legislators. In a vicious circle legislators appoint judges, and judges authorise donations. A massive tax reduction for the wealthy followed in 2017.[9] More generally, public policy in the United States serves the interests of the rich, while those of ordinary voters have almost no influence at all.[10]

A third form of corruption is not only legal but laudable. An 'economy of favours' basks in the virtue of reciprocal exchange. 'Do as you would be done by' generates a glow of virtue.[11] A favour granted instigates a requirement to reciprocate and sets off a cycle of mutual regard.[12] Reciprocity accords with intuitions and norms. It

---

[2] Steffens, *Shame of the cities*, 13.   [3] Rose and Peiffer, *Paying bribes*; idem, *Bad governance*.
[4] Rose-Ackerman, 'Democracy and "grand" corruption'.
[5] Owen, 'What would Madison say?'
[6] Craig et al., 'Cuomo's office hobbled ethics inquiries'; Hamilton and Vielkind, 'Bharara ends probe'; *New York Times* editorial board, 'Gov. Cuomo's broken promises'; Weiser and Wang, 'He was Governor Cuomo's closest aide'.
[7] Miller, 'Walker and the Kochs make Wisconsin corruption-friendly'.
[8] Davey and Confessore, 'South Dakota legislators seek hasty repeal of ethics law'.
[9] Ferguson et al., 'How much can the U.S. Congress resist political money?'
[10] Edsall, 'After Citizens United'; Gilens and Page, 'Testing theories'; McGuire and Delahunt, 'Predicting United States policy'.
[11] Elster, 'The Valmont effect'.   [12] Offer, 'Between the gift and the market'.

gives rise to affinity and a sense of shameless entitlement.[13] In the words of George Washington Plunkitt, a New York political boss of the gilded age, 'If I have a good thing to hand out in private life, I give it to a friend. Why shouldn't I do the same in public life?'[14] A less flattering description is croynism. Corruption was rife in Communist Europe, but the move to democracy felt like a retrograde one from reciprocal 'do me a favour' into the furtive 'give me a bribe'.[15]

In the 1980s the World Bank and the IMF began to promote their own and commercial bank credit for emerging economies, to be serviced by export surpluses. To make sure of export revenues, borrowers had to undergo 'structural adjustment' to liberalise and marketise their economies. This script, conforming to a 'Washington Consensus', was followed quickly by an uncalled for 'corruption eruption'.[16] But Washington was unfazed and urged more of the same: 'any reform that increases the competitiveness of the economy will reduce incentives for corrupt behaviour'.[17] Chicago economist Gary Becker went further: 'If we abolish the state, we abolish corruption.'[18] The opposite is actually the case: ungoverned failed states are corrupt and big-state Scandinavia is upright. Privatisation in developing countries created rent extraction opportunities, and privatisation of state-owned enterprises subverted their integrity and promoted corruption.[19]

Corruption is not easy to measure or even to define but indicators were soon compiled, conferences assembled, books and articles published, an anti-corruption movement set in motion.[20] In the space of a decade from the mid-1980s corruption references in the *Economist* increased fivefold and almost doubled in JSTOR, the academic journal database.[21] Corruption undermined the Washington Consensus promise. If one imagines market outcomes to be ethical

[13] Murray and Frijters, *Game of mates*; Krastev, *Shifting obsessions*, 59–67.
[14] Plunkitt and Riordon, *Plunkitt of Tammany Hall*, 5–6. [15] Krastev, *Shifting obsessions*, 7.
[16] Celarier, 'Privatization: A case study'; Naím, 'Corruption eruption'; Williamson, 'Short history of the Washington Consensus'.
[17] World Bank, *World development report 1997*, 15.
[18] Tanzi, 'Corruption around the world', 26.
[19] Reisenberg et al., 'Bad governance'.
[20] Abed and Gupta, *Governance, corruption*; Hough, *Corruption, anti-corruption*; Krastev, *Shifting obsessions*, ch. 1.
[21] Glynn et al., 'Globalization of corruption', 21.

then corruption rewarded insiders and crooks. The promise itself was a con: 'Not one of the democratic governments that launched market-oriented reforms ran on a platform of free trade, price liberalization, and privatization. The drastic reforms of elected governments almost uniformly surprised Latin American voters.'[22]

IMF and World Bank economists working on corruption were handicapped by theory. Their neoclassical models were driven by agent greed and their theories of asymmetric information endorsed cheating.[23] Subsequent decades of research on corruption have had little positive effect, perhaps even the opposite.[24] For the World Bank the touchstone of corruption was 'the abuse of public office for private gain'.[25] Corruption was governments' fault. However nuanced their findings, international agency economists typically endorsed marketising agendas. In 2000 the World Bank President declared: 'If you are against the structures of the sin that plague our world – corruption, nepotism, collusion, protectionism – you must go for structural adjustment, like it or not.'[26]

In 1970 the United States had a legacy of statutes which imposed a duty of integrity on public servants without defining it very precisely. From that decade onwards the courts worked to narrow its scope. In 1971 Lewis Powell, a lawyer for corporate tobacco, was raised to the Supreme Court by President Nixon. Two months earlier he had delivered a confidential document commissioned by the US Chamber of Commerce. It advocated a strategy of aggressive fightback against New Deal values in the media, universities, public opinion, among shareholders, and pointed out 'neglected opportunities in the courts'.[27] Supreme Court cases *McCormick* (1989) and *Sun Diamond* (1999) defined corruption narrowly as consisting only of quid pro quo, which paved the way for *Citizens United*.[28] If no executive action followed on a bribe, it no longer counted as corrupt.

[22] Naím, 'Latin America: post-adjustment blues', 135.
[23] Offer and Söderberg, *Nobel factor*, 26, 247–249.
[24] Krastev, *Shifting obsessions*; Hough, *Corruption, anti-corruption*.
[25] World Bank, 'Helping countries combat corruption', 8.
[26] Camdessus and Naím, 'A talk with Michael Camdessus', 35.
[27] Powell, 'Confidential memorandum'.
[28] Teachout, *Corruption in America*, chs. 12–13; idem, 'No such thing as a free Rolex'.

This narrowing of scope might be considered as being corrupt in itself.

Bob McDonnell, ex-governor of Virginia, was sentenced in 2015 to two years in prison for trading favours in return for $177,000 in loans, vacations, and gifts from a wealthy family friend.[29] In the Supreme Court McDonnell argued that gifts constituted free speech and the court concurred. Only official government action counted as payback. Favours did not count even in return for money or gifts. As in *Citizens United* money spoke and bribes were sanitised as free speech.[30] The Supreme Court was similarly relaxed about itself. In 2016 Justice Scalia died on a junket paid for by a business crony, one of several such trips and friendships. In at least two cases the host had been involved in a case before the court. Justice Thomas was not above suspicion either.[31]

Lower courts had already set the course. From the mid-1970s onwards, in a sequence of cases, New York regulators and courts shifted their rulings from the spirit of the law to its narrowly interpreted letter. Banks exploited loopholes to get around the ban on insider trading, took advantage of clients and traders, and worked to shape case law in their favour. Officials moved freely in and out of the firms that they regulated. In response to financial crises, collapses, swindles, bankruptcies, and scandals, regulators offered firms negotiated settlements which imposed modest penalties, with no admission of wrongdoing and unenforced promises to reform. Individual wrongdoers were punished only very rarely. Attempts by judges to enforce integrity were blocked by higher courts at the insistence of regulators.[32]

The United Kingdom also has corruption in high places. It is not often pay for play but that happens too. Several inquiries since the 1970s each issued similar detailed recommendations. Those of the first two were never implemented and not even debated in

[29] Steinhauer, 'Bob McDonnell, Ex-Governor of Virginia, is sentenced'.
[30] Liptak, 'Supreme Court vacates ex-Virginia governor's graft conviction'.
[31] Blum, 'Case for impeaching Clarence Thomas'; Burton, 'Antonin Scalia's death during secret junket'; Lindorff, 'Supreme court junket king'; *New York Times* editorial board, 'Justice and junkets'.
[32] Ally, 'Understanding financial wrongdoing'; Coffee, *Corporate crime and punishment*; Eisinger, *Chickenshit Club*; Garrett, *Too big to jail*; Keefe, 'Why corrupt bankers avoid jail'; Rakoff, 'The financial crisis'.

Parliament. Lower-level reports by the National Audit Office, the Audit Commission, and the Parliamentary Public Accounts Committee tend to be ignored with no official or media response.[33]

2.2 THE INTEGRITY REVOLUTION OF THE NINETEENTH CENTURY

If corruption is an improper partiality, then the solution is its opposite. Impartiality has emerged out of corruption once before, in the integrity revolution of the nineteenth century. What was it and how did it come to pass?

In the *ancien régimes* of eighteenth-century Europe, public office was a gift of patronage from the Crown or the Church, from whence it percolated down the ladder of authority. Once bestowed, patronage congealed into property. Public office was a licence for enrichment, an asset to be bought, sold, leased out, bequeathed, or held plurally with other ones. Obligations could be delegated for profit, 'having one duty done by one person whilst another enjoys the emoluments'.[34] Officials speculated with government's idle funds and lent them out privately. Some Members of Parliament were elected by 'rotten' or 'pocket' boroughs with few or captive voters. Other voters were bribed. Professors did no teaching, army commissions were sold and had to be paid for, Anglican clerics had 'livings' which could be bought, sold, given away, and contracted out. Church tithes were paid even by those who chose to worship elsewhere. Bishops sat in Parliament by right. Unelected notables governed the cities. Judges grew wealthy while lawyers drew out cases to swell their fees. Ministers of state, government officials, military contractors, the Bank of England, all had lucrative privileges protected by law. Government had become a bundle of private assets. Every country in Europe had its own variants

Reform came in two pulses; the first under the *ancien régime*, the second in the nineteenth century, and by 1870 it was complete across most of north-western Europe.[35] The method was to replace patronage with expertise. In 1831 an activist wrote: 'Intelligence, not patronage, is to form the pivot of public authority: the idea is a grand

---

[33] Doig, 'Politics and public sector ethics'. [34] Burke, *Speech*, 41. [35] Neild, *Public corruption.*

one, – it is worthy of the age, and we wait in hope to see it practically realized.'[36] Prussia, Austria, France, Britain, and most of the minor powers, reformed their public services, the judiciary, the armed forces, the Church, the universities, and the professions.[37]

Bureaucracy replaced patronage. What this entailed was explained by the German sociologist Max Weber.[38] Administration was no longer handed down as a personal privilege: it was undertaken by qualified and empowered officials, selected by competitive examination after a course of university-level study certified by diploma or degree. Competition was keen: in the Indian civil service every appointment held out 'nothing less than an honourable social position, and a comfortable independence for life',[39] not only material rewards, but also the prospect of an ethical calling and a profession. The model was first developed by reforming monarchs in Prussia, Denmark, and Austria. They expected total devotion. Joseph II of Austria, an 'enlightened despot', defined the official's vocation as requiring 'a burning enthusiasm for the good of the state and a complete renunciation of himself and of every comfort'.[40] Tenure was commonly for life. Officials were ordered by rank and took their lead from immediate superiors. Tasks were handled impartially in conformity with impersonal rules. Experience built up over years of service. A mastery of procedure and detail underpinned the discretion that officials acquired by virtue of their expertise.

This eighteenth-century innovation was adopted widely in the nineteenth, according to Weber, due to its 'purely technical superiority over all administrative forms'.

A strictly bureaucratic administration – especially a monocratic administration run by trained, individual *Beamte* [officials] – produces an optimal efficiency for precision, speed, clarity, command of case knowledge, continuity, confidentiality, uniformity, and tight subordination. This is in addition to minimization of friction and the costs associated with materials

---

[36] Wade, *Extraordinary black book,* vi.
[37] Main powers: Neild, *Public corruption*; Judson, *Habsburg Empire,* 58–62; minor ones: Rotberg, *Corruption cure,* ch. 7.
[38] Weber, 'Bureaucracy'. Written in 1911–13, published posthumously in 1921.
[39] Macaulay et al., 'Report on the Indian Civil Service', 120.
[40] In 1783. Judson, *Habsburg Empire,* 61.

and personnel. The opposite is true for all other forms of administration, such as collegial, honorary, or adjunct administration.[41]

For the same reasons, business corporations adopted similar command structures.[42]

In wartime, pretensions are exposed to brutal reality.[43] Following a century of military conflict in the eighteenth century, Europe had two more decades of warfare after the French Revolution. Imperatives of political survival drove a quest for efficiency.[44] Flimflam was brushed aside by necessity. In the nineteenth century, imperial ambitions and economic growth pushed the cities outwards. Paving, illumination, piped water, sewers, energy supply, and urban transport were needed. In Britain, evangelical moralising may have done something for integrity, as well as the Enlightenment quest for truth in scholarship and natural philosophy.[45]

Each country reformed at its own pace. Eighteenth-century Prussia strove to leverage the military weight of its middling economy and population. It adopted the disciplined form of standing army created in the previous century by Gustavus Adolphus of Sweden and Cromwell's New Model Army.[46] To support it, the Prussian kings built up a meritocratic corps of civilian officials with high privilege and social rank. A standing commission selected them by competitive examination. 'Hard work, sober living, thrift, honesty and careful accounting became official gospel in the Prussian state service', which offered attractive careers for the sons of landowners, officials, and merchants.[47] The courts underwent a similar reform. A second wave began on the rebound from defeat by Napoleon in 1806. Careers were thrown more open to talent, albeit socially exclusive and expensively educated. The machinery of government set up originally to support autocracy eventually broke free from it. Rulers lost authority to the competence of their officials.

In 1789 the *ancien régime* in France collapsed under the weight of privilege. For revenues, the king sold titles and public offices, a form

[41] Weber, 'Bureaucracy', 96. [42] Ibid., 83, 87; Chandler, *Visible hand*.
[43] Dixon, *Psychology of military incompetence*. [44] Neild, *Public corruption*.
[45] Halevy, *Philosophic radicalism*; Harling, 'Rethinking "Old Corruption"', 153–154; Mokyr, *Enlightened economy*.
[46] Roberts, *Cromwell's war machine*; Duffy, *Army of Frederick the Great*.
[47] Neild, *Public corruption*, 24.

of royal borrowing that had to be serviced with salaries and tax exemptions. The revolution that followed had an impulse to rationalise. Napoleon suppressed its excesses only to embark on some of his own, but he brought the rationalising impulse into a lasting settlement:

Centralized power; formalized rule by detailed laws and decrees; an imperial structure of government operated through prefects (the successors of the *intendants*) acting as guardians of law and order in their departments and implementing orders received from Paris; a large public service with all school teachers, the staff of universities and research institutes, judges and postmen on the payroll of the central government; and a professional civil service with a technocratic-cum-legal tradition, with education and training the key to entry. In short, a highly professional system of government.[48]

A set of selective post-graduate training institutions for officials was modelled on eighteenth-century military and technical academies. These *grandes écoles* ensured a common indoctrination and a high level of academic achievement among the elites. Their training, recruitment, and retention still followed highly selective patterns in the 1960s.[49]

In Britain, reform also went through two distinct phases. In the 1770s and 1780s the Whig opposition attacked mismanagement in the failed American war. In a brilliant speech in Parliament, Edmund Burke advocated a programme of 'economical reform' and set in motion a commission of inquiry which worked from 1780 to 1787. As Burke explained, the benefits of reform were widely diffused, while their cost fell on a powerful few who had the means and motives to resist.[50] As ever, inspiration came from the past. Reformers invoked a seventeenth-century idea of 'the public interest' (as opposed to the king's) as the norm for government office, of official corruption as a breach of the people's trust.[51] Alone among British revenue departments, the Excise (which administered the largest single source of revenue) had evolved an effective Weberian-type bureaucracy. The commission took it for its model.[52]

---

[48] Ibid., 42. [49] Fulton, 'The civil service'. [50] Burke, *Speech*.
[51] Harling, *Waning of 'Old Corruption'*, 47; Knights, 'Old Corruption', 13.
[52] Torrance, 'Social class and bureaucratic innovation'.

Subsequent wars with France provided new opportunities for enrichment. William Cobbett coined the term 'Old Corruption' for the web of entitlements of the British political-administrative elite, and John Wade listed them in their thousands in 850 pages of the *Extraordinary black book: An exposition of abuses in church and state, courts of law, representation, municipal and corporate bodies, with a precis of the house of commons past, present and to come* (1831). Unlike France, reform was gradual and spun out over decades.[53] Sinecures were abolished as their incumbents died out. The Church of England's tithes were bought out in the 1830s and pluralities reduced.

The Northcote–Trevelyan report of 1854 laid out the pattern of civil service reform. Instead of patronage it proposed competitive examinations in 'history, jurisprudence, political economy, modern languages, political and physical geography, and other matters, besides the staples of classics and mathematics'.[54] Ability would replace connections. Academic achievement was difficult to make and difficult to fake. But promotion by merit was never fully achieved. The intention was to create a body of public servants with core values of 'integrity, propriety, objectivity and appointment on merit, able to transfer its loyalty and expertise from one elected government to the next'.[55] Implementation was piecemeal but in retrospect the report was foundational.[56] Civil servants came to regard themselves as 'a true profession. We profess an ethic regulating our work; and we possess knowledge and know how specific to that work.'[57]

2.3 BUREAUCRACY AGAINST MODERNITY

Weberian bureaucracy came into conflict with two other agents of modernity, democracy and markets.[58] Nineteenth-century officials largely came out of the old elites: reform was meant to preserve social

---

[53] Harling, 'Rethinking "Old Corruption"'. [54] Northcote and Trevelyan, 'Report', 14.
[55] Hennessy, 'British Civil Service'.
[56] Reprinted in Fulton, 'The civil service', Appendix B; Lowe, *Official history*, vol.1, introduction, ch. 1.
[57] Derek Morrell, a senior civil servant, in 1969. Hennessy, *Whitehall*, 205.
[58] Lynn, 'Myth of the bureaucratic paradigm'; Thompson, 'Bureaucracy and democracy'; Van Riper, *Civil service*.

rank by other means.[59] When Northcote–Trevelyan replaced the dim with the bright they meant to reinforce privilege.[60] Civil service examinations (except for specialist roles) covered the academic syllabus in Britain, law and management ('cameralism') in Germany, and more specialised post-graduate training in France. At the time only a few went to university. Candidates studied the core texts of their culture and the most accomplished expositors were appointed: 'the youth who does best what all the ablest and most ambitious youths about him are trying to do well will generally prove a superior man'.[61] In its turn, the syllabus was adapted to the needs of bureaucracy.[62]

By placing reason above passion, Weber thought that bureaucracy came into potential conflict with democracy. He read in Thucydides of the conflict in Athens between aristocracy and democracy, how Alcibiades the demagogue harangued democracy into a bad war with Syracuse. In Germany such forebodings were prescient. Ostrogorski described how mass parties worked for leaders rather than followers. Michels formulated an 'iron law of oligarchy' – mass movements had to muster as hierarchies under leaders and office-holders.[63] For Weber, democracy did not signify the general will but a spectacle for the masses: 'Democracy tries to replace the arbitrary ordinances of the superior "Ruler" with the equally arbitrary rule by the citizens, which really means replacing the Ruler with the party bosses who then dominate the citizens.'[64]

Rule by credentialed and qualified experts also came into conflict with the market. Officials, wrote Weber, had an exalted 'calling' (*Beruf*), not a labour market contract of employment. In contrast, for the Austrian school of economics (hostile to bureaucracy), the market was unknowable and uncertain.[65] 'Spontaneous order' emerged out of market exchange. In Anglo-Saxon and French ('neoclassical') economic theory market exchange gave rise to an optimal order (i.e. even better) by means of all-knowing, self-seeking agents. Both doctrines regarded markets as templates for society. Neither had a role for government, except as an afterthought.

[59] Harling, *Waning of 'Old Corruption'*.
[60] Weber, 'Bureaucracy', 123; Lowe, *Official history*, vol. 1, 30–31.
[61] Macaulay, 'Report on the Indian civil service', 123. [62] Lowe, *Official history*, vol. 1, 30–31.
[63] Michels, *Political parties*; Ostrogorski, *Democracy*. [64] Weber, 'Bureaucracy', 125.
[65] Reinert, 'Austrian economics'; Introduction.

If market ideology rejected despotism (by no means always), it was in other respects no less conservative than bureaucracy. Its immoveable core was the sanctity of property.[66] Inheritance and initial endowment were ethically deserving and market payoffs too. Weberian bureaucracy is founded on probity, but the market norm is the opposite, 'let the buyer beware'. Cheating is permitted, but not being caught. In the asymmetric information version of market doctrine (I call it 'bad faith economics'), anything goes. The norm is opportunism, 'self-interest seeking with guile'.[67]

Weber pointed out that big business depended on bureaucracy no less than government. Corporate managers regarded themselves as having a similar calling (*Privatbeamte*). This internal command structure of business has puzzled economists: if competition is efficient, why is it not applied inside companies as well? why are firms hierarchical?[68] Weber wrote that command worked better with economies of scale, for example in the railways of his time. General Motors' annual turnover is more than twice as large as Bulgaria's GDP.

Orthodox economic theory disregards increasing returns to scale because it leads to monopoly.[69] But dominance by one or a few firms is common. In Chapter 1 we argued that the truly competitive domain is limited, that many of the firms even within that domain have large market power, and that a good deal of business activity requires government support.

Governments coerce. Officials do as they are told. Bureaucracy can be captured. In Nazi Germany and Soviet Russia, bureaucracies inflicted monstrous atrocities. Official power can expose people to insecurity and harm. After decades of abuses, the British East India Company (which governed that country for Britain as a franchise) sought legitimacy by means of integrity and established an honest and competent system of oppression.[70] Its reformed system of staff

---

[66] Friedman and Friedman, *Capitalism and freedom*, 161–162.
[67] Williamson, 'Opportunism and its critics', 97; Offer and Söderberg, *Nobel factor*, 164–169.
[68] Williamson and Winter, *Nature of the firm*.
[69] Weber, 'Bureaucracy', 95; Reinert, *How rich countries*, 5–7.
[70] Macaulay, 'Report on the Indian civil service'; Mason, *Men who ruled India*, vol. 2, *The guardians*.

selection complemented the Northcote and Trevelyan reform at home.[71]

In north western Europe official integrity was largely in place by 1870. What it takes to be corruption-free is administration by disinterested experts. They are qualified by means of impersonal procedures and are bound by written codes. Once in office, their proficiency is difficult to monitor, so they have to be trusted. Think of professors or judges. Trustworthiness is sustained by having something to lose. Hence, professional incentives are aligned with the future: career progression, job security, recognition and honours, a generous pension.

Expert authority commands an asymmetric power which is easy to abuse. It would be costly to match such opportunities with sufficiently high pay. Instead, experts are overseen by superiors and peers. Professionals submit to a dual authority, a chain of command, and a code of conduct. Violation can be punished with disgrace. At stake is the licence to practice and all that it stands for. Recruitment and promotion by merit is found to be associated with less corruption and more economic growth in many countries. Just paying officials more rarely had the same effect, even in poor countries.[72]

Professional identity implies a loyalty to something larger than oneself. In generalist training this is the ethical content of the literary, legal, and historical canon. Britain had a notion of gentility, of privilege justified by duty, of an inner superiority founded on self-restraint – at least that was the ideal. If bureaucracy upheld elite rule, at least it aspired to integrity and fairness.[73] In literary depiction a gentleman was expected to place duty ahead of personal interest.[74] In Germany righteousness rested on an education in law, in France on reason and science, on respect for the truth. To qualify was difficult, with a real chance of failure. Leonard Woolf for example, later husband of the writer Virginia and a luminous writer himself, underwent a long and arduous preparation at St. Paul's School and Trinity College Cambridge but still failed to enter the British home civil

---

[71] Fulton, 'The civil service', Appendix B.

[72] Barfort et al., 'Sustaining honesty in public service'; Charron et al, 'Careers, connections and corruption risks'; Evans and Rauch, 'Bureaucracy and growth'; Ornaghi, 'Civil service reforms'; Rauch and Evans, 'Bureaucratic structure and bureaucratic performance'.

[73] Mason, *English gentleman*. [74] Berberich, *Image of the English gentleman*, 10.

service in 1903. Instead, he excelled in his second choice as a colonial official in Ceylon.[75]

Once qualified and admitted, experts are committed (sometimes explicitly by oath) to a code of conduct. Officers to king and country, professors to disinterested truth, doctors to do no harm, judges to justice, officials to the public interest. Because they all have so much discretion, honesty is fundamental: a study in Denmark found that honest applicants self-select for public service, so that raising their salaries does not increase their honesty.[76]

In Britain in the 1880s the Fabian Society of left-leaning intellectuals (Beatrice and Sidney Webb, George Bernard Shaw, H. G. Wells) laid out a vision of government by disinterested experts, and with lasting effect. In his novel *A modern utopia* (1905) Wells depicted a society administered by an order of ascetic 'Samurai'. In his influential stratification scheme for post-war British society the sociologist John Goldthorpe named the two upper classes (out of seven) 'the service class'. The term came from the Austrian statesman-scholar Karl Renner, with a clear affinity to the Weberian model. By 1982, when Goldthorpe wrote, demand for impartial administration had expanded so much that the 'service class' accounted for almost a third of the male labour force in Britain and Europe. Many were severely under-qualified, not reliably expert, and not as grounded in righteousness as the nineteenth-century elites.[77] Its very success made this diluted elite a tempting target for attack.

---

[75] Woolf, *Growing*. [76] Barfort et al., 'Sustaining honesty in public service'.
[77] Goldthorpe, 'On the service class', 173–177.

CHAPTER 3

Plutocratic Blowback

3.1 DEMOCRACY AND CORRUPTION IN THE UNITED STATES

In the United States the forces of democracy and the market stood up to bureaucracy and integrity. Weber had American democracy in mind when he laid down his model. The country has a multitude of jurisdictions and separation of powers. In consequence it is more corrupt than other wealthy ones. Male suffrage came earlier than in Europe, at least among the whites. It was deformed, however, by 'machine politics' in the great immigrant cities. Tammany Hall in New York and its equivalents in Boston, Chicago, Philadelphia, and elsewhere harvested votes in immigrant communities in return for inclusion and an ear for grievances.[1] Party bosses skimmed off the outlay on civic services in shameless cronyism and grand corruption, with the petty kind also thrown in.[2] George Washington Plunkitt became rich by 'honest graft' (his term):

They didn't steal a dollar from the city treasury. They just seen their opportunities and took them ... The books are always all right ... All they [critics] can show is that the Tammany heads of departments looked after their friends, within the law, and gave them what opportunities they could to make honest graft.[3]

The decline of corruption only began at the point where it ended in Europe, around 1870, and continued up to the First World War.[4] A delegation of American urban reformers and businessmen steamed

---

[1] Ostrogorski, *Democracy*, vol. 2, chs. 6–7; Steffens, *Shame of the cities*.
[2] Garrigues, *You're paying for it*; Glaeser, 'Public ownership'.
[3] Plunkitt and Riordon, *Plunkitt of Tammany Hall*, 5.
[4] Glaeser and Goldin, 'Corruption and reform: Introduction', 13–18.

57

over to Britain in 1907 to a see whether private or public ownership was better for urban services. By disposition they inclined to private except for water and sewage, 'when the temptation for profit might produce disastrous results'.[5] This begs the question as to why temptation should be any less elsewhere. Following the logic of franchise, they wanted business monopolies to be disciplined by a right of compulsory purchase for the city. The United States eventually settled on private regulated monopolies (themselves prone to regulatory capture), and the UK followed after a very long delay in the 1980s.[6]

It took the slow slog of progressive reform and the New Deal to achieve a modicum of integrity. Lawlessness remained, especially in the South, in the form of bootlegging (distilling untaxed liquor) and lynching. Federal civil service reform was fitful and slow – officials had lower status, prospects and pay than in Europe. In the upper reaches of government administration, thousands of posts were kept for the incoming President's patronage.[7]

The most blatant preference for democracy and money, and disdain for expertise and permanence, was the practice of electing judges for fixed terms, i.e. shifting them out of the bureaucratic order and into the political one. Currently judges are elected in thirty-nine states. Elected judges rely on donors to finance their campaigns and often defer to business.[8] Corporations invest heavily in their election. In 2004, for example, more was spent in the race for a single seat on the Illinois Supreme Court than on half the US Senate races. In one case, two Pennsylvania judges pleaded guilty to accepting $2.6m in kickbacks for sending juveniles to private prisons.[9] In a notorious case the CEO of a coal company in West Virginia spent $3m on election ads against a State Supreme Court Justice. The incumbent lost and the winner swung a decision that overturned a $50m verdict against the company. He would not recuse himself.[10] That this was

[5] National Civic Federation, *Municipal and private operation*, 23.
[6] Offer, 'Why has the public sector grown so large'.
[7] Neild, *Public corruption*, 48–51; Van Riper, *Civil service*.
[8] Associated Press, 'Supreme court tells judges'; Baumann, 'Permission to encroach the bench'; *New York Times* editorial board, 'Judges and justice for sale'; Shepherd and Kang, 'Skewed justice'; Smith, 'Continued stealth takeover of the courts'.
[9] Urbina, 'Suit names two judges'. [10] Baumann, 'Permission to encroach the bench'.

wrong was decided in the US Supreme Court in *Capteron vs. Massey* (2009) but only by a partisan 5–4 majority.[11] The US Chamber of Commerce spent at least $100m to elect judges, in line with the plan it commissioned from Lewis Powell (who became Supreme Court Justice soon afterwards) to turn around universities, the media and the courts in favour of business. In the 1970s an emerging 'law and economics' movement argued that economic efficiency (i.e. market outcomes) trumped other judicial priorities. The right-wing Olin Foundation paid for scores of university chairs and departments to disseminate this pro-business teaching.[12] This is the spirit in which the Supreme Court is appointed today. *Citizens United* has lifted the limits on contributions to judicial races as well, which are now in the gift of deep pockets. Judicial independence is a form of the rule by experts. The clamour against it is heard in Britain as well. In 2016 the *Daily Mail* shouted, 'Enemies of the People' when the Supreme Court ruled that the Brexit referendum result required parliamentary approval.[13] More than 800 lawyers, including former judges and academics, have sent a letter to the press to protest against the verbal abuse of judges by the Prime Minister and the Home Secretary.[14]

American democracy is also rife with voter suppression. Drawing boundaries to bias the vote and disqualifying the other side's supporters have both withstood judicial scrutiny. In *Shelby County vs. Holder* (2013) the Supreme Court 'gutted the central provision of the Voting Rights Act and opened the door to rampant voter suppression, most of it targeted at Democratic voters'.[15] In a 2014 survey of electoral integrity worldwide, the United States ranked 26th out of 73, the lowest score among Western nations. In 2019, it was ranked 57th out of 167.[16] Under British and American first-past-the-post systems it is common for governments to be formed with a minority of the popular vote.

[11] Associated Press, 'Supreme court tells judges'.
[12] Smith, 'Continued stealth takeover of the courts'; Smith, 'William Black'.
[13] Slack, 'Enemies of the people'. [14] Bowcott, 'Lawyers call for apology'.
[15] *New York Times* editorial board, 'The Republican party's Supreme Court'.
[16] Norris et al., 'The year in elections 2013'; Norris and Grömping, 'Electoral integrity worldwide'.

3.2 FIDUCIARY SELL-OUT

Another form of corruption, fiduciary sell-out, arises when expert professionals take advantage of lay clients. It is common in finance.[17] Mortgages were mis-sold in the United States and Britain, albeit in different circumstances. After the financial crisis of 2008, financial institutions and intermediaries in the United States successfully resisted the imposition of a fiduciary duty towards their clients.[18] Fiduciary obligation can also be misdirected. Auditing firms appear to favour their corporate clients over the investors that it is their nominal duty to protect. Arthur Andersen, a 'Big Five' accountancy firm, was forced to disband after covering for Enron corporation, and for its own malpractices. The remaining Big Four exemplify the franchise system, their cartel founded on the legal requirement for accounts to be audited.[19] These firms routinely sent staff to undertake free work for MPs and for the three main political parties in the UK.[20]

Professional vows and market incentives do not mix well, as shown in the record of American healthcare and its divergence from European norms of universal access. In subsequent chapters market-liberal norms will be shown to impede education, pensions, and housing for all. Healthcare, another pillar of the welfare state, also relies on long-term provision. Market relations in the health sector rely on a franchise which depends on monopoly, subsidy and revenue guarantee.

Doctors vow to do no harm, and this has made it easier for society to grant them a monopoly of medical practice.[21] In return for this power, the healing professions tried to refrain from abusing it: 'The organizational culture of medicine used to be dominated by the ideal of professionalism and voluntarism, which softened the underlying

---

[17] Ally, 'Understanding financial wrongdoing'; Anon. and Harper, *License to steal*; Lewis, *Liar's poker*; Martens, 'Insiders tell all'.

[18] Duckworth, 'Isn't honesty the best policy?'; Eichelberger, 'Lobbyists secretly wrote house Dem's letter'; *New York Times* editorial board, 'Rules to make retirement investment safer'; idem, 'Democrats undermine efforts to protect retirement savers'.

[19] Brooks, *Bean counters*; Syal et al., '"Big four" accountants "use knowledge of Treasury to help rich"'.

[20] Sabbagh, 'KPMG abandons controversial lending of researchers'.

[21] Arrow, 'Uncertainty and the welfare economics of medical care'.

acquisitive activity.'[22] From a market point of view professional power is a restrictive practice. Market liberals do not believe in good faith or the common good. Their solution to unequal power is to place the duty of care on the patient, and let the buyer beware (*caveat emptor*). The vendor's duty is only to himself.

In 1962 Milton Friedman advocated free entry into medical practice.[23] By the 1970s he was one of the two most cited economists in the world and likely the most famous.[24] In *Goldfarb vs. Virginia State Bar* (1975), the Supreme Court ruled that professional codes of practice were not exempt from anti-trust. The case applied to the legal profession, but doctors embraced the ruling too and relaxed the anti-competitive strictures in their codes.[25] *Goldfarb vs. Virginia* undermined the professional code of practice, a core component of the integrity settlement. Competition was not enhanced: the profession continued to control standards and admission. But fees were quick to rise: American doctors are the best paid in the world by far.[26]

When prices are set by corporations there is less room for a duty of care. At the point of contact with the patient, however, there is an incentive for indulgent, lucrative and futile overtreatment.[27] Unlike the doctors' ethical code, health insurance providers retained their immunity from anti-trust, even as they came to dominate many of their territories.[28] Healthcare providers increasingly charged as much as the patient could bear, and more than that for the one-seventh of the population who remained uncovered. Obama's healthcare reform reduced that proportion somewhat.

With no restraint doctors can be venal. Top ones get kickbacks from drug companies and ordinary ones benefit too.[29] 'Marketing and administration' is by far the largest cost in drug production. Salesmen press drugs for purposes for which they are not approved: in

[22] Starr, *Social transformation of American medicine*, 448.
[23] Friedman and Friedman, *Capitalism and freedom*, ch. 9.
[24] Offer and Söderberg, *Nobel factor*, 111, 133.
[25] Relman, 'What market values are doing'; idem, *Second opinion*, ch. 1; Friedman opposed professional monopolies but had no compunction about corporate ones.
[26] Laugesen and Glied, 'Higher fees paid to US physicians'. [27] Gawande, 'Letting go'.
[28] American Medical Association, 'Competition in health insurance'.
[29] Healy, *Pharmageddon*; Kassirer, *On the take*; Nguyen et al., 'Dollars for docs'; Ornstein and Thomas, 'Memorial Sloan Kettering leaders violated conflict-of-interest'; Pear, 'U.S. to force drug firms to report money'.

2017 some 72,000 deaths were attributed to the wrongful prescription of opioids. Overall life expectancy in the United States is declining.[30] Drug companies slant and even ghost-write medical research. Doctors commission tests from labs which they own. Medicare, the public health insurance agency for the elderly, is overcharged. Anti-fraud control is outsourced to private contractors who sometimes cheat themselves.[31] American healthcare is 'criminogenic'.[32] Insurers and doctors discriminate among patients, doctors overcharge, insurance companies undercompensate, patients resell subsidised drugs.[33] Fraudulent billings alone are estimated by the Federal Bureau of Investigation (FBI) to cost between 3 and 10 per cent of total health expenditures or approximately 0.5–1.7 per cent of national income.[34]

Healthcare costs in the United States are at a level which threatens macroeconomic stability. At around 17 per cent of GDP they are almost twice as high per head as in comparable countries (and much more than that in absolute terms) but outcomes are the worst among the top developed countries (Figure 3.1).[35] American medicine shows how market incentives can upend the norm of disinterested expertise.

3.3 ONSLAUGHT ON EXPERTISE: THE NEW PUBLIC MANAGEMENT

In the name of democracy and markets, the neoliberal reaction of the 1980s set out to replace official expertise with self-interest, cunning, and flair. It strove to diminish the scope of government except as a safeguard for business. Politicians (both right-wing and centre-left) denigrated official integrity, knowledge, and competence. If the objective was to capture control for a privileged few, it has largely succeeded.

[30] Angell, 'Opioid nation'; Case and Deaton, *Deaths of despair*, ch. 9.
[31] Dartmouth Atlas Working Group, 'Dartmouth Atlas of Health Care'; Forden, 'Why Medicare can't catch the fraudsters'; Gawande, 'The cost conundrum'; Leap, *Phantom billing*; Lefcourt, 'A corporate "culture of fraud"'; Pope and Selten, 'Public debt tipping point', 19–22.
[32] Leap, *Phantom billing*, ix, 3, 11.
[33] Pear, 'Report on Medicare cites prescription drug abuse'; Rashbaum, 'A $250 million fraud', and reader comments; Smith, 'Are cheating doctors running bill scams'; Terhune, 'Many hospitals, doctors offer cash discount'.
[34] Leap, *Phantom billing*, ix, 3, 11. [35] Offer, 'Warrant for pain', fig. 1, table 1.

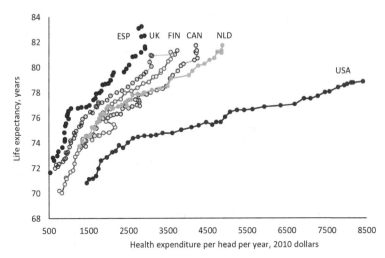

Figure 3.1 Life expectancy at birth and health expenditure per capita in six
countries 1970–2015.
Source: Roser, 'Link between health spending and life expectancy'.

Public administration presents a 'trilemma', a triple dilemma,
a trade-off among effective governance, democratic responsiveness,
and competitive market efficiency. Weberian bureaucracy is unavoid-
ably elitist. But it provides 'some degree of stability, legality, predict-
ability and continuity to a country'.[36] Democracy cares for equity,
even at the cost of efficiency and probity. It also values integrity – and
achieved it for much of the twentieth century.[37] For bad reasons and
good, voters remain a long way from power. How to give everybody
a voice, and is everyone competent to use it? Voters delegate to
politicians, and politicians must delegate too. Markets provide
a third handle. If democracy is equitable in theory, the market is
efficient in theory. But efficiency is a delusion: the term is used in
economics in a technical sense and only applies under impossible
conditions. It does not mean that markets guarantee more for less.[38]

[36] Pierre and Rothstein, 'Reinventing Weber', 410.
[37] Argued by Johnston, *Corruption, contention and reform.*
[38] Offer and Söderberg, *Nobel factor*, 18–19, 181–182.

Table 3.1 *Corruption instances reported in* Private Eye, *two issues every year, 1975–2011*

	Parliament	Public–private	Local govt.	Public bodies	Law & order	Govt. depts.	Total
Numbers	273	264	204	193	76	38	1,048
Per cent	26.0	25.2	19.5	18.4	7.3	3.6	100

Source: Private Eye, two issues a year (one each in March and November). Compiled for me by Danyal Arnold.

Market doctrines do not aspire to equality or honesty. Whether they can even work independently of bureaucracy is our next question.

First, some words of caution: corruption is not captured in official datasets. The most popular measure (Transparency International's corruption perception index) is based on an annual survey of business people's perceptions. Other indices of corruption are also indirect, as they have to be.[39] We rely on the press and on public-interest reports from non-governmental organisations (NGOs) and government. Some social scientists dismiss journalism as hearsay (for others it is 'the first draft of history'). Journalists aspire to ethical norms and newspapers are legally bound to tell the truth. Strict libel laws in the UK see to that, though maybe less so in the United States. *The Financial Times, The Guardian, The Times,* occasionally the *Daily Telegraph,* are the sources used here for Britain, and the *New York Times* for the United States.[40] The British satirical magazine *Private Eye* reports more than twenty instances of corruption every fortnight. It has beaten off libel suits time and again. Summary findings over more than three decades are presented in Table 3.1. Most instances of corruption occur in Parliament, followed closely by the private–public interface and local government. Very few take place in ministries, thus confirming that Weberian bureaucracies stand up to corruption. *Private Eye* provides about 350 instances of credible, newsworthy corruption reports a year for the UK.

[39] Hough, *Corruption, anti-corruption,* 16–20. [40] Copies have been kept of every item cited.

The dismal 1970s reflected badly on Weberian expertise. Inflation, de-industrialisation, economic stagnation, industrial unrest, war in Vietnam and terrorism in Northern Ireland all acted to discredit social-democratic regimes, and carried Thatcher and Reagan into power. Once in power it was easy to blame a hidebound civil service, class-ridden financial institutions, obstructive trade unions, haughty professionals. Business was also lacklustre but that did not count. The Thatcher whirlwind originated in North America with its culture of freewheeling individualism. In the words of Lincoln Steffens, the gilded age muckraker: 'The spirit of graft and of lawlessness is the American spirit . . . The typical business man is a bad citizen.'[41]

In the UK version the vision was 'liberationist': the 'full potential of business energies released and stimulated for the social good, through the operation of a free-market economy, with a minimum of state control and a maximum of resources in private, not public hands'.[42] The ideas came from several different sources, from Hayek's Mont Pèlerin Society and its British offshoot the Institute of Economic Affairs, from an energetic minority of business leaders, and from ideologues inside the Conservative Party.[43]

Government, said Reagan, is the problem and not the solution. It should recast itself as a business. Once elected Thatcher appointed 'a hatchetman', Derek Rayner, Joint Managing Director of Marks & Spencer, to knock heads together by means of an 'efficiency unit'.[44] In America word went out that the next big thing was 'entrepreneurial government'.[45] The movement counted on the inducement of managerial payoffs, implying that ability was otherwise withheld. It distrusted and even vilified the experienced civil servant. The archetypal mandarin Sir Humphrey Appleby appeared on television for twenty-one episodes of the serial 'Yes, Minister' between 1980 and 1984 and sixteen more ('Yes, Prime Minister') between 1986 to 1988, frustrating reform with his smooth command of procedure. Thatcher extended distrust to teachers, academics, doctors, and lawyers. With no one to trust, the movement worked to diminish other sources of

[41] Steffens, *Shame of the cities*, 12, 16. [42] Boswell and Peters, *Capitalism in contention*, 17.
[43] Cockett, *Thinking the unthinkable*.
[44] Haddon, 'Reforming the civil service'; for the term 'hatchetman', ibid., 6; Hennessy, *Whitehall*, ch. 14.
[45] Osborne and Gaebler, *Reinventing government*, xix.

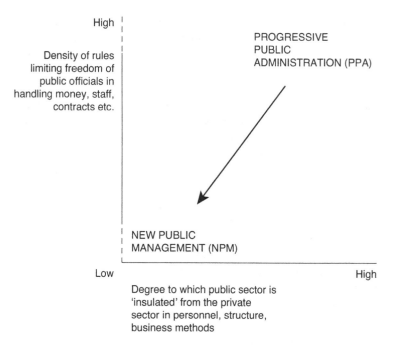

Figure 3.2 From Weberian bureaucracy to the New Public Management.
Source: Dunleavy and Hood, 'From old public administration', 10.

independent authority, local government and universities, to replace professional and administrative hierarchies with quasi-markets driven by incentives of performance rewards.

Almost from the outset it set out to downgrade the Weberian machine by replacing long-term career incentives with short-term performance targets and bonuses for delivery. This protean movement has gone under the title of 'the New Public Management'.[46] It is captured nicely in the diagram in Figure 3.2.

Instead of a ministerial-departmental hierarchy of accountability, public services were spun out into autonomous ('Next Step') agencies, packaged for privatisation, responding to targets, with managers driven by pay. Users were no longer entitled citizens but 'customers'

---

[46] Christensen and Lægreid, *New public management*; Ferlie et al., *Oxford handbook of public management*.

to win over from the competition.[47] Civil servants were placed in an adversarial relation with the citizens they served. For example, the Child Support Agency was set up in 1991 in order to get separated fathers to pay for their children. Generous performance incentives for successive directors failed to overcome resistance from the parents.[48]

In the Weberian model expertise built up slowly through qualification, experience, a record of competence, minutes of deliberation, impartiality, honesty, and commitment. It drew on open science, technology and published data. In Weber's teaching, charismatic leaders were followed by bureaucrats. The New Public Management reversed this sequence: rational management reverted to charisma. Despite their technocratic trappings the methods used had an opacity akin to magic: what counted was not procedure but results. Objectives were achieved by means of protean leadership, personality, private knowledge, and confidential deal-making. A good manager could master anything (not all that different, it should be admitted, from the versatility claimed for Weberian mandarins). No longer deliberate and genteel, the culture became abrasive, assertive, and adversarial. Tony Blair moved from Cabinet government to huddles on the sofa.[49] If lip service was still paid to integrity, the reward, as under 'Old Corruption', was private gain with no apologies.

Government and private interests intermingled. Private-sector managers embarked on stints in the public service alongside officials and even in charge of them. Officials left early for private employment. Thousands of military officers joined arms firms. High-flying careers were no longer a lifetime vocation but a succession of short spells in government, the academy, NGOs and business.[50] A 'revolving door' between Whitehall and the private sector operated both ways. Hundreds of the most senior civil servants went into corporate employment after truncated careers. Their counterparts in business came for periods in Whitehall, sometimes to draft contracts

[47] Lowe and Pemberton, *Official history*, vol. 2, chs. 5–7; Panchamia and Thomas, 'Next steps initiative'.
[48] King and Crewe, *Blunders of our governments*, 83–94 and passim.
[49] Hastings, 'The sofa government of Blairism'; Oborne, *Triumph of the political class*, 144–151; Rawnsley, *End of the party*, 287–292.
[50] Davis, *Reckless opportunists*.

with their own firms.[51] Senior procurement officials even worked part-time in the private sector. There was a palpable shock when this came to light.[52] More than half of the top 200 posts in the civil service were filled from the outside.[53] Every government accounting unit was given a board on the corporate model, staffed with hundreds of 'non-executive directors' drawn from business, and placed in positions to acquire inside knowledge.[54] Ministers brazenly handed out these directorships to political supporters and party donors.[55] In September 2020, Conservative Health Secretary Matt Hancock exercised ministerial discretion to appoint his lover Gina Coladangelo to a paid directorship of this kind.[56]

In the United States revolving doors were even more accommodating. Every incoming President appoints thousands of officials. Notionally non-partisan think tanks (including the august Brookings Institution) are funded by corporations, and look after donors' interests.[57] Secretaries of the Treasury come out of Wall Street. Financial firms pay large secret bonuses to senior staff who make a temporary sacrifice to go into government.[58] At the Securities and Exchange Commission officials moved in and out of the firms they scrutinised, and the Chair, Mary Jo White, was accused by Elizabeth Warren, the Democratic Senator, of 'extremely disappointing' leadership, with page after page listing cosy understandings with finance.[59]

Under the New Public Management budgets were meant to be transparent, with costs attributed to outputs not inputs, and continuous monitoring of results. Organisations were seen as clusters of low-trust principal–agent relationships rather than fiduciary ones. Purchasing (both internal and external) replaced planning and provision, with procurement open indiscriminately to public agencies, firms and

[51] Barret, 'Fixing the revolving door'; Brooks and Hughes, 'Public servants, private paydays'; Hopkins et al., 'MoD staff and thousands of military officers'; Quinn, 'Dozens of arms firm employees on MoD secondments'; Wilks, 'Revolving door'.
[52] Syal and Walker, 'Cameron's "insurgents" under scrutiny'. [53] Wilks, 'Revolving door', 33.
[54] Ibid.; Wighton, 'Greensill risks long-term damage'.
[55] Grylls and Wright, 'Tories make donors and friends directors'.
[56] *Express & Star*, 'Row reignited over appointment'.
[57] Lipton and Williams, 'Researchers or corporate allies?'; Lipton et al., 'Think tank scholar or corporate consultant?'
[58] Dayen, 'Wall Street pays bankers to work in government'.
[59] Ally, 'Financial wrongdoing', ch. 10; Project on Government Oversight, 'Dangerous liaisons'; Warren, 'Letter to Mary Jo White'.

NGOs.[60] Expertise was hollowed and sourced out. 'The Department of Transport spent 70% of its total staff costs on consultants; the figure for Education was over 50% and for the Home Office 40%.'[61] Whitehall, said a minister, was infantilised by its reliance on consultants.[62] Consultants earned billions from overseas aid and raked it in from Brexit and Covid.[63] Price Waterhouse, an accounting firm, had a contract from the regulator to assess water pricing, and also audited water supply firms and advised them. Water bills have risen about 40 per cent in real terms since privatisation.[64] The 'commissioning state' lost its capacity to specify purchases and monitor their quality. Ministry of Defence officials routinely resigned and came back as consultants.[65] One reason for outsourcing is that when civil service lost its expertise, power passed back to the ministers, and management consultants were not bound by the civil servants' independence, impartiality and the professional commitment to the public interest. The author of 'Yes, Minister' later rued the effect of his television series.[66]

Despite the fetish of results, no systematic performance audit ever took place, and only rarely for individual projects. The New Public Management had promised 'a government that works better and costs less'. This has proven difficult to measure. The best effort so far has found that:

UK central government 'cost a bit more and worked a bit worse' over the thirty years considered here [to 2014]. That conclusion is strikingly at odds both with the heady drumbeat of political and managerial rhetoric surrounding successive makeovers of central government and with the common academic view that NPM and many of the changes that went along with it had major consequences (positive or negative) for government performance.[67]

This is in line with a similar finding that privatisation has made little difference to productivity and efficiency (Introduction), the reason being that neither ownership nor management incentives have much

---

[60] Dunleavy and Hood, 'From old public administration', 9. [61] Wilks, 'Revolving door', 36.
[62] Dunhill and Syal, 'Whitehall "infantilised"'; Craig and Brooks, *Plundering the public sector*.
[63] Greenwood and Kennedy, 'Management consultancy firms reap the rewards'; Jolly and Syal, 'Consultant fees'; Syal, 'Brexit drives government consultancy fees'.
[64] Plimmer and Pickard, 'PwC's role in advising Ofwat'.
[65] Norton-Taylor, 'Ministry of Defence cuts programme'. [66] Chorley, 'Yes minister creator'.
[67] Hood and Dixon, *A government that worked better*, 183.

effect on performance. How well an enterprise performs depends on middle-ranking managers or technicians who face the same incentives under all systems. Public service costs actually rose in those three decades, mostly due to outsourcing and private provision.[68]

Integrity itself became a performance target. An external scaffolding of integrity rose up with at least fifteen different bodies operating at national level as ethical watchdogs. In 2010 an Act of Parliament finally placed the civil service 'and its core values of integrity, honesty, objectivity and impartiality' on a statutory footing.[69] This was worthy of King Canute commanding the waves to recede. A round of civil service reforms in 2011–15 exemplify the notions involved and their unintended consequences.[70] Civil servants were no longer the generalists of yore, but mostly social science graduates imbued with the 'me-first' doctrines of rational choice. The reforms were inspired by the same 'liberationist' cravings, namely to make the civil service more like a private corporation, but the minister in charge (Francis Maude) admitted cheerfully that 'I don't know how all this gets to happen'.[71] Every post in the civil service would be thrown open to competition to create a marketplace in talent, and to encourage lateral movement within departments and beyond. The bottom 10 per cent of civil servants would be disciplined, hectored, and maybe sacked. Within seven years the effects were evident: no promotion in post, hence no reward for performance – for promotion it was necessary to compete sideways for another post. Turnover increased to as high as 20 per cent a year, and higher in some departments, with the consequent loss of expertise and institutional memory.[72]

Why then is the civil service still in place? If reformers were in earnest, why did they fail to sweep it away? Maude introduced his reforms by saying how much he admired the tradition of 'permanence, political impartiality and meritocracy'.[73] Weber said that there was no other way to do it. The public service that emerged from the New Public Management reforms was controlled by a thin layer at the top

---

[68] Ibid. [69] Heywood, 'Integrity management', 475. [70] Thanks here to Damien Shannon.
[71] Maude, 'Speech to civil servants'.
[72] Hood and Dixon, *A government that worked better*, 163–173; Sasse and Norris, 'Moving on'.
[73] Maude, 'Speech to civil servants', 2.

(politicians and senior officials) moving from post to post, coming in from business, leaving for the private sector, not staying long enough to master briefs, getting out before being found out.[74] The real work, in both the civil service and in its outsourced and offshored satellites, was done by demoralised functionaries bedevilled by performance targets, intimidated by managers and ministers, with incentives to look after themselves, not their assignments.[75] Since there is no other way to do the work, it tends to be done badly, hence the endless sequence of policy failures, of which the PFI described in Chapter 1 is one instance, and Covid-19 management the latest one.[76] It is telling that the only organisations in Britain to come out of Covid with credit were Oxford University which developed a vaccine, and the NHS which delivered it efficiently and rapidly. The costly private sector 'track and trace' organisation was a dismal failure.

3.4 CORRUPTION AT THE TOP

Politicians are not bound by the same codes of impartiality as their officials. In English-speaking societies the two main parties have largely been captured for the business drive to weaken government and to hollow out its machinery.[77]

Robert Rubin, former US Treasury secretary [under Clinton], helped introduce a law that allowed banks to merge with insurance firms, something lobbied for by Citibank. He left the Treasury the day after the law was passed and, three months after that, was hired by – you guessed it – Citibank. He earned $126 million (£91 million) over eight years as the bank loaded up on risk, then used his connections to secure $45 billion in taxpayer bailouts when it failed.[78]

Under President Trump, propriety appears to have been discarded altogether: 'over 200 companies, special-interest groups and foreign

---

[74] Davis, *Reckless opportunists*; in the USA, Frank, *Listen, liberal*; Oborne, *Triumph of the political class*.
[75] Boffey, 'Public sector workers need "discipline and fear"'.
[76] King and Crewe, *Blunders of our governments*.
[77] Chayes, *Everybody knows*; Farnsworth, 'British corporate welfare state'; Geoghegan, *Democracy for sale*; Mayer, *Dark money*; Oborne, *Triumph of the political class*, 151–153; Wilks, *Political power of the business corporation*; Wilks, 'The corporate elite'.
[78] Seyd, 'Our economy is increasingly sick'.

governments ... patronized Mr. Trump's properties while reaping benefits from him and his administration'.[79] In Britain today, a government minister fast-tracks government hardship money to his prosperous constituency and boasts about it, he signs off planning approval worth £45 million to a Tory donor in defiance of official advice. A London mayor favours his undeclared mistress with grants and speeches. He is already Prime Minister when she spills the beans. He raises government cronies to the House of Lords, and his closest adviser breaks Covid lockdown rules with impunity. Nothing happens. Sleaze becomes the norm.[80] In the Covid-19 crisis propriety was cast to the wind and vast procurement contracts were awarded without tender to a 'chumocracy' of ministerial cronies.[81]

The great and the good are not above petty corruption either. In a scandal of March 2010, five former New Labour ministers (then still MPs) agreed to work in secret for a fictitious political lobbying firm for fees of up to £5,000 per day. A former transport minister described himself as a cab for hire, while a former defence minister looked forward to 'sort of translating my knowledge and contacts about sort of international scene into something that bluntly makes money'.[82] Four other former ministers were implicated during those years, two from New Labour and two Tories.[83] In 2009 the media were full of the parliamentary expenses scandal. Most MPs made claims that were fraudulent, exaggerated, inappropriate, or grotesque. Improprieties extended over accommodation, tax avoidance and evasion, overclaiming for food, and misuse of the 'no receipt' upper limit of £250. Large sums were repaid, apologies were made, inquiries were launched and dropped, and a few offenders went to prison.[84] Tony Blair emerged from office a millionaire many times over, while Gordon Brown was the highest earner in Parliament, at

---

[79] Confessore et al., 'The swamp that Trump built'.
[80] Murphy, 'Robert Jenrick says he regrets'; Parris, 'Smirking ministers don't care'.
[81] Bradley et al., 'Waste, negligence and cronyism'; GB NAO, 'Investigation into government procurement'; Kinder et al., 'Watchdog criticises government'; Pegg, 'Fifth of UK Covid contracts'.
[82] Quotes and list of newspaper sources, Wikipedia, '2010 cash for influence scandal'.
[83] Helm and Syal, 'Storm over Blunkett role'; Newell et al., 'Jack Straw and Malcolm Rifkind'.
[84] Daily Telegraph, 'The complete expenses files'; Wikipedia, 'United Kingdom parliamentary expenses scandal'.

close to £1m a year.[85] The Clintons' moneymaking is legendary, while even the civic-minded Obama yielded to the lure of $400,000 per speech, his annual salary in the White House. Of recent US presidents, Carter alone has resisted.[86]

Senior civil servants were not immune. The watchguard of official probity, the Auditor General, practised grand corruption on a grand scale. Shielded by the freedom from oversight accorded to his office to ensure its independence, he wined, dined, and travelled overseas in luxury, often with his wife, with the tab being picked up by the department and by private firms. Taxes on these benefits were also paid by the office. He frequently gave the pass to New Labour projects, including the PFI, and the academies described in the next chapter. 'The man with the job of preventing taxpayer's money being wasted was in fact wasting it on himself.'[87] Despite being outed he was never brought to book. The financial ombudsman, protector of the little man (but funded by the banks), showed a systematic bias against the million complaints it received every year.[88] The accountancy regulator was captured by the firms he oversaw.[89] Heads of the Serious Fraud Office gave excessive pay-offs to retiring executives and tried to cover their tracks.[90]

Mark Britnell, Director General of Commissioning in the Department of Health, moved to work for a company bidding for health contracts three months after leaving, and at least three departmental contracts followed for his new company. His successor did not even require approval for the same move a year later.[91] Dave Hartnett, Director of Her Majesty's Revenue and Customs, left before retirement age after making indulgent tax deals with several large corporations. He then took up posts with two of the firms he had dealt with.[92]

[85] Malnick et al., 'Revealed'; Pickard, 'Former foreign secretaries caught'.
[86] Lynch, 'Clinton's accumulation of wealth'; Shear and Kelly, 'Obama balances civic-minded side with lure'.
[87] Brooks, 'The Bourn complicity'.
[88] Jones and Hurley, 'Financial ombudsman "sided with banks"'.
[89] Frean, 'Accountancy watchdog should be scrapped'; Marriage, 'UK accounting regulator'.
[90] Kelly, 'Bosses at Fraud Office used secret emails'.
[91] Barrett, 'Fixing the revolving door', 5; Brooks and Hughes, 'Public servants, private paydays, 21.
[92] Brooks and Hughes, ibid., 24; Houlder, 'Did light touch tax become soft touch?'; Neville, 'Deloitte appoints official criticised over "sweetheart" tax deals'.

As this book went to press, a new scandal emerged, involving Prime Minister David Cameron and Cabinet Secretary Jeremy Heywood, which might have been commissioned for this chapter. In 2012 Heywood was permanent secretary of the Cabinet Office and close to the Prime Minister. He promoted a private–public scheme whereby his previous American employer (the same Citibank) would discount supplier invoices, i.e. pay their government invoices early at a discount and get full payment from the government ('supply chain finance'). This lucrative scheme, a classic 'franchise' for a government-secured revenue flow, was promoted by a crony of Heywood's, a young Australian financier (Lex Greensill) whom he had met at Citibank. Overriding civil service objections, Greensill was given official status ('Crown agent') as an adviser with a desk in the Prime Minister's office, and the scheme went ahead, without tender, for pharmacy invoices to the NHS in the first instance. Cameron formally endorsed it in a public event. Eventually it was transferred from Citibank to Greensill's own company, which subsequently employed the Prime Minister and gave him stock options after he resigned. Another crony, former head of the Crown Commercial Service, Bill Crothers, began to work for Greensill while still a civil servant, and later became a director in Greensill's bank. Cameron lobbied four ministers to support Greensill and its borrowers, with some measure of success. Greensill collapsed in March 2021 and Cameron never got to cash in his options.[93] This scandal is still unfolding as I write. In the meantime, the current Prime Minister is embroiled in a scandal regarding clandestine contributions for refurbishing his official residence.

3.5 CONCLUSION

A 'New Corruption' has emerged to match the eighteenth century's old one. For decades now politicians have vented impatience with officials for standing in their way. 'People in this country have had enough of experts' said Michael Gove during the Brexit campaign of 2016.[94] He is now a minister in the Cabinet Office where another shakeup of the civil

---

[93] Pogrund and Collingridge, 'David Cameron and the toxic banker'; idem, 'David Cameron, Jeremy Heywood'.
[94] Mance, 'Britain has had enough of experts'.

service is being prepared. It is destined to fail like the previous ones because it is driven by the same notions.

The 'New Public Management' episode confirms the time horizon constraint laid out in this book. Activity which extends beyond the private break-even horizon (governed by the interest rate) cannot be undertaken by business alone (Chapter 1). A good deal of business activity requires the sanction of the state. From this perspective the government is a prior entity with the power to coerce. But dependence on government provides business with incentives to capture it.[95] Neoliberal writers perceived this already in the 1970s as part of their project to discredit the state.[96] Academic support for this business takeover of government was both overt and subtle. Some of it was grotesquely misguided.[97]

The New Public Management has not been a success. Likewise privatisation and financialisation. By the crudest measure of economic growth, the years of its hegemony since 1980 were worse than the social democratic decades that preceded them. The great financial crisis of 2008 put paid to the notion that 'free markets' are a cure for boom and bust. In the Covid-19 crisis of 2020 the outsourced 'test and trace' system was an expensive shambles.[98] The National Health Service response, both in treatment of the sick and the rollout of vaccination, was exemplary, even world-leading.

Why has market liberalism failed? Maybe the premises are wrong. Its advocates would answer that it has never been tried properly. But that would be impossible. A free market in everything cannot work. It would be a reversion to a pre-civilised state, if such has ever existed.[99] Worship of the market has become unmoored from its roots in economic theory (where there was no public sector or finance) to become a cult, an obsession. Its disastrous consequences were seen in the collapse of excessively responsive market electricity systems in California in 2001, and in Texas in 2021, inflicting physical suffering and hardship.[100]

---

[95] Wilks, *Political power of the business corporation*.
[96] Buchanan and Musgrave, *Public finance and public choice*; Mirowski, 'Postface'; Musgrave, 'Leviathan cometh'.
[97] Krugman, *Peddling prosperity*; Offer and Söderberg, *Nobel factor*, 164–169.
[98] GB NAO, 'Government's approach to test and trace'.   [99] Cordelli, *Privatized state*.
[100] Borenstein, 'Trouble with electricity markets'; Galbraith, 'Cold truth'; Krauss et al., 'Texas's drive for energy independence'.

The integrity revolution of the nineteenth century succeeded, but no one is claiming this for its unwinding. Things are not going well. Economic growth, productivity, income and wealth inequality, private debt, access to healthcare, life expectation, all these have worsened during the decades of market liberalism. If things have still muddled along, it is due to the persistence of expertise, to the embattled survival of Weberian bureaucracy and its virtues of impartiality, honesty, integrity, and competence. When President Trump attempted to overturn the election results in 2020, public servants saved the day for democracy, with some of the elected ones showing civic courage in the face of political risk.[101]

But what if the public good is not the appropriate test? Another view is that the market liberal turn was a plutocratic move to transfer wealth and power from the many to the few.[102] Enforcement agencies are deliberately underfunded so that corporate crime goes unpunished.[103] Liberal critics regard the modern corporation as an anti-social monopoly.[104] Directors of multinationals have been tasked by the Treasury to design the taxation of their own companies.[105] American and British governments have reduced their tax scrutiny of the rich and provided them with special deals.[106] The United States and the United Kingdom are among the leading international tax havens.[107] The European Union has long tolerated tax avoidance by international companies making use of haven policies in Ireland and Luxembourg.[108] Seen in this light, market liberalism has succeeded.

The public mood is sour: social trust is low and even before the pandemic, only a minority in the US (43 per cent) and the UK

---

[101] Goldberg, 'The MAGA revolution devours its own'.

[102] Chayes, *Everybody knows*; Dickinson, 'Inside the Koch Brothers' toxic empire'; Frank, *Wrecking crew*; Klein, *Shock doctrine*; MacLean, *Democracy in chains*; Mayer, *Dark money*.

[103] Coffee, *Corporate crime and punishment*.

[104] Hutton, *How good we can be*, ch. 3; Mayer, *Firm commitment*; Philippon, *Great reversal*.

[105] Brooks, *Great tax robbery*, loc. 2848; Chakrabortty, 'Tories are allowing big business to design their own tax loopholes'; Houlder and Parker, 'Osborne appoints former bank lobbyist to untangle tax code'.

[106] Brooks, *Great tax robbery*; Brooks, 'Tax, lies and videotape'; Rappeport, 'Under Trump'; Syal, 'UK's super rich appear to get special deal'.

[107] All Party Parliamentary Group on Responsible Tax (APPG), 'A more responsible global tax system'; Cummins, 'Hidden wealth'; Shaxson, *Treasure islands*; Zucman, *Hidden wealth of nations*;

[108] Shaoul, 'Corporations reached secret deals'.

(27 per cent) believed that they were going to be better off in five years' time.[109] If the scheming has been covert the results are there to see: high and growing inequality, less taxes for the rich, economies dominated by a few financial and digital firms, governments captive to corporations, stagnant living standards, a squeeze on housing, and a simmering dissatisfaction which has fed into a social and political crisis with no end in sight.

[109] Edelman Intellectual Property, 'Edelman Trust Barometer 2020', 7–10.

CHAPTER 4

Creating Humans

People are born, mature, raise their own children, grow old, and pass away. The life cycle is a long-term project. Rugged individualism is not enough: it requires prior investment, social collaboration, and mutual support. As lifespans increased over the nineteenth and twentieth centuries, sustaining them became a task for local and national governments. Since the 1980s, however, market advocates have attempted to reverse this trend, to privatise education and old age. This effort has not succeeded. Raising children to adulthood takes much longer than the break-even period of a commercial loan. The market can support these parts of the life cycle but quality is not good and cost is high. It can only be done well at affordable cost by means of collective action.

4.1 WHERE DO CHILDREN COME FROM?

In economics the labour force comes out of nowhere. Children underpin emotional, economic, and personal security, and become the workers of the future. But in the corporate economy they are an anomaly: produced not in factories or farms, but at home using artisanal methods. The scale of the family economy is also challenging: the value of unwaged housework ranges between one and two-fifths of GDP.[1]

It didn't have to be that way. North American slavery reproduced itself for more than a century and a half under capitalism. But the production of slaves was too uncertain to be financed by credit. About 15 million slaves had to be abducted and brought over from Africa by force. Once landed, slaves were a cash commodity. It was

---

[1] Offer, 'Between the gift and the market', 458–459.

impossible to borrow in order to raise them to maturity. Credit for slave purchase 'rarely had terms of longer than twelve months'.[2] Rather than credit underpinning slavery, the opposite was the case: slaves served as collateral in the cotton and sugar economies, easily seized and their money value realised.[3]

Children can be raised successfully outside the family. In Britain the top tiers of society have long sent their boys (and some of their girls) to boarding schools. These schools were typically well-endowed not-for-profit tax-exempt institutions (the 'public schools' Eton, Harrow, Winchester, Westminster, and many of lesser renown) and the parents paid expensive fees. On Israeli kibbutz communities for most of the twentieth century, children boarded together and only saw their parents for a few hours a day and sometimes only weekly.

The kibbutz community, which was not wealthy, could still take a longer view than each set of parents on their own.[4] Both the English and the kibbutz systems provided a solid education and a distinctive and positive experience for many: I was brought up on a kibbutz myself and have taught many British 'public school' graduates at university.[5] Both systems are short on parental intimacy, but can protect and nurture young people when the family does not. Such a nurturing quality is notoriously absent in social care, another form of collective upbringing which is available as a last resort when parents fail.

Communal upbringing is not an exotic outlier. As soon as toddlers are ready to read, and often earlier, they are released into a social setting. Thirteen years of kindergarten to secondary school education ('K–12' in the USA) are undertaken in partnership with society. The family provides board, lodging, and nurturing while schools impart a range of skills. When time comes for college the family pitches in with funding and out-of-term accommodation. Colleges and universities, even those that are nominally private, are collective rather than commercial undertakings. They obtain support from governments, do not seek profit, and pay no tax. In higher education only

[2] Kilbourne, *Debt, investment, slaves*, 52.
[3] Ibid.; Martin, 'Slavery's invisible engine', and references therein.
[4] Hakim, *Kibbutzim in Israel as a public good*.
[5] Abramitzky, *Mystery of the kibbutz*; Bamford, *Rise of the public schools*; Spiro, *Children of the kibbutz*; Walford, *Life in British public schools*.

narrow vocational training such as secretarial schools, language schools, and low-grade vocational private 'universities' in the United States are run for profit. Commercial institutions do not undertake a broad range of teaching and research in the arts, sciences, and professions. A British attempt at for-profit higher education, the New College of the Humanities, opened in 2012, and recently had to be sold to an American private not-for-profit university. It never rose above 300 students, and depended on the public University of London for facilities and resources.[6] American for-profit universities are massive scams which do not provide useful qualifications and rely for their fees on student funding from government loans.[7]

4.2 EDUCATION

Each person embodies an intrinsic endowment. It requires a period of investment to build up, and then pays off over a longer period. Transforming young people into earning adults needs to be funded. They may provide emotional satisfaction but not the means to feed, house, and educate themselves. As a financial investment children are less attractive than housing (Chapter 6). Any financial payoffs are remote and uncertain. They mainly go to the child and to society more broadly with much less financially for the parents. During the industrial revolution children often paid for themselves: they went to work in large numbers throughout the nineteenth century, and earned around a third of family incomes, much more than working mothers. Child labour diminished from the middle of the nineteenth century and onwards. Humanitarian regulation and compulsory schooling instigated an 'adulting' of the workforce.[8] Literacy was in the public interest and parents could not be trusted to pay so education became free. In the transition to modern affluence children lost their economic value and gained an affective one, becoming 'economically worthless, but emotionally priceless'.[9]

---

[6] Wikipedia, 'New College of the Humanities'.
[7] Armona et al., 'How does for-profit college attendance'; Halperin, *Stealing America's future*; *New York Times* editorial board, 'Predatory colleges, freed to fleece students'; Wikipedia, 'Trump University'.
[8] Cunningham, 'Decline of child labour'; Humphries, 'Child labor: Lessons'.
[9] Zelizer, *Pricing the priceless child*, 209.

Child-rearing in the United States and Britain requires a large financial outlay, equivalent to almost half of a woman's potential lifetime earnings, or the value of a medium-priced house. Parental care is a vital input into personal development. When marriages break down, the risk of educational, behavioural, and emotional disorder rises. In return for care and attention, children provide parents with a meaningful role and recurring pleasure. In North America at least, offspring get more than they return. In the aggregate, this intergenerational exchange can be seen as delayed or indirect reciprocity. Offspring and kin reciprocate by caring for old and infirm parents.[10]

Education can occupy a fifth of the modern lifespan, between kindergarten and a PhD. This requires foresight beyond the capacity of the average family. When children turn five or six society takes them over and makes the requisite investments in teachers and classrooms. Competent teachers require extended training and job security. Classrooms, once built, will last for decades. The content of education, knowledge, science, scholarship, and the arts are open ended. Money and time have to be invested long before there is any return.

4.3 MOCK MARKETS IN EDUCATION

If commercial finance cannot do it, it has not been for the lack of trying. Privatisation can be seen as a licence to extract private rents from public services. As in the case of the Private Finance Initiative (Chapter 1), it required a nominally centre-left government in Britain to explore the potential of privatising public education.

Starting in 2000, secondary schools were gradually taken out municipal control and vested in 'academies' funded directly by central government with no local government oversight. One justification was to inject variety and pluralism into education. Another was the opposite, namely to control the syllabus more tightly. An abiding slogan was 'choice'. Privatised schools continue to be funded by government and remain free at the point of use. Now if choice is costless, why would anybody choose anything but the best? Choice,

---

[10] Offer, 'Between the gift and the market', 457–462; idem, *Challenge of affluence*, chs. 11, 14.

however, was a euphemism, a signal to more privileged voters that they would be allowed to separate themselves from the less desirable.

School choice originated in the United States as a strategy by Southern state governors to preserve racial segregation.[11] Sweden has gone further than most countries in privatising schools. It turns out that the choice of secondary schools is made more by students than the parents, and they prefer to stick with their kind. Students from well-to-do homes are more capable of identifying the best academic schools. The effect is to increase inequality and segregation by class, religion, and ethnicity.[12]

Neoliberal regimes, whether centrist or right-wing, took the profit-seeking company as their model, and strove to mimic it in the public services. Privatised schools were not meant to make a profit and to pay dividends, although some of them eventually did. But their independence of government regulation and norms allowed them to pay high salaries to managers, to squeeze their workers, and to monetise the real estate they inherited from the community. They came under different names – charter and voucher schools in the USA, free schools in Sweden and the UK (different types of organisation), and the academies already mentioned.

This movement is in violation of credit time horizons. Its schools are a 'franchise' with a revenue flow guaranteed by society, and an incentive for managers to place their personal interests first. Three decades of experience show that charter schools, academies, and free schools are rife with corruption and failure.[13] In Britain, for example, 'state-funded academy chains have paid millions of pounds to closely associated business, directors, trustees and their relatives'.[14] As in the case of privatisation more generally, state schools are not necessarily inferior. The incentives of ownership and management do not seem to matter much because teachers are not exposed directly to them. Whenever privatised school examination results have been better

[11] Schneider, *School choice*, ch. 3. [12] Holm and Lundahl, 'A stimulating competition'.
[13] Mansell and Savage, 'Top academy schools sound alarm'; McInerney, 'Academy dream is in freefall'; Perraudin, '40,000 children trapped'; idem, 'Collapsing Academy Trust'; Woolcock, 'Academies accused'.
[14] Quote, Benn and Downs, 'Who runs our schools?', 4; Boffey, 'Academy chain under fire'; Thomson, *School scandals*, ch. 5; Warrell, 'MPs say loopholes in regulation'; Weale, 'Government system "fails to address …"'.

(itself a problematic quality measure) it is due to the exclusion of weaker students. There is no educational benefit in entrepreneurial management of public schools.[15]

Imposing simulated market incentives on the public school system has long been promoted by would-be reformers from among the wealthy. This is in line with the 'win–win' ideology of corporate social responsibility which seeks to mitigate social problems without disturbing the rich.[16] For the billionaires, it provides a façade of progressive and technocratic reform and distracts attention from their privileged position. It is a form of ideological money laundering, 'a semblance of being on the right hand of change'.[17] By imposing economic incentives on education, the wealthy insinuate their acquisitive values to help legitimate their wealth. Facilitators were not shy of profiting directly. Of the two candidates who emerged for the American presidential election of 2016, Trump's business empire was running a bogus for-profit 'Trump University', while Hillary Clinton's husband Bill earned some $18m in seven years as 'honorary chancellor' of Laureate, a chain of for-profit, hard-sell, high-charging post-secondary institutions mostly in Latin America.[18] The chain had earned the 'social responsibility' kitemark of being a public spirited 'B-Corporation'.[19]

In spite of advocacy by political promoters and billionaire would-be reformers all the way from the right to the centre-left, there is little to show for thirty years of effort. Charter schools have only captured a small minority of students in the United States, and have mostly not become commercial entities in Britain. A massive and lucrative regime of annual testing in the United States was implemented in 2001 (the No Child Left Behind Act) in order to expose teachers to competitive incentives and punishments. The results are inconclusive – test results

---

[15] Baker, 'Exploring the consequences of charter school expansion'; Lubienski and Lubienski, *Public school advantage*, chs. 4–5; Lubienski, 'NEPC review', 7–9; Ravitch, *Slaying Goliath*, chs. 6–7. For the UK, e.g. Adams, 'Lauded academy chain'; Weale, 'Free Schools policy under fire'.

[16] Giridharadas, *Winners take all*.

[17] Giridharadas, *Winners take all*, 121; quote, ibid. 120; Street, 'The shell game'; West, *Billionaires*, ch. 3.

[18] Kimes and Smith, 'Laureate, a for-profit success'; Nelson, 'Bill Clinton's $18 million job'; Wikipedia, 'Trump University'.

[19] Giridharadas, *Winners take all*, 253.

did not improve, and schools on the whole withheld the rigours of the incentive regimes from their teachers. In Sweden schools were converted to parental choice and free private entry in the early 1990s. The trend of examination performance has been sharply down. Internationally comparable PISA examination results (first administered in 2000) fell precipitously. No other country experienced a steeper decline, and Sweden moved in ten years from a position around the OECD average to one much lower down.[20] Truly private schools (e.g. the UK 'public schools') are only superior when parental fees allow them to spend more on every student than the taxpayer is willing to allocate.

4.4 HIGHER EDUCATION

One of the benefits of European welfare states is cheap access to universities. In the United States the public universities used to offer similar benefits. New Labour in Britain followed a two-step policy of higher education reform: replacing an administrative model of universities with a corporate one, and then shifting their public finance away from direct grants and into student loans. Universities were no longer funded centrally, but had to compete for student fees. Similar movements took place elsewhere in the neoliberal world. Institutions were meant to compete with each other and to respond to student choice. But universities did not compete on price: funding from student debt allowed fees to rise much faster than inflation at both public and private universities.

As in the case of infrastructure (Chapter 1) and housing (Chapter 6), public debt was a means for private enrichment: it captured a growing share of household income for decades of loan service, the actual risk being underwritten by government. Marketising education justifies the market ethos more widely. The burden of student debt was socially regressive and the outcomes were inequitable. The rich could pay up front and avoid the credit cost.

As in the old Soviet Union, debt finance creates a 'soft budget constraint': there is no hard limit on expenditure.[21] When students

---

[20] OECD, 'Improving schools in Sweden', 26–30; Trumberg, 'Market reforms in Sweden'.
[21] Kornai et al., 'Soft budget constraint'.

can borrow as much as the colleges charge, the limits on spending become elastic. A weak budget discipline encourages gold-plating with expensive facilities and high pay for those in charge. As in charter schools, there is also an incentive to exploit and casualise junior staff. Universities began to work like corporations, managed by means of rewards for achieving performance targets. Publication quotas took precedence over open-ended free enquiry in scholarship and science.[22]

When American states cut back on their support of public universities, fees went up. Private colleges and universities raised the cost of first degrees to levels that approach the capital cost of housing, and with similar consequences. A generation being priced out of home ownership was now saddled with high college debts. With large loans to service, newly graduated doctors, lawyers, and executives demanded higher incomes, pushing the cost of professional services beyond the reach of ordinary people, and exacerbating the inequality already caused by financialisation in other sectors. With everyone striving for high-income qualifications (business studies became the most popular undergraduate discipline) these credentials would no longer be paying so well, while socially necessary and culturally worthwhile activities in the arts, humanities, and social sciences were left to languish. When only those who win the race can aspire to the basic decencies of a house, a car, and an education for their children, financialisation drives a ruthless social competition.

Like private healthcare, private higher education is expensive. Paying for higher education in the United States has created a debt burden second only to housing, and interest rates are high. Congress has blocked the escape route of bankruptcy. The total liabilities are currently around $1.6 trillion. That sounds like a lot – it is about 8 per cent of GDP – but is mostly owed to the federal government hence not a threat to financial stability. It has blighted lives and amounts to debt servitude, negating the freedom of choice which market education was meant to confer.[23]

[22] Collini, *What are universities for?*; Mirowski, *Science Mart*; Newfield, *Great mistake*; Sayer, *Rank hypocrisies.*
[23] Akers and Chingos, *Game of loans*; Best and Best, *Student loan mess*; Kantor, 'The $1.6tn US student debt nightmare'; Zaloom, *Indebted.*

British universities used to be free or very close to it and students were also given living grants. Numbers were low. From the 1960s onwards participation rose consistently, and New Labour aspired to a goal of 50 per cent. To pay for this, student fees rose to £9,000 a year by 2010, covering the full cost of tuition. For three years of studies the cost in fees alone is more than a year's median wage. The principle of free access, however, was maintained: the fees would count as a loan, to be paid for over thirty years as a percentage of income, at a high interest rate (with forbearance for low incomes). In 2017 the student debt book was sold off to private investors; according to the Parliamentary Public Accounts Committee, 'government received too little in return for what it gave up'. The *Financial Times* wrote politely: 'Selling off student loans makes next to no sense.'[24] In line with PFI and the privatisation of energy, water, and railways, the debt was serviced through the tax system and guaranteed by government. Income was transferred from working people, whose spending drives economic activity, to rentiers who lend it out again. The privatised loans company soon began to frighten students into needless early repayments by giving them a misleading 'demoralising, damaging and dangerous' picture of their debts.[25]

The life cycle has two extended periods of dependency: before entering the workforce, and after leaving it. Markets are based on immediate exchange, but life and livelihood need to be sustained for long periods without labour earnings. Markets find it difficult to finance such long periods beyond their short break-even horizons. The rich have assets way beyond their needs, and do not face such problems. For everybody else, the solutions that have emerged during the twentieth century depend on reciprocity and government. Childhood, adolescence, and young adulthood depend on a combination of family altruism and government or not-for-profit education. The attempts to introduce the profit motive and economic incentives by means of charters in the USA has largely failed and not for lack of trying. There and elsewhere public education

[24] FT View, 'Selling off student loans'; GB Public Accounts Committee, 'Sale of student loans', 3.
[25] Lewis, 'Martin Lewis accuses'.

predominates, though full cost fees for university education has created gross inequalities and enduring debt servitude.

Effort and ability drive the economy. Withdraw them and the economy collapses. And yet their supply is not part of the market economy. They are conferred on capitalism by the combined efforts of altruistic families and self-effacing teachers. Market competition can produce and reproduce the capital input into production but not the hands and the heads. Markets need to make a profit for somebody in a short and specified time. Bringing up children cannot be done for profit because it cannot be financed with commercial credit. Parents give without being sure of receiving; while society and government know that investing in all will raise the welfare of all.

CHAPTER 5

Exit from Work

In the course of the life cycle every person goes through periods when they cannot provide for themselves. Infancy and childhood, motherhood, education, illness, unemployment, disability, and old age are all time-consuming and costly. How to provide for people when they cannot earn? Social institutions help: family, charity, mutual assistance, or insurance associations (i.e. 'clubs', which provide benefits only to members), employers, legal trustees and fiduciaries, governments, house property, financial companies, insurance payouts, and tort awards. Money can be laid aside for future contingencies. But finance alone cannot provide.

The best provision is to be one of the rich. Their risks are diversified, their income exceeds their consumption. Edmund Burke wrote, 'all the classes and descriptions of the Rich – they are the pensioners of the poor'.[1] The wealthy demand care and attention without having to provide them in return. That is what it means to be rich.

Whatever the arena – health care, education, work, leisure – on one side of the velvet rope is a friction-free existence. Red tape is cut, appointments are secured, doors are opened. On the other side, friction is practically the defining characteristic, with middle- and working-class Americans facing an increasingly zero-sum fight for a decent seat on the plane, a college scholarship, even a doctor's appointment.[2]

In an unequal society the many serve the few, with no confidence of being cared for themselves.[3] Those who attend to the rich cannot all be rich themselves. The fewer the rich, the more secure they are in being looked after.

---

[1] Burke, *Details on scarcity*, 2. [2] Schwartz, 'When it's this easy at the top'.
[3] Schwartz, *Velvet rope economy*; Segal, 'Inequality as entitlements'.

Everyone faces a period of dependency whose timing and extent are unknown. For society as a whole, however, the scale of dependency can be predicted actuarially. There is no need to set aside savings for an uncertain future. The dependent and old can be supported by those in work. The risks of dependency are pooled. Over time everyone gives and everyone will receive. The method is pay-as-you-go taxation (henceforth PAYGO). How much to transfer comes out of political negotiation.

When people provide for the future on their own they need to transfer buying power to their future selves by means of financial middlemen. PAYGO transfers buying power from one group to another today. No contracts have to reach beyond the financial time horizon. Financial claims do not have to be kept in being for decades. The agreement is current and is always open to revision. It does not have to lock in the future. PAYGO systems are robust, durable, and affordable. There is no other viable way of supporting everybody who is old.

Under PAYGO the main risk is that producer incomes in the future will not be sufficient to provide the transfer payments expected. But this risk affects financial contracts as well, which are meant to be honoured after decades in quite different conditions. Using PAYGO, and assuming that inter-generation solidarity is preserved, one solution is to link the growth of payouts to labour incomes, or to the growth of the economy. Aggregate labour income tends to be stable from one year to another and this places PAYGO on a predictable basis.

In the nineteenth century trade unions of skilled workers sometimes supported their retired members. This provided a template for the universal pension systems established in developed countries during the twentieth century, which were designed to pay out a modest retirement income for life. Under PAYGO pensions are paid out of earmarked payroll deductions and employer contributions, or directly out of general taxation. By the 1970s such basic pensions were firmly established in most countries as offering a secure if frugal safety net for workers and their families. The payments ('replacement rates' expressed as a fraction of pre-retirement incomes) were low, but outgoings in retirement were also low.

Despite being a pioneer of the welfare state, the British old-age pension replacement rate in the 1970s was only some 20 per cent of average incomes. Support was also provided through medical and housing benefits, as well as separate means-tested income for those whose contribution record did not give access to a state pension. In the United States a full working life of payroll tax deductions provided about twice as much. These levels were low in comparison with most countries in Europe and remain so today.[4] In Britain in 2019, the state pension replacement rate was the lowest in the OECD (at 25 per cent), and the American one, though still twice as high, was in the lower third (Figure 5.1).

5.2 FROM SOCIAL INSURANCE TO 'PERSONAL RESPONSIBILITY'

In United States the Social Security system was set up as part of Franklin D. Roosevelt's New Deal in 1935. PAYGO was always a thorn in the flesh of American conservatives. Welfare state recipro-city was challenged from the 1960s and onwards by the re-emergent doctrine of market liberalism.[5] The rich have done well out of market competition and urge it on the rest. They sought to cast off social obligation and to lower their taxes.[6] It was also a bid by finance to capture the revenues of social insurance and extract a profit.

In *Capitalism and freedom* (1962), their own neoliberal manifesto, Milton and Rose Friedman asked: 'What conceivable justification is there for taxing the young to subsidize the old regardless of the economic status of the old?' Inefficient government bureaucracies, they argued, were taking business away from competitive insurance companies.[7] The couple came back in *Free to choose* (1980). Social

---

[4] GB Pensions Commission, 'Pensions: Challenges and choices', ch. 3.
[5] Buchanan, 'Public choice'; Friedman and Friedman, *Capitalism and freedom*; Musgrave, 'Leviathan cometh'; Prasad, *Politics of free markets*, chs. 1–2.
[6] Chait, *The big con*; Mankiw, 'Optimal taxation'; Saez and Zucman, *Triumph of injustice*.
[7] Friedman and Friedman, *Capitalism and freedom*, 184. See 182–189. The answer: if the poor pay more of their income for social security, they also get back more of their income in benefits.

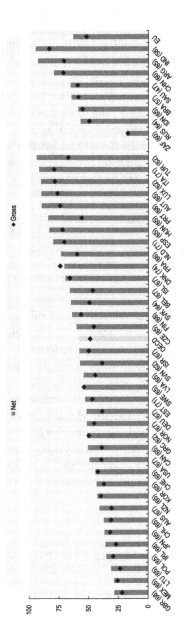

Figure 5.1 Net pension replacement rates per cent, mandatory pensions, average earners in the OECD.

Source: OECD, *Pensions at a glance 2019*, fig. 5.4, 155. Retirement age in brackets.

Note: Full contribution record from age 22. These involve combinations of PAYGO and other forms, but are effectively guaranteed by the state. The cluster of countries on the right have a high take-up of voluntary pension schemes.

security did not provide a fair return on the payroll tax contributions that funded it. They proposed to 'unwind Social Security while meeting present commitments, and gradually requiring people to make their own arrangements for their own retirement'.[8]

A relentless, deliberate, gradualist programme of ruthless ('Leninist') subversion was mounted to replace the social security PAYGO pension with investment in the stock market.[9] In a candid talk in 1986 Edwin Feulner, President of the neoliberal Heritage Foundation (a top conservative think tank) said that 'the ideal solution [for social security] is privatisation'.[10] In an interview in 2006, Stuart Butler, a vice-president of the same organisation, made no bones about it:

What we say is 'Let's essentially privatize the risk management for health or retirement.' You give people other vehicles to manage the risk of living too long or being sick. You wean people gradually off social insurance risk management into private risk management without making them fearful about it. You have to do it in steps and have some government protection, at least in the beginning.[11]

As ever in the United States, the rich could call on clever academics. In 1974 the young Harvard Professor Martin Feldstein stated that the existence of a social security retirement programme depressed personal savings by 30 to 50 per cent, which would lower the national 'capital stock' by 38 per cent in the long run, implying a big loss of prosperity and economic growth.[12] Feldstein's influential assertion (very damaging to social security) was exposed a few years later as incorrect due to what Feldstein claimed was a computational error. The balance of evidence shows that PAYGO pensions do not reduce savings, and that stock market investments do not increase them. People save for many reasons and not only for retirement.[13]

---

[8] Friedman and Friedman, *Free to choose*, 105, 120.
[9] Brief account in Russell, 'How the Koch brothers'; detail in Laursen, *People's pension*; Butler and Germanis, '"Leninist" strategy'; Ferrara, *Social security*; Hacker, *Great risk shift*, ch. 5.
[10] Fuelner, 'Comments on "Marketing the Free Market", Mont Pèlerin Society St. Vincent Meeting, September 1986, Hoover Institution Archives, Mont Pèlerin Society papers, MPS 26.7, fos. 3–4.
[11] Interview with Stuart Butler, 11 May 2006, in Hacker, *Great risk shift*, 56.
[12] Feldstein, 'Social security'.
[13] Lesnoy and Leimer, 'Social security and private saving'; Minns and Sexton, 'Too many grannies', 17.

Feldstein was a rising star in economics, second only to Milton Friedman as an intellectual foe of the welfare state.[14] As in the case of education, the driving force were billionaire reformers and their foundations, of whom the most persistent was Peter Peterson, a big figure in Wall Street and Republican Party politics. Rolling back the welfare state became his personal crusade, in support of which he wrote eight books and co-founded a 'Concord Coalition'.[15] The potential prizes were large even for billionaires: a surge in asset values and lucrative financial business, tax cuts for themselves, and more dependence for everybody else, as market risks were shifted on to those least able to bear them. The rhetoric was of 'personal responsibility'.[16]

Martin Feldstein was President and Chief Executive Officer of the National Bureau of Economic Research (NBER) from 1978 to 2008, and also chief economic adviser to President Reagan and chairman of his Council of Economic Advisors (1982–1984). The NBER is the most prestigious academic outlet in the United States for economic empirical and policy work. Under Feldstein it supported funded retirement with almost 150 papers (30 by Feldstein himself) and several research monographs, of which he himself edited *Privatizing social security* (1998).[17]

In 1996 he gave the keynote Richard Ely Lecture to the American Economic Association, summarised for the libertarian Cato Institute as 'Privatizing Social Security: The $10 Trillion Opportunity'. The opportunity was this: the rate of return on stock market equity was much higher than the implicit rate of return on social security contributions (of which the residue not paid out was invested in low-yield government bonds).

Each generation now and in the future loses the difference between the return to real capital that would be obtained in a funded system and the much lower return in the existing unfunded program. Shifting to a privatized system of individual mandatory accounts that can be invested in a mix of stocks and bonds would permit individuals to obtain the full real

[14] Horioka, 'Life and work of . . . Feldstein'. [15] Laursen, *People's pension*, passim.
[16] Berry, 'Austerity, ageing', 9–11, 15–16; Hacker, *Great risk shift*, 26–28.
[17] Laursen, *People's pensions*, 278; NBER, 'NBER Aging Program'; Feldstein, 'Privatizing social security'.

pretax rate of return on capital. This would mean a larger capital stock and a higher national income.

Equities have outperformed fixed-income securities consistently for more than a century.[18] This 'equity premium' is the prime justification for entrusting entitlements to financial markets. On the face of it there was a dollar bill lying unclaimed on the pavement. But that was wrong and misleading. Social security is not an investment plan to maximise returns on investment by taking on risk. It is an insurance scheme for reducing the risks of old age by pooling them. Feldstein compares stock market returns today with PAYGO pensions at retirement. High returns today might not translate into higher returns at retirement because neither asset prices nor commodity and labour costs are going to remain the same. Equity returns might be higher than those of bonds, and also higher than economic growth overall, but that is primarily a reward for the risk of holding uncertain claims, and does not represent the genuine productivity of the whole economy, which is what pensions have to be paid from. Some of these stocks are going to underperform and others will fail. That savers earn more now does not mean they will be better off as pensioners.[19] Gross returns are misleading. The volatility of equity returns is very high, and the probability of earning less even than the risk-free rate (on government bonds) increases over time. The equity premium compensates for that.[20] For investment, the equity premium is a cost and not a benefit. What matters is the rate of return adjusted for risk and for management costs

The dollar bill on the pavement was an illusion. The real rate of return to savers was much lower than the headline yield rates because of management costs. For example, if the return to bonds is 2 per cent and of a judicious mix of equities 3.5 per cent, then a typical (and conservative) management charge of between 1.5 per cent and 2.0 per cent would nullify the difference. The financial crisis of 2008, for example, destroyed five decades of equity advantage.[21]

[18] DeLong and Magin, 'The U.S. equity return premium'; Dimson et al., *Triumph of the optimists*; Siegel, *Stocks for the long run*.
[19] Baker, 'Saving social security with stocks', 23–5; Gollier, 'Intergenerational risk-sharing'; Laursen, *People's pension*, 399–400.
[20] Bodie, 'Risk of stocks in the long run'. [21] Authers, 'Is it back to the fifties?'

There should not be any free lunch.[22] Holding stocks for long does not reduce the risk. It merely makes the loss greater when it finally occurs.

Feldstein was appealing to an intuitive model ('loanable funds') in which the source of capital expenditure is household savings. This is contested and arguably incorrect. In 'endogenous money theory' (now endorsed by central banks) commercial lending is not constrained by household savings but by the supply of credible borrowers.[23] No worthwhile project should go without a loan. The stock market (where Feldstein's savings were meant to go) does not raise capital for productive investment, but for speculation in assets already created by the retained profits of firms. It also allows managers to cash in their outsize rewards. It does provide an incentive for venture capitalists to make their initial speculative investments.

From the 1980s onwards retirement savings increasingly flowed into the American stock market. This did not feed a surge of capital investment in the economy but a stock market boom, high asset values, and low interest rates and asset yields. After the financial crisis of 2008 'quantitative easing' to bail out commercial banks grossly inflated liquidity without increasing investment. Finally, there is no relation between the rate of return on assets and economic growth.[24]

5.3 A SECOND TIER: WORKPLACE AND PRIVATE PENSIONS

Old-age pensions were also introduced in the nineteenth century by large firms and governments for their higher earners. Once universal pension systems were established, these workplace benefits added a second tier of 'occupational pensions' to the basic state pension, a tier for which both workers and employers made regular contributions. Such benefits attracted good workers, helped to retain them into their sixties, and then made it easier to let them go. This intergenerational reciprocity operated as a 'club' for insiders within each corporate workforce, except that in parts of the public sector and in some companies (especially in the USA) the funding was

---

[22] Furman, 'Would private accounts provide?'
[23] Offer, 'Market turn', 1,057–1,058 and references therein.
[24] Minns, *Cold War in welfare*, 110–114.

entirely by employers. By the 1970s about half of all workers in both countries were enrolled for such benefits but these supplementary pensions provided only about 15 per cent of total retirement earnings.[25] The pensions were typically 'defined benefit', i.e. they promised (like the state PAYGO pension) a fixed regular post-retirement payment for life, determined by years of service and level of pay. The contributions (and sometimes the pension asset revenues as well) were tax-exempt, the tax being postponed to retirement, when the benefits were often taxed at lower rates than those paid by active workers.

On the face of it this pension promise was a big risk for the companies involved. What allowed the providers to take it on was their 'franchise' status, i.e. strong market power by virtue of a government concession or guarantee, or some lasting technological or natural advantage. For example, the railways which pioneered this approach began as natural monopolies and eventually moved into state ownership. By the time the car manufacturers in the USA set up generous pensions after the Second World War, they had formed an effective cartel of three.

These business franchises lasted for decades, and their defined benefit pensions worked well. But they were embedded in a dynamic capitalist mode of production whose driving force is 'creative destruction'. Over the decades required for pensions to mature, the franchises turned out to be not durable enough. The fortunes of the companies that offered them rose and then declined.

American regulators identified this risk in the 1970s, and strove to insulate the benefits as much as possible from the solvency of their corporate sponsors, with two separate approaches.[26] Regulation was tightened and a central insurance fund built up against corporate default. The other approach was to detach pensions from employers and move them into funds invested in the financial markets, in order to pay out regardless of corporate solvency. Britain followed this lead about twenty-five years later.

In the quest for lower taxes, neoliberal governments in Britain and the United States began to reduce pension tax reliefs by restricting

[25] Munnell and Sass, *Social security and the stock market*, 71.
[26] Hacker, *Great risk shift*, 107, 109–110.

the ability of corporations to over-fund their pension in good times. In 1997 the New Labour government withdrew the tax immunity for pension fund revenues altogether, dealing a heavy blow to defined benefit occupational pensions, which hastened their demise.[27]

Some of the pillars of the Fordist productive economy were cracking: the railways, automobile makers, steel companies, and surrounding ecosystems all declined sharply in both countries, to be replaced by burgeoning services with mercurial outputs, an educated and mobile labour force, and managers more focused on financial extraction than on production.[28] All of these trends undermined the long-term viability of defined benefit arrangements in the corporate sector, which were closed to new entrants or completely wound down.[29] Those that remained were often manipulated by companies which (cheered on by economists) made the welfare of managers their prime objective. Historical defined benefit systems were often plundered by the corporations that owned them, enabled by loose regulation and scheming lawyers and accountants. One method was a temporary bankruptcy to shake off creditors, including pension obligations. Other companies invested company pension funds in their own shares. When Enron collapsed in 2001, its workers lost all of their retirement savings.[30] Worker benefits fell while those of managers rose.[31]

Governments, which had made these corporate franchises possible, now spurned them in favour of the financial ones. Large parts of the public sector, the franchise of franchises, invested pension contributions in financial assets that were meant to pay the benefits. Local governments in the United States largely went this way, and university systems too. Revenue assumptions were absurdly optimistic, contribution levels were set too low, and many American cities found themselves in deep pension deficits, especially depressed ones like Detroit and Chicago.[32]

If corporations could no longer guarantee a stable retirement decades hence, another solution emerged at the end of the 1970s.

---

[27] Brummer, *Great pensions robbery.* [28] Mayer, *Firm commitment.*
[29] Munnell, 'Employer-sponsored plans'; GB Pension Commission, 'Pensions: Challenges and choices', ch. 3, sec. 4–5.
[30] Hacker, *Great risk shift,* 99–102. [31] Schultz, *Retirement heist.*
[32] Pew Charitable Trust, 'The trillion dollar gap'.

This was for individuals to take charge of their own savings with some employer support. Clause 401(k) in the USA tax code shielded such savings from tax. Pensions of this kind were called 'money purchase', or 'defined contribution': retirement income depended on investment performance. Regular contributions were made to a fund which invested in the stock market. On retirement the workers received the balance accumulated. All the risks, of investment performance, volatility, fraud, and living too long, were borne by savers on their own. If a saver persisted in saving a fixed share of their income (with modest employer input as well), they might accumulate retirement entitlements comparable (or indeed superior) to those promised by a defined benefit scheme with the same inputs.[33] The final balance could be invested in an annuity to provide a regular income in retirement. That was the theory.

From the 1980s onwards defined contribution pension schemes replaced defined benefit schemes in the United States and in Britain too. What this meant was relying entirely on a personal hoard for retirement, with no sharing of risk among savers and employers, with no insurance for longevity, and no guaranteed support for survivors. Personal balances depended on stock market movements. By the early 2000s, and despite two previous decades of booming stock prices, this arrangement was 'coming up short' (the title of a book by the foremost expert).[34]

Economists prefer to understand outcomes as arising out of personal choices ('methodological individualism') and they also assume that people make the best of information currently available, i.e. that they are rational. After thirty years it is now clear that 401(k) has failed to provide secure and adequate pensions for retirement. Employers (even very large ones) often failed to keep up their contributions.[35] But the main reason was the premise of saver rationality. People acting on their own do not have the motivation and skills to secure their old age for themselves, or even to do so as a group. About a quarter of those eligible did not even enrol. Savers were allowed to withdraw funds from their balances for other life-cycle contingencies. Immediate needs were more compelling than a remote retirement, and such withdrawals were the main

---

[33] Munnell and Sunden, *Coming up short*, 30–31. [34] Ibid. [35] Ibid., 32.

reason that pensions fell short. Such a cash withdrawal option under-mined other social insurance, and its mere existence would have acted to raise the price of urgent outlays like healthcare, vehicles, higher education, and housing.

Savers lacked the competence to devise good investment strategies, a problem that defeats even professionals. The payout was a lump sum, which was rarely invested in an annuity, so even if 401(k) savers made the same contributions as in defined benefit schemes, they still faced the risk of living too long. Annuities tended to be overpriced. The median saving in all retirement accounts of USA households aged 56–61 in 2010 was $91,000, rather less than twice the median annual wage.[36] For 401(k) plans in 2001, at age 55–64 the median assets (at $42,000) were only 15 per cent of the simulated potential, the one that matched or exceeded defined benefit plans.[37] These inadequate personal savings formed more than half (56 per cent) of all retirement assets in the USA in 2010.[38] Half the savers saved less than the average.

Market savings rely on the habit of thrift. But inequalities in the United States, and the daily economic insecurity of living there, are such that savings are grossly inadequate. In 2012, for example, less than half the labour force (itself less than 60 per cent of adults) even had defined contribution (401(k)) plans, which do not build up sufficient savings, and incur heavy overheads. More than a third of households had no retirement savings at all. Those facing retirement within a decade (aged 55–64) had a median of $120,000 in all retirement accounts with a median overall net worth of $179,000. For those who relied on their home equity, the financial crisis of 2008 wiped out some $6 trillion, comparable to about a third of national income. Those aged 50 and older owned 3.5 million houses worth less than their mortgage debt.[39] For all of these people, the default support in old age remained the reviled social security system.

Stock market values are driven by very short-term incentives, a combination of gut feelings and new information, and are very

[36] Sabadish and Morrissey, 'Retirement inequality chartbook', fig. 12.
[37] Munnell and Sanden, *Coming up short*, table 2–5, 36.
[38] Sabadish and Morrissey, 'Retirement inequality chartbook', fig. 5.
[39] Munnell et al., 'Pension coverage problem'; Trawinski, 'Nightmare on Main Street'; *New York Times* editorial board, 'Road to retirement'.

volatile. Even a stable and steady record of contributions did not lead to steady accumulation, but to balances that varied unpredictably. A simulation of retirement income based on stock market returns over more than a century has shown that pension revenue as a proportion of working income (the 'replacement rate') varied by a factor of three depending on the year of retirement, between less than 20 per cent and almost 80 per cent at age 70.[40] These are gross returns. Savers received much less since market investment incurs commissions, management fees, and trading costs that take a large slice out of the contributions made.

It is misleading to infer from levels of participation in workplace pension plans to the adequacy of coverage. Workplace pensions, whether defined benefit or defined contribution, only benefit a minority of workers, roughly speaking the fifth or so of the labour force who have regular well-paying jobs and build up assets.[41] This minority also benefits disproportionately from tax subsidies.[42] For the vast majority of workers, in both the United States and in Britain, retirement incomes continue to depend primarily on the pay-as-you-go pension arrangements of the basic safety-net state pension, and despite vast inequalities, PAYGO and defined benefit pensions still provide most of retirement income in the United States. In 2010, for retirees in the aggregate (aged 68–79), this was by far the largest source of income.[43]

Social security and defined benefit pensions had a strong equalising effect on wealth inequality in the United States, while defined contribution pensions had the opposite one.[44] Pension wealth increased to about half of all wealth (Figure 5.2), while about two-thirds of non-pension wealth was made up of housing, most of it people's own homes. Stock markets are for the better off, whose basic retirement is secure, and who own the bulk of stock market assets.

How much saving is enough? Actual levels of assets in private pension savings accounts are inadequate as a main resource for retirement. In the UK private sector in 2004–5, more than half the

---

[40] Burtless, 'Social security privatisation'.
[41] Sabadish and Morrissey, 'Retirement inequality chartbook', figs. 18–22.
[42] Minns and Sexton, 'Too many grannies', 16, n. 38.
[43] Sabadish and Morrissey, 'Retirement inequality chartbook', figs. 6–7.
[44] Wolff, *Century of wealth*, 366.

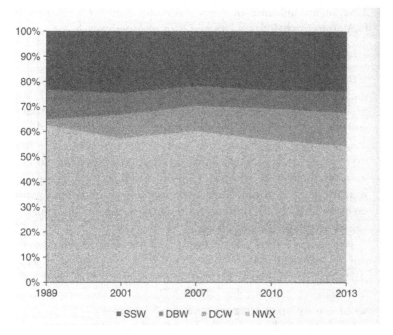

Figure 5.2 Pension and other household wealth, all households USA 1989–2013.

Source: Wolff, *Century of wealth*, figure 8.3a, 342. Copyright: *A century of wealth in America* by Edward N. Wolff, Cambridge, MA: The Belknap Press of Harvard University Press, Copyright © 2017 The President and Fellows of Harvard College. Used by permission. All rights reserved.

Note: SSW: Social security wealth; DBW: Defined benefit pension wealth; DCW: Defined contribution pension wealth; NWX: Market household wealth excluding DCW.

workers were making no pension contribution at all.[45] In the USA almost half of all retirees in 2012 had no retirement savings, and even the top quarter of those aged 50 to 64 had median retirement savings of only $52,000.[46] Subsidies for saving went largely to high earners:

---

[45] Apart from National Insurance contributions, Turner et al., 'Implementing an integrated package', slide 2. A good survey of British pension system in 2005 in GB Pensions Commission, 'Pensions: Challenges and choices', ch. 3.

[46] Saad-Lessler and Ghilarducci, '"Near retirees" defined contribution account balances'.

'Overall, around three-quarters of defined contribution pension and IRA assets are held by the richest fifth of Americans.'[47]

5.4 THE POLITICS OF PENSIONS

President Bill Clinton led the way in market solutions to social problems. He endorsed private–public partnerships in education and enacted a punitive welfare reform that required mothers to seek paid work rather than look after their children. His solution to black mens' under-employment and under-education was to throw more of them into prison.[48] Clinton flirted with investing social security reserves in the stock market, and with individual pension savings accounts, but this impinged on the well-being of mainstream America, and he did not persist.[49]

His successor President George W. Bush was bolder: he pushed for private retirement accounts, to be funded out of the social security payroll tax. It was part of his election campaign of 2004, but it gained little traction. Likewise his successor Barack Obama set out to curb social security (appointing the bipartisan Simpson–Bowles Commission for this purpose) but eventually he held off too.[50] With such powerful support, why were these reforms not implemented? Mostly because the scheme affected the great majority of Americans. It was bad for savers and was effectively resisted in Congress, just as the charter school movement in education repeatedly failed. Privatising social security did not succeed because the scheme was impractical and could not secure a retirement for everybody. Popular pressure was strong enough to prevent it.

America is more of a democracy than Britain. In the UK as well, neoliberal governments worked to shift pensions away from welfare state reciprocity and towards financial institutions, and with greater success. The state pension provided a replacement rate of somewhat above 20 per cent of average earnings in the 1970s. This made up some 60 per cent of retirement income in 1979.[51] On coming to

---

[47] Hacker, *Great risk shift*, 112, citing congressional testimony by Peter Orszag, 2004.
[48] Alexander, *New Jim Crow*, 56–57. [49] Laursen, *People's pension*, 374, and chs. 26–27.
[50] Laursen, *People's pension*, Pts. VI–VII.
[51] Munnell and Sass, *Social security and the stock market*, 70–71.

power in 1980 the Thatcher government removed the linkage with wage levels, and pegged pension updates to prices, which rose more slowly. It also reduced the benefits of the income-related extension (SERPS), intended for those without second-tier workplace pensions. In 1986 it encouraged savers to move away from workplace pensions to private ones by means of tax incentives. Insurance companies and other financial intermediaries piled in with misleading advice, and the same government later felt compelled to require them to compensate several million people for pension 'misselling'.[52] The successor New Labour regime attempted to nudge low earners into inferior private schemes ('stakeholder pensions') which they could ill-afford, but these found few takers among workers or insurance companies.[53]

The UK is one of very few countries in the world to impose the risks of individual private pension accounts on its lowest earners. Second-tier occupational pensions were declining down to about half of all workers in 2012 when the UK government imposed compulsory saving in individual accounts on everybody not otherwise provided for, albeit with a low level of contribution. This latest iteration of marketisation had been set in motion by New Labour in the previous decade with its Turner Report of 2005.[54] The government had to set up its own management company (National Employment Savings Trust – NEST) to administer the funds for less than conventional insurance company management charges. It was yet another genuflection to the delusion of funding, a device to squeeze the low paid in order to reduce taxes on the better off, cynically imposing the virtue of thrift on those who could ill afford it, and who were barely going to benefit.[55] In consequence, defined contributions rose from less than 10 per cent of workplace pension participants to more than a third, but the median wealth held in these accounts was derisory.[56] More than three decades after the 'personal responsibility' pension

---

[52] Black and Nobles, 'Personal pensions misselling'; GB HC, Select Committee on Treasury, 'Ninth report'; GB Pensions Commission, 'A new pension settlement'; Pemberton et al., *Britain's pension crisis*; Ward, 'Personal pensions in the UK'.

[53] GB Pensions Commission, 'Pensions: Challenges and choices', 92.

[54] GB Pensions Commission, 'A new pension settlement'.

[55] Sass, 'U.K.'s ambitious new retirement savings'.

[56] GB Office of National Statistics (ONS), 'Employee workplace pensions', fig. 1, 3; GB ONS, 'Pension wealth', fig. 6, 12.

revolution in Britain, four-fifths of active pension wealth remained in defined benefit pensions, and that has not changed over time.

5.5 THE DELUSION OF FUNDING

From the 1980s onwards, as social democracy and its values went into eclipse, PAYGO was increasingly derided, and the view took hold that 'funded' provision was superior to pay-as-you-go. In 1981 Pinochet's Chile (advised by Milton Friedman) converted its PAYGO pensions to a system of individual accounts invested with competing private fund managers. It took some time for performance quality to emerge, but the reform was aligned with Washington Consensus marketising policies worldwide, and its example was forcefully commended by the World Bank as a Chile-type 'second pillar' of mandatory privately managed and invested pension systems.[57] This was particularly influential in Latin America and Eastern Europe.[58]

Pre-funding one's own pension has an aura of prudence, of frugal thrift for rainy days. 'Personal responsibility' sounds virtuous. But it is an illusion. A person on an average income cannot provide on their own for all the risks of retirement. Credible commercial insurance is not available for purchase for the average person. What savers lay aside is not provisions, but financial claims. It is impossible to store up subsistence for the future. You cannot bake bread now to eat in forty years' time. Real estate can be hoarded or lived in, but sits exposed to regulation, taxation, and financial markets. Housing has had long booms, but has also suffered slumps, massive destruction (in wartime), and expropriation by both government and finance (see Chapter 6). Pensioners have to be supported by what workers currently produce, whether their pensions are funded or not. What they can buy has to be provided today by current work and the existing stock of physical capital.[59] The choice of funding or PAYGO does not in itself change the resources available overall, though it might affect the distribution between the active and inactive in ways which cannot be predicted in advance. An ample progressive PAYGO

[57] World Bank, *Averting the old age crisis.* [58] Morris, *Management and regulation*, section 2.4.
[59] Crawford, 'Big pension lie', 39.

provision might actually drive up demand, employment, and prosperity. Or for savers (the inactive) to get more, workers (the active) might need to get less. Current workers might be able to drive a hard bargain that would devalue pensioners' financial claims.

Headline yields are not for the saver, who receives much less. Financial entitlements have to be kept alive, and transaction costs absorb much of the outlay. Initial marketing, commissions, administration, trading charges, taxes, returns on company capital, salaries, and bonuses all have to be paid. A pension saver faces several types of cost: a management charge, portfolio trading costs, shifting between providers (few investors stay the course with one firm), and the taking out of an annuity. The management cost is expressed as a percentage of the current balance in the fund.[60] It grows absolutely as the asset grows. The 'charge ratio' is the percentage by which management and transaction costs reduce the total accumulated. As a rule of thumb (assuming a fund return of 5 per cent real), a management fee of 1 per cent translates into a charge ratio of 20 per cent, i.e. reduces the total accumulated by that magnitude.[61] For the same result, a 1 per cent management charge reduces the 5 per cent yield by 1 percentage point to 4 per cent, i.e. 20 per cent absolutely. Typical management charges on equity-based private-account pensions range between 1 and 2 per cent of assets every year.[62] Charge ratios vary widely, e.g. between about 10 per cent (Bolivia) and 35 per cent (Australia, Mexico, UK). Extra transfer and annuity costs, as well as dealing charges, are not included. In the UK in 1999, taking all costs, and based on the first decade's experience of personal private pension accounts, the average charge ratio, estimated conservatively, came to 43 per cent. This is consistent with published trade assumptions.[63] Some funds charged much more. The cost of investing in managed equity trusts and life offices in the UK came, implicitly, to about one-third of the final payoff: an investment of £1.50 was required to obtain the market rate of return on £1.[64]

[60] Murthi et al., 'The charge ratio'.
[61] Whitehouse, *Paying for pensions*, 77; Orszag, 'Administrative costs', table 1, 7.
[62] Mitchell, 'Administrative costs', table 10.10.
[63] Murthi et al., 'Administrative costs', 308–335, at 331, 324.
[64] James, 'Price of retail investing', 5, 7.

The New Labour government in Britain treated such levels of costs as reasonable – its voluntary 1999 'stakeholder pension' for low earners permitted management costs (before dealing charges) of up to 1.5 per cent, implying a charge ratio of more than 30 per cent (the public stayed away). The most recent compulsory pension plan for low earners (NEST) is similarly handicapped. Its charges are not low: 1.8 per cent of every contribution plus an annual 0.3 per cent on the total. Nevertheless, the insurance industry successfully lobbied for a cap of £4,400 contributions per year, to prevent 'unfair competition'.[65]

John C. Bogle, a senior American financial market insider, railed for decades about the cost of market investment. As the founder and long-time head of Vanguard, a low-cost index fund company, he may have been partial – but his rant was for real. He pointed to additional costs of herd behaviour (bad market timing, bad stock selection), survivor bias (some firms fail), up-front and redemption fees, manipulative and costly marketing, and excessive churning, which generates brokerage fees and tax liabilities. The average investor received only 54 per cent of the nominal market yield and 33 per cent of the fund's final gross value.[66] Corporate managers in listed companies manipulated returns so as to maximise their own payoffs at shareholder expense.[67] Intermediaries and agents, whether fund managers or corporate executives, did not act as fiduciaries, but were in it for themselves. Bogle wrote of a 'a skimming operation', 'fleecing machine', 'giant scam', 'looted funds'.[68] Another insider account is called *A license to steal.*[69]

Savers are easily misled.[70] Taking interest rates at 5 per cent, market horizons are only twenty years, and shorter at higher rates.[71] Life cycles and contracts are longer than that. Stock-picking funds underperform the index and are five times more costly than passive index tracking ones, but most private savers choose these active funds, largely in response to marketing.[72] As entitlements build up, savers can face decades of moral hazard – the firm has a steady income stream and a standing temptation to defect. For example, income

---

[65] Bureau of Investigative Journalism, 'Insurance lobby weakens pension plan'; NEST, *All the facts*, 21.

[66] Bogle, *Battle for the soul*, ch. 7, and table 7.3, 167. [67] Ibid., part I, esp. pp. 22–28.

[68] Ibid., pp. 212, 229. [69] Anon. and Harper, *License to steal*. [70] Schwartz, *Paradox of choice*.

[71] For life insurance, Schleef, 'Joint determination', 620.

[72] Aaron, 'Social security', 71; Bogle, *Battle for the soul*, 94, 202.

protection single-premium policies were widely bundled with insurance and credit in Britain. The Financial Services Authority found that half the policies restricted the ability to claim, or provided very limited cover. Premiums were several times higher than payouts. The regulator fined some companies, had premiums repaid, and, after much delay, has phased the contract out.[73] Financial intermediaries and corporate managers take advantage of outsiders, e.g. by means of 'market timing' (selling outside market hours using breaking information).[74] Even insiders are alarmed. Warren Buffet has described mutual fund directors who buy management services from themselves as looters.[75] The practice is pervasive and legal, but criminal fraud and mismanagement are also endemic. Maxwell in Britain, Enron, Tyco, Worldcom, Global Crossing, Madoff, and Stanford have all stolen money directly from pensioners, savers, and shareholders.

When the time comes to claim, clients may find themselves disqualified by small print.[76] Insurers resist claims aggressively as a matter of policy.[77] Corporations threaten claimants with litigation, and (like several American airlines) can escape from pension liabilities by temporary bankruptcy.[78] Contracts can be used to offload risk. An investor who loses the stock market gamble has no recourse, while managers are protected by limited liability and bankruptcy. Government guarantees for bank deposits, pensions, and life insurance attempt to correct this asymmetry, but in doing so provide opportunities for corporations to take on even more risk.

5.6 STOCK MARKETS ARE TOO SMALL

Another problem with funding has been overlooked.[79] The stock of financial capital is not large enough to provide the scale of revenues

---

[73] Cumbo, 'FSA Steps up campaign'; GB Financial Services Authority, 'FSA update on Payment Protection Insurance (PPI)'.

[74] Bogle, *Battle for the soul*, ch. 7.

[75] Buffet, 'Chairman's Letter', in Bogle, *Battle for the soul*, 228–29.

[76] E.g. Abelson, 'Many with insurance'.

[77] Baker, 'Insurance fraud'; Feinman, *Delay, deny, defend*; Grow et al., 'Fresh pain for the uninsured'; Henry, 'Fortune 500'; Terhune, 'Wrangling over "reasonable" fees'.

[78] Kaplow and Shavell, *Fairness versus welfare*, ch. IV, section B/I; Stein, 'When you fly in first class'.

[79] E.g. Feldstein, *Privatizing social security*.

required. Financial markets are typically too small. It is not widely appreciated that stock markets are not large enough to carry the weight of social insurance and have little spare capacity to take on this role. They do not generate enough revenue. Between 1992 and 2013, 70 per cent of financial wealth in the USA belonged to the top 5 per cent, and 93 per cent to the top quintile. The Gini coefficient of financial wealth was 0.9.[80]

Financial assets are already spoken for and are not available for transfers. In the USA, with the second largest stock market after Britain among rich societies, and the smallest welfare state, the total corporate earnings reported to the equities market was less than half the level of government welfare transfers. In the USA, average government transfer payments (11.4 per cent of GDP, most of it pensions) from 1989 to 2005 were more than twice as large as the average flow of stock market earnings (4.6 per cent of GDP).[81] Over the period 1960–2000, average annual stock market realised rates of return (4.06 per cent) were only slightly higher than the annual growth of real government transfers per capita (3.69 per cent), but their volatility was three times as high (Figure 5.3). Net of management and transaction costs, stock market returns would have been much lower. Asset prices already embody investor *net* revenue expectations, so the rate of return reported here (and assumed by Feldstein) is much too high.

With the government pension and workplace defined benefit schemes a person could be fairly confident of their income in retirement. For defined contribution 'money purchase' personal account savers, whether income will be sufficient or not depends on the state of the stock market at the point when they happen to or choose to retire. Figure 5.3 shows how volatile it can be. The stock market is no longer an inventory of assets which allows an external investor to earn the real rate of return on capital, whatever that really is. In other words, the Feldstein proposal, like a good deal of right-wing economics, was a deception.[82]

---

[80] Wolff, *Century of wealth*, table 2.2, 56.
[81] Level of earnings of S&P 500 extrapolated to whole of stock market capitalization. Beck et al., 'Financial Institutions and markets'; Shiller, 'Stock market data'.
[82] Offer and Söderberg, *Nobel factor*, 33–41, 157–173.

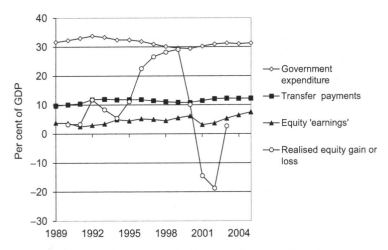

Figure 5.3 USA government and welfare expenditures, stock market equity earnings, and realised equity gain or loss, 1989–2005.
Sources: Beck et al., 'Financial Institutions and markets across countries', chs. 3–4; Carter, 'Historical statistics of the United States'; US, Bureau of Economic Analysis, Industry Economic Accounts Information Guide, 'Annual industry accounts', http://www.bea.gov/industry/iedguide.htm#aia; Shiller, 'Stock market data'.

In 2000, around the time of our calculation of stock market earnings, the USA stock market represented about 150 per cent of GDP (175 in the UK) and even that fell a long way short of providing the necessary cash flows. But that year was a high point. Stock markets were typically much smaller thus limiting their capacity to generate the requisite returns (Figure 5.4). The number of quoted firms in the American stock exchanges also peaked around the year 2000. Since then their numbers have fallen by about one-half, with a great deal of capital exiting public markets into private equity. Although pension funds invested in private equity, this has none of the liquidity and transparency of stock markets. The service fees were high (typically 20 per cent of the profit plus a service charge of 2 per cent of assets) and the promised rates of return impossible to sustain. Hedge funds, another refuge, charge at least 2 per cent management fees but their performance after 2008 has fallen a long way below a typical institutional portfolio comprising 60 per cent

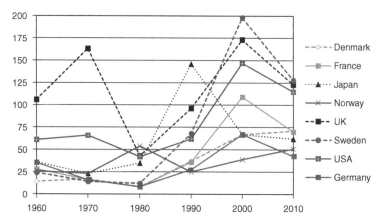

Figure 5.4 Stock market valuations as percentage of GDP, 1960–2012.
Source: Hedberg and Karlsson, 'Internationella och nationella börshandelns', 212.

American equities and 40 per cent Treasury bonds.[83] Bonds would seem
to be another, safer option. But social security revenues are already
invested in government bonds or guaranteed by government. Their
rates of return are low because they are immune to default. Net of risk all
bonds offer the same rate of return so market bond holdings do not
provide any advantage.[84]

Very few countries have embraced full funding. Chile, Australia,
Israel, and Denmark have all installed mandatory funded pension
systems on top of the first-tier PAYGO safety net system, and the
Netherlands have one effectively. The first three have made use of
'money-purchase' defined contribution personal accounts. All of these
countries are small, and thus do not face the constraint of the domestic
stock market – they can hold assets overseas. Nevertheless, returns are
low, management costs are high, and the systems have not bedded
down well. Experience in Latin America and Eastern Europe was
poor.[85] In some Latin American and East European countries there
has been a partial return to PAYGO.[86] In Chile the system has failed.

[83] *Economist*, 'A losing bet'. [84] Munnell and Sass, *Social security and the stock market*, 5–6.
[85] World Bank, 'Economic growth in the 1990s', 186–192.
[86] Australia: Morris, *Management and regulation*, section 2.4; Israel: Spivak, 'Pensions in Israel';
abuses: Bar-Eli, 'It is time to tell the truth'. Chile and the Netherlands, see this section.

The private sector funds made exorbitant profits from high management charges, while investment performance was poor. Most of the assets were government bonds or government-guaranteed; only about a tenth were invested in equities. Only about half the workers contributed, and a large proportion of those failed to build up adequate savings. Four-fifths of pensions fell below the minimum wage, and 44 per cent below the poverty line. In 2008 and again in 2016 there was a phased return to PAYGO. In two rounds of urban riots in Chile in May and December 2019, pensions were by far the largest grievance.[87]

PAYGO pensions face the risk of inadequate revenues to support the promised benefits because of insufficient contributions and increased longevity. The solution is to avoid pre-funding, but to index the benefits to output. For example, the Swedish system specifies a contribution of 16 per cent of wages into a pension account. Sweden had a legacy of state-sponsored funding for second-tier pensions since the 1960s. Under the influence of neoliberalism it introduced a thin layer of mandatory direct contribution funds (2.5 per cent on top of the compulsory 16 per cent contribution to the PAYGO system). Initially private funds proliferated but eventually most savers chose the default public one. Contributions are recorded individually and receive a rate of return equal to the growth in the national wage bill – this is not very different from the contribution record on which most PAYGO pensions are based. Pensions are paid out of tax revenue on a PAYGO basis. The link to the wage bill keeps the risk under control.[88] In the Dutch system a foundation PAYGO layer pays a flat rate pension at 50–70 per cent of the minimum wage. The next layer is effectively a mandatory funded pension for occupational clusters managed by not-for-profit foundations. The entitlements are not individual but pooled, which means that investment and longevity risks are shared. Although funded, these are effectively defined benefit schemes. With economies of scale and not-for-profit administration, the cost is very low. But funding is exposed to market risks: even this prudent scheme,

[87] Arza, 'Noncontributory pensions'; Borzutzky and Hyde, 'Chile's private pension system at 35'; *Economist*, 'Remodelling the model'; Hyde and Borzutzky, 'Chile's neoliberal retirement system'; Laursen, *People's pension*, ch. 20.

[88] This is the core provision. The other components are the small mandatory funded pension as described, separate occupational pensions, and a means tested safety net (Chłoń-Domińczak et al., 'First wave of NDC reforms'; Hagen, *Swedish pension system*).

which used to have assets valued at twice the level of its obligations, went into deficit after the financial crisis of 2008.[89]

The actual work of stock markets is not to raise capital for productive activities but mostly to speculate on existing asset prices. In consequence volatility is very high.[90] Funding pensions in the stock market creates a grotesque mismatch of time horizons. Retirement is decades hence. In the stock market, returns are immediate and depend on a thousandth of a second. A great deal of investment has gone into long-range fibre-optic communications by brokers in order to beat competitors by a split second.[91] In 'high speed trading' low margins produce high profits by means of large volumes. Most trading is currently done that way.

Feldstein was as brilliant an economist as they come, though perhaps too biased even for the Nobel Prize committee.[92] His high citation record tracks that of another outstanding Harvard non-winner on the left, John Kenneth Galbraith.[93] He would surely have understood that the stock market was not big enough to replace social security revenues. Indeed, he recommended that only one-fifth of the payroll tax should be invested there, an effective acknowledgement that financial market funding as advocated by Friedman was impossible. One-fifth was sufficient, however, to boost the assets of wealthy people like himself, and the business of the financial firms on whose boards he sat.[94] He took the financial crisis of 2008 as a unique opportunity to inflict pain on ordinary people: 'painful cuts in government pensions and in public payrolls as well as increases in personal taxes may only be possible while there is a sense of crisis throughout Europe'.[95]

5.7 CONCLUSION

The obligations of social insurance extend for decades and are therefore largely ruled out by credit time horizons from 'free market' solutions.

---

[89] Broeders and Ponds, 'Dutch pension system reform'; Dutch Association, 'The Dutch pension system'.
[90] Haldane, 'Patience and finance'.　[91] Lewis, *Flash boys*.
[92] Offer and Söderberg, *Nobel factor*, ch. 5, and fig. 6.8, 139.　[93] Ibid., fig. 6.8, 139.
[94] Mitchell, 'Martin Feldstein should be ignored'.
[95] Feldstein, 'Double dip is a price worth paying'.

Governments and financial corporations began to provide support for old age ever since the middle of the nineteenth century.[96] After almost two centuries, the experience is this. As in the case of education, the rich and the better off can provide for themselves – they can lay aside savings and pay financial intermediaries. They also take the lion's share of the tax benefits. In the developed world, most of those who retire receive basic old-age pensions by means of government PAYGO schemes which often extend to a higher tier of earnings-based provision as well. The replacement rates vary considerably from one country to another. To provide a universal and safe retirement pension there is no viable substitute for the basic pay-as-you-go system, and that is why it persists. In most countries there is also a middle layer provided by financial corporations, professional associations, or voluntary organisations. Some of them are conducted frugally and efficiently, others enrich managers and intermediaries. Much of the British middle-class pension solution of terminable life insurance was undertaken by mutual insurance societies. Equitable Life, the largest and most important of these, collapsed with serious recriminations in 2000.[97] These associations are not 'free market'. Many are not-for-profit. They mostly fall into the 'franchise' category: they depend on a range of fiscal incentives and regulation. Both savers and providers have an implicit government bailout which makes sure that a pension will be paid come what may, though not always up to the expected level.

Milton and Rose Friedman wrote in 1962 that social security had 'given birth to a large bureaucracy that shows tendencies of growing by what it feeds on'.[98] But government pay-as-you go systems are between one and two orders of magnitude cheaper to run than private stock-market investment accounts. In the USA in 1999, social security administrative expenses amounted to 0.5 per cent of benefit payments.[99] This was about 1/50th of the management charges on

---

[96] Hannah, *Occupational pension funds*.
[97] GB HC, 'Equitable Life Inquiry'; GB Parliamentary and Health Service Ombudsman, 'Equitable Life'.
[98] Friedman and Friedman, *Capitalism and freedom*, 189.
[99] United States Social Security Administration, 'Annual statistical supplement 2000', table 4. A1, Old-Age and Survivors Insurance, 1937–1999, 136; 0.7 per cent according to Mitchell, 'Administrative costs', 406.

private pension accounts. Government creates large risk pools, it deals uniformly with large numbers of people, and it does not need to sell: it can mandate participation to suppress free riding. A similar advantage of public over private was found in health: private insurance administrative costs in the USA were estimated at 12 per cent of spending, compared to 1.3 per cent in the tax-financed health service in Canada.[100]

There is good deal of alarm about the future solvency of American and European welfare systems.[101] But if the taxpayers cannot pay, then they won't. Long before collapse, the terms will be revised. American social security payouts were raised under Nixon and lowered under Reagan, in both cases in line with changing actuarial expectations. They are reasonably secure now, and provide quite substantial replacement rates. They form the bulk of retirement income for most people. They will be revised again if necessary.

A contract for delivery decades hence is uncertain. For a pension contract the risks include: market volatility, costly annuities, inflation, outlived savings, mismanagement, opportunism, default, regulatory and political risk. This still embodies a considerable overestimate of the payout, which assumes no charges, transaction costs, or taxes. A worker might invest more privately to get a higher return, but the volatility would not change. A financial balance is a hoard. Once spent, it is gone. In contrast, a public pension entitlement continues for life with some inflation protection. PAYGO is a claim on 'the community's indestructible real tax base'.[102] In effect, it is a claim on a share of GDP – how much to be revealed when it comes up for payment.

Dependents have little to trade with. So how can they compel delivery? Despite being a minority their bargaining power is not zero. Their needs are salient in a way that claims in the remote future are not. The elderly are here, present, and able to speak and to vote. Welfare entitlements often rely on a record of contributions. The

---

[100] Woolhandler, 'Costs of health care'; American health costs are far higher than in OECD countries, and health outcomes are substantially inferior (Angrisano et al., *Cost of health care*; Garber and Skinner, 'Is American health care uniquely inefficient?').

[101] Largely an American trope, directed against both American social security, and European welfare states, e.g. Kotlikoff and Burns, *Coming generational storm*; Peterson, *Gray dawn*.

[102] Samuelson, 'Exact consumption-loan model', 482, n. 23.

old, the ageing, and parents vote disproportionately. From 1964 to 2006, of those aged between 18 and 24, less than a third voted in congressional elections, about one-half of those aged 25 to 44, and 62 per cent of those older than 45.[103] An implicit contract rests on the norm of reciprocity. The old have paid taxes in the past and fairness entitles them to something in return. The young who pay now can expect to benefit in the future. If there was no social insurance families would have to carry much of the burden and PAYGO insures against this liability.[104] Family dependency risks are 'lumpy' and today's family webs too thin and frail to carry them. The government's promise may be a 'soft' one, but the spuriously 'hard' contracts of financial service companies are no more robust.

The contract gets modified to reflect voters' changing level of generosity. Entitlement was not abandoned but it was tightened. In Britain, as the state pension declined, contribution-based entitlement was replaced by a means-tested one, still an entitlement by another name (in this case, 'minimum income guarantee' and 'pension credit'), with no requirement for a record of contributions. It has remained a good deal. Paul Samuelson considered that PAYGO beneficiaries could not expect more than the increase in national income per head in return for their contributions.[105] Arguably, according to Modern Monetary Theory, so long as the economy is short of full employment tax revenue is not a constraint. It does not seem to be. Overall, in 2003, for £32bn that were paid in that year as National Insurance contributions, UK pensioners received £46bn retirement pensions, a notional 'rate of return' of 43 per cent. The total of contribution-earned transfers was £58bn (a notional return of 81 per cent) with means-tested benefits on top of that.[106] If distribution was still dire, it was because of rising inequality and poverty in Britain during the Thatcher years.

The well-off campaign to expose public employees to the same market rigours experienced by private sector ones.[107] As in the case of private education, the push to pre-fund pensions by means of

---

[103] US Census Bureau, 'Voting and registration', Table A-1, 'Reported voting and registration by age'.
[104] Offer, *Challenge of affluence*, 88–9. [105] Samuelson, 'The exact consumption-loan model'.
[106] In 2003. GB ONS, *United Kingdom national accounts 2003*, table 13 (App. 1).
[107] Goff, 'Public sector staff set for wealthier retirement'; Miles, 'Gold-plated pensions'.

financial assets has likewise not succeeded. It works well for the better-off due to extensive tax subsidies. It is also in their interests as lenders and taxpayers. For the rest it provides inadequate retirement income at excessive cost. Historically, the only way to provide an adequate retirement for all is by means of PAYGO, which does not require speculating on a distant future. Funded retirement is in perpetual crisis; most of the world, most of the time, prefers versions of pay-as-you-go and continues to rely on mutual insurance by means of defined benefit pensions. The experience of several decades confirms the durability of collective education and retirement arrangements, and confirms that market competition is only efficient when time horizons are short.

CHAPTER 6

Housing and Democracy

What could be more private-sector than home ownership? In England, 'My home is my castle'. In Europe, North America, and Australia most households own their dwellings, and most of those who don't aspire to ownership. Housing is financed, constructed, and owned privately, is traded in markets, and serves as collateral. To achieve ownership there is an obstacle to overcome. Dwellings can last for a century or more but lenders expect their money back much sooner, a hurdle to ownership that requires collective action to overcome.

6.1 THE ARGUMENT

In the nineteenth century most city dwellers in Europe lived in rented accommodation, on short-term contracts with private landlords. Much of the housing was expensive or bad. Since late-Victorian times housing provision has gone through three stages: petty capitalism, social democracy, and financialisation. From the end of the First World War and up to 1980 governments increasingly strove to provide housing for all by controlling rents, enabling owner-occupation, and constructing it themselves. Everybody gained. After 1980 they turned over housing finance to commercial banking, creating losers as well as winners.

House values rise as the economy grows. Much of the time they grow even faster than the economy, with no effort on the part of the owner.[1] In the nineteenth century these windfalls went to proprietors. In the twentieth century social democracy distributed them

[1] Offer, 'Ricardo's paradox'.

progressively in the form of security for renters and capital gains for owner-occupiers. By converting renters into owners social democracy provided them with a 'nest egg' source of economic security as an alternative to the welfare state. Mass home ownership made everybody into a capitalist, accustomed them to large financial transactions, turned them against redistribution, and shifted political views to the right.[2]

Home ownership provided a constituency for neoliberalism. But housing markets cannot handle short break-evens on their own, and continue to rely on government support. Free-market delusions in recent decades have stoked up a new housing crisis that threatens the foundations of democracy.[3]

6.2 HOUSING SUPPLY 1870–2008

Construction is paid for up front over the time that it takes to erect a dwelling, which then provides shelter for a century or more.[4] Housing then has to be paid for out of recurrent income. There is a mismatch between the high initial cost and what the dwellers can afford to pay every week or month. How much they can afford depends on how long they or the landlord are given to pay back a mortgage, or conversely, how long the owner or lender can wait to make a profit. The longer these periods, the less needs to come out of current income, even if the total is larger. What determined the length of the break-even period was the rate of interest. Shelter was not cheap in the nineteenth century because the cost was loaded up front and had to be paid off during a few initial years. Break-even rarely took more than a dozen years, for an asset that can last ten times longer. To make housing affordable repayment had to be extended somehow. The small mortgagee and house landlord could not afford to do so and the task eventually shifted to deeper pockets, initially to philanthropy and voluntary associations, and then to local and central government. This shift released large economies of scale in finance and administration which made it possible to reduce the monthly cost of housing even more.

[2] Harris and Hamnett, 'Myth of the promised land', 175–176; Ansell, 'The "nest egg" effect'.
[3] Offer, 'Market turn'.   [4] Tarbuck, *Handbook of house property*, 167.

Up to the First World War (and up to the Great Depression in North America), housing finance and construction were undertaken by small business. The financial turbulence of wartime disrupted the stability that such enterprise required. After 1918 governments facilitated longer repayment periods with several initiatives. They pushed effective interest rates down below market levels and provided security to lenders by building dwellings on their own account, supporting voluntary associations, encouraging not-for-profit credit, and introducing loan guarantees, subsidies, and tax reductions. Repayment periods were stretched out to twenty-five years in the UK and thirty in North America, which made housing at least twice as affordable. Rent control put an end to the pre-war property cycle.

Even a single borrower's default was a large risk for a petty capitalist. When risks were pooled into large bundles after the First World War defaults turned out to be low because long tenures were aligned with the life-cycle objectives and resources of households. By the 1970s, government interventions had cleared away the worst slums and extended home ownership to majorities of households in English-speaking countries. Combined with full employment, owner-occupation became the bedrock of democratic consent for mixed-economy capitalist economies, but large groups, about a third of households, were still left out. In Scandinavia and the German-speaking-countries ownership levels were lower, but rental more secure.

In the 1970s this private–public collaboration came under pressure. De-industrialisation diminished manual worker electorates, while additional years of education and white-collar work gave rise to self-reliant and opportunistic voters. Academic economists in the expanding universities advocated market efficiency and de-regulation, notions then transmitted into business and government by their graduates.

In Britain lenders kept mortgages on their books all the way to maturity. After 1980 credit controls were relaxed and commercial banks, taking housing as collateral, moved in to capture the finance of housing.[5] In the United States mortgage originators sold the loans on to government-supported agencies which enhanced them with

[5] For the UK, Offer, 'Narrow banking'; Butzbach, 'British building societies', fig. 2, 138.

federal guarantees, securitised them in large batches, and sold them on to investors. In the 1990s commercial banks began to forsake these guarantees in order to lend to less creditworthy borrowers. Rising house prices created a speculative opportunity which turned into a frenzy in the early 2000s, everybody pushing prudence aside in pursuit of yield and capital gains. Borrowers took on more debt than they could service and when prices turned down, the financial system seized up. In response, American and British governments bailed out the banks at previously unimagined cost, and continued to pump them up for years. In the United States, however, millions of people lost their homes, while British ones suffered the ensuing shocks of recession and austerity. These household traumas played a part in the political crisis of Western democracies which has emerged since 2008.[6]

6.3 NINETEENTH-CENTURY HOUSING

The land surface of central London is owned by a small number of noble families, notably the Bedford, Cadogan, Eyre, Grosvenor, Portman, and Howard de Walden estates. Aristocracy has a dynastic outlook. Landed property (both rural and urban) was not owned outright, but was held in legal trust for future generations.[7] From the seventeenth century onwards these London estates laid out ample residential squares for well-heeled tenants, with exclusive gardens in their centre. Land was let out on ninety-nine-year building leases which reverted to the owners with houses intact, and was then re-let on residential leases. Three centuries later the elegance and grandeur of these squares testifies to the vision of the owners.[8] This cycle was only partly disrupted in recent decades by a circumscribed right to convert leasehold into ownership. The Crown, the City Corporation of London, and several charities hold ground on similar terms. The National Trust, set up in Britain at the end of the nineteenth century, acquired the mansions of hard-up

---

[6] For the United States, e.g. Immergluck, *Preventing the next mortgage crisis*; an encompassing view, Muellbauer, 'When is a housing market overheated'.
[7] Thompson, *English landed society*, 64–70; English and Saville, *Strict settlement*.
[8] Anon., *Great estates*; Olsen, *Town planning in London*.

landowners and opened them to the public. The former owners remained in residence. This tenure combined dynastic permanence with popular access to preserve the timeless appeal of great palaces and gardens.

For everyone else their tenure was often secure for no more than a few days at a time. In England and Wales housing was typically rented by the occupiers, not owned, for periods of time that increased with the rent. Labourers occupied by the week, skilled artisans might rent by the month, while the middle classes (in the British sense, i.e. the top fifth or so) took their houses for a quarter, a year, or, in the case of the well-to-do, on leases for a few years.

Housing as a business was a lot of work. Dwellings were run up by builders and sold on to investor-managers who borrowed in order to buy. These 'landlords' let out the dwellings and managed them. Builders, owners, and lenders worked mostly on a small scale. Lenders were typically private individuals: savings were aggregated and lent out locally either by one person directly to another or by local solicitors (i.e. lawyers).[9] In the 1890s the yield of government bonds ('consols') fluctuated around 2.7 per cent, and mortgages typically yielded 4.5 or 5 per cent a year, i.e. almost twice as much, but with much less security.[10]

The business of housing in Britain depended on credit. Small savers invested in mortgages because exit looked easy and the yield was more than on government bonds. If the loan was called in, the borrower could re-mortgage easily, and if not, they were able to sell: London at least had an auction facility with rapid turnover.[11] Money was lent out for a term of six months initially, and once that time was up could be called in at three months' notice. Mortgage loans were typically of between one-half to two-thirds of market value. This is confirmed in the aggregate too: the flow of mortgages was about three-quarters of housing sales and leases: taking off rural mortgages and industrial ones, the scale of mortgage finance was between one-half and two-thirds of sale and lease transaction values.[12] Investors in property expected to earn 7 to 9 per cent a year, i.e. up to twice the cost of credit.[13] The margin above loan service was required to cover

---

[9] Offer, *Property and politics*, 142–144.
[10] Tarbuck, *Handbook of house property*, 123; Samy, *Building society promise*, fig. 2.3, 60
[11] Offer, *Property and politics*, 254–259. [12] Ibid., 68–69. [13] Ibid., 278.

profit, management, repairs, and replacement. Both new construction and buy-to-let responded to the interest rate. Rents, however, could not rise much. They were capped by income levels, which rose only slowly.[14] Stable rents made housing akin to a fixed-income security. When interest rates increased, the fixed rental stream was worth less, depressing the asset value. Conversely, when interest rates declined, house values rose. Landlords aspired to pay off the mortgages and own their property outright. Mostly they succeeded. Death duties indicate that between 1896 and 1914 mortgage debt on housing and business premises was only a quarter of their value, for which somewhat more than a third was pledged as collateral.[15]

This financial system underpinned the cyclical growth of the great British cities, but in the last peacetime decade before the First World War it went through its terminal disruption. In the 1890s interest rates fell about 14 per cent, which set off an unprecedented construction boom in dwellings, commercial buildings, and taverns. Public investment in paving, drains, schools, gas, electricity, and tramways had to follow, which drove up municipal taxes (known as 'rates'). Early in the twentieth century interest rates turned up again and house values began to fall. Stagnant wages, unemployment, emigration, and more legal security for tenants also worked against landlords.[16] Around 1903, a deep depression began to settle on the housing market, the Edwardian property slump. Nothing like it has ever happened since.

Mortgage interest rates did not change very much: credit was regulated by quantity rather than price. When house prices fell, it appears that old mortgages were not recalled, but that new ones were not extended. Instead of mortgages, savers looked elsewhere, to municipal and overseas bonds, which offered better returns than domestic ones. Overseas investments were also secured or subsidised by governments. Some 93 per cent of capital exports from Britain, France, and Germany between 1880 and 1913 went into government or government-supported entities.[17] Hence, even before the First World War, free-market housing was squeezed by the superior security of government.

[14] Ibid., 264–268; Samy, *Building society promise*, fig. 2.2, 59.
[15] Offer, *Property and politics*, 138–139. [16] Ibid., 224–227; Daunton, *House and home*, chs. 5–7.
[17] Offer, *Property and politics*, 144–147; Bent and Esteves, 'Government-supported industries', table 3.

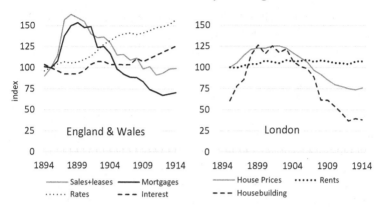

Figure 6.1 The Edwardian property slump: property market activity in
England and Wales and London, 1894–1914.
Sources: House numbers (Great Britain), Stamp, *British incomes and property*,
table H.D, 141. Sales and mortgages, Great Britain, *Inland Revenue annual
reports*, in Offer, *Property and politics*, table 4.2, 66–67 with explanatory notes.
Rates and interest rates, Mitchell, *British historical statistics*, 'Public finance
11', 609–610; ibid., 'Financial institutions 13', 678. London house prices and
rents, Samy, 'Indices of house prices and rent', Table A.3.1–2, 41, 43;
Housebuilding, Weber, 'A new index of house rents', 131–132.
Notes: 'Rates' are local taxation. Index (1895=100) with house numbers kept
constant at 1895 level. 100 equals £140m (sales and leases), £104m (mortgages),
£40m (rates), 2.7% (yield on British perpetual bonds), £39 (median rent), £325
(median price). Housebuilding index, 100=mean 1900–1909. Calendar year up to
March. Interest rate calendar year lagged -1. Chapter 6, Appendix 1 for more detail.

Figure 6.1 shows how sensitive credit was to interest rates and taxes.
In 1895, for every increase of 10 per cent in the yield on government
bonds (consols) (e.g. from 2.7 per cent to 2.97 per cent) the flow of
mortgages in England and Wales would have fallen by about
23 per cent (i.e. by £24m). The elasticity was about the same for
local taxation.[18] New construction was even more sensitive and rose
and fell more sharply. By the First World War, compared with 1895,
interest rates had risen by about a quarter and local taxation by half.
During the Edwardian period London house prices fell about

---

[18] Chapter 6, Appendix 1.

40 per cent below their peak. The flow of mortgages, which peaked in 1899, fell by more than half from that peak. When credit dried up, so did British housing supply (Chapter 6, Appendix 1 for more detail). Effectively, public long-term investment (municipal and overseas) crowded private housebuilding out of the credit market by means of higher taxes and guaranteed foreign bonds.

When house prices fell they no longer provided sufficient collateral for the credit they secured. In these circumstances it would be risky for lenders to call in the loans and to advance new ones. The number of transactions and their values both fell.[19] If landlords had to sell they faced big losses. With rents capped by sluggish demand it was difficult to make a profit. The size of the housing stock was not affected much; it continued to grow. What collapsed was market liquidity, the ability to attract investment and to sell it on quickly if necessary. A very high rate of return (*c.* 14 per cent) kept the market turning over, albeit at a much lower level of activity and prices. Such figures signified a very high risk – a break-even time horizon of seven years or so, but even that may have been too long. The mode of production anticipated its own collapse.

Our model of interest rates and time horizons (Chapter 1, 1.2–1.3) specifies that the higher the rate, the shorter the wait, and the more difficult it is to finance long-term assets. House prices fell sharply during the Edwardian period. The same happened to the volume of sales and to new construction, and, at the national scale, to the flow of mortgages.

'Years Purchase' was a late-Victorian measure of value (going back before Adam Smith and still in use today) for land and house prices. It was calculated by dividing the price by the annual rent and is precisely the same concept as our own 'payback period', namely the number of annual rental payments that add up to the purchase price.[20] Its main use was as a common measure for heterogeneous properties: 100 divided by years purchase gives the yield. Table 6.1 shows that between 1892 and 1912 Years Purchase of London properties fell almost by half. This decline is also expressed as a rise in the

---

[19] Offer, *Property and politics*, 270.
[20] Smith, *Wealth of nations*, Bk. II, ch. 4, 358; Tarbuck, *Handbook of house property*, 125; Marshall, *Principles of economics*, 593.

Table 6.1 *The Edwardian property slump: Years Purchase of London house property, 1892–1912* (yield in brackets)

	Freehold	Leasehold	Mean Rents
1892	11.8 *(8.5%)*	8.7 *(11.5%)*	£39.20
1897	10.9 *(9.2%)*	8.3 *(12.0%)*	£37.40
1902	11.8 *(8.5%)*	8.7 *(11.5%)*	£40.70
1907	9.6 *(10.4%)*	6.6 *(15.1%)*	£37.90
1912	7.4 *(13.5%)*	5.2 *(19.2%)*	£39.40

Source: London Auction Mart, in Offer, *Property and politics*, 278. Rents, interpolated five-year figures from Samy, 'Indices of house prices', table A.3.2.

Note: The rate of return is net of local taxation, but includes repairs and management costs. Assuming a mortgage for 60% of the value and a rent of 8.5% (as in 1892), the rate of return on the landlord's capital (i.e. all landlord functions bought in) would be 10.1% (9.9 Years Purchase). In 1912 this would rise to 21.6% (with value falling to 4.6 Years Purchase).

gross yield of houses from 8.5 per cent to 13.5 per cent, suggesting a very high-risk premium. On the landlord's capital alone (over and above the cost of debt service) the rate of return would rise to 21.6 per cent, a Years Purchase of 4.6 (Table 6.1, note). The requirement to break even in 4.6 years on an investment with an economic life of 100 can be compared to fever in a patient.

The Edwardian property slump was the terminal crisis of the petty capitalist system of housing supply. Free markets in buy-to-let housing did not survive the First World War. War is an indeterminate open-ended project that only governments can fund. The long-horizon imperative of national survival destroyed the short-term system of free-market housing supply. New construction stopped when war began. For those who stayed behind work was easy to find and wages high. Workers crowded into the centres of war production. Prices rose faster than wages. Soldiers' families became indigent. In 1915 Parliament froze rents and mortgage interest at their pre-war level.[21] Not only in Britain: combatant countries and most of the others too implemented

---

[21] Stafford and Doling, 'Rent control'; Rider, *Ten years' adventures*.

rent controls, which effectively froze the pre-existing systems of housing supply. Laissez-faire in housing never recovered.

6.4 COMMUNITARIAN ENTERPRISE

A housing crisis had been brewing for decades. You cannot have a free
labour market and a free housing market concurrently: the better off will
crowd out the poor, and unskilled workers will compete wages down
below subsistence. More than three-quarters of households in Britain
were made up of manual workers, about a third of them in poverty at
any time. Skilled workers as well could be laid off for the season and
unskilled ones sometimes had to seek work every day. Travelling into
town was costly, making it necessary to live near work, and inner-city
rents were high. Trapped in a low-wage/high-rent equilibrium, the most
insecure workers lived in squalor.[22] Contemporaries understood: 'I do
not deny that artisans have good dwellings in many towns,' said Arnold
Toynbee in a resonant lecture in 1881, 'but I assert that the dwellings of
the great mass of the people are a danger to our civilization'. Interest
rates were too high, he said. The Home Secretary and expert testimony
in 1875 had 'all declared that the great mass of labourers cannot be
provided with decent houses at a remunerative price'. The solution was
'for the community to step in and give the necessary aid'.[23]

A new housing form began to appear in the 1860s, 'model dwellings', solid and spartan apartment blocks erected by philanthropists
(notably by an American banker's Peabody Trust in London), and
many of them are still there today. 'The Peabody Trustees keep their
interest at three percent gross, thirty or forty percent below that of
other companies.'[24] These 'other companies' were early types of
social   enterprise,   limited   liability   companies   committed   to
'5 per cent philanthropy'. They capped their rate of return, and
bundled investment opportunity with social virtue. Five per cent
was the historical usury cap in Britain, only recently abolished. It was
comparable to returns on investments with similar risk profiles
(though much less than what private landlords took).[25] With

---

[22] Daily News, *No room to live*; Jones, *Outcast London*; Wohl, *Eternal slum*.
[23] Toynbee, 'Are Radicals socialists?', 234, 236. [24] Ibid., 236.
[25] Morris, 'Market solutions', 538.

government bonds at around half this yield, 5 per cent provided a twenty-year break-even (on the payback method) which allowed an affordable rent and a reasonable rate of return.

But this was not a market answer to the housing question. To keep costs low, model dwelling companies insisted on punctual payment and respectable lifestyles. They cherry-picked precisely those tenants sought after by private landlords. Pools of well-meaning investors and reputable tenants were not large enough. Philanthropic and commercial housing associations together put up about 36,000 dwellings in London over three decades, more than a tenth of new working-class housing; of this, about three-quarters was provided for profit.[26] From the middle of the 1890s interest rates began to rise, depressing asset values. The return (including capital gains) began to fall short of the promised 5 per cent and then turned negative in the Edwardian period. Local government began to build to similar designs in Liverpool in 1869. The London County Council inaugurated its well-designed and well-built model dwellings in 1899. Those that were privatised in the 1980s command premium middle-class rents today.[27]

6.5 AFTER THE WAR: GOVERNMENT TAKEOVER

In 1915 the number of dwelling houses in Great Britain was 8.2 million. Between 1919 and 1939 some 4.4 million new houses were added, the largest surge of housebuilding in Britain ever, either before or since. This was not achieved by rugged individuals (apart perhaps for the actual workmen), but by not-for-profit institutions, both voluntary and governmental. Figure 6.2 plots the magnitudes of the three British housing regimes. In the first laissez-faire period up to the First World War, new construction averaged 2.8 a year per thousand people, put up by local building firms, then sold on to investors using short buy-to-let mortgages with low loan-to-value ratios (50–66 per cent). In the second period, from 1920 to 1980, construction was twice as high at 5.85 per 1000 (excluding the Second World War). Housing was subsidised and regulated. One million new houses were rented out by local authorities while most of the rest

---

[26] Ibid., 530, 533. [27] Boughton, *Municipal dreams*, 8.

Figure 6.2 New dwellings per year per 1,000 people in Great Britain,
1856–2014.
Sources: 1855–1980, Mitchell, *British historical statistics*, tables Building 5, 7,
pp. 390, 392. 1980–2014, GB ONS, Table 209. House building: permanent
dwellings completed.[28]

were built for owner-occupation. Building firms were much larger
and built about 3.4 million houses for sale between the wars.

Buy-to-let in Britain could no longer be revived after 1918. Most of
the existing stock was on controlled rents. Yet it was still worth
holding on to: interest rates were high, the assets still returned
a revenue (the same as in 1914), and the pound recovered its pre-
war value. So private rental remained the most common tenure until
after the next war, but could not attract new investment. Instead (and
apart from public housing), the subsequent housing booms up to
1980 were of owner-occupation, financed by building societies.

These mutual societies had their origins in Victorian times, but came
of age under interwar conditions. Unlike individual mortgage lenders
before the war, the societies were financial institutions, and some of
them grew to be very large. As mutual societies, owned by their

[28] https://www.gov.uk/government/statistical-data-sets/live-tables-on-house-building.

customers, they did not have to pay dividends and got by with a surplus half as large as the banks, 'a steady ratio of net profits to total capital and reserves of 5%, compared to a highly variable 10.1% for banks'.[29] In comparison with lending money out on mortgage, saving with a building society was safer, for the same rate of return, and with immediate and costless exit if required. For borrowers, monthly payments were lower: building societies offered repayment terms of up to 25 years, and loan-to-value ratios of up to 95 per cent. They knew their customers and had very low rates of arrears and bad debts. Owner-occupation was like a self-service checkout – passing the cost of management on to the customer. The saving was large: it could take about a third off the borrower's interest payments (i.e. the monthly cost net of capital repayments) while the lender's break-even remained almost the same (Figure 6.3). And after twenty-five years there was no more to pay.

Everyone was in it for the long term: neither depositors, nor lenders, nor borrowers were likely to walk away. Building society loan maturities coincided with the typical duration of child rearing in

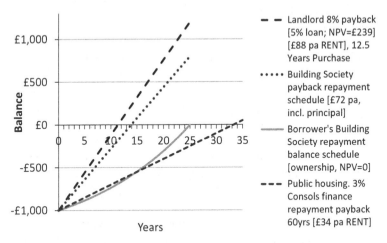

Figure 6.3 Affording a house, England and Wales post 1920, mortgage interest at 5 per cent.
Note: Exclusive of local taxation which was payable by the occupier.

---

[29] Samy, *Building society promise*, 33.

small, stable families. To extend tenure from weeks or months to decades was a remarkable innovation.

Figure 6.3 shows the annual payment under different credit regimes, all at the same prevailing mortgage interest rate of 5 per cent. An 8 per cent gross return to landlords would have been a typical level before the First World War. The landlord's markup of 3 per cent over credit cost covered profit, management, and repairs. Taking this markup as the cost of loan service on the landlord's own capital, the combined lenders' (mortgagee and landlord) break-even was 12½ years, requiring the cost of the house to be front loaded, i.e. high in weekly or monthly terms. Building societies spread the payments over 25 years (i.e. twice as long) and that included repayment of principal. Their break-even, however, was only two years longer than the landlords' and actually about the same, since they had no repair costs and management was cheaper. The annual cost to the occupier was 18 per cent lower, with full ownership at the end. Public housing was the cheapest, since it had the benefit of low government borrowing rates. The annual rent of public housing was about half of building society mortgage repayments, even including repayment of principal (in sixty years).[30]

Building societies were prudent: they were pure intermediaries which only took deposits and lent them out. The money was genuinely all withdrawn from consumption, and the supply of housing credit was therefore self-regulating and non-inflationary.[31] So despite the massive building boom of the 1930s, house prices remained stable. The building societies passed on government subsidies to the savers in the form of tax concessions. Cyclical factors also helped, a steep decline in interest rates after 1932, falling prices, the low price of materials, and high unemployment which kept labour costs down.[32]

The final turning point came in 1980 when governments embraced neoliberalism. The new Conservative government invited local government tenants to buy their houses at knock-down prices and halted the construction of new ones. After 1945 public housing made up about half of new construction, so new housebuilding fell sharply from 1980

---

[30] Needleman, *Economics of housing*, 119–120.
[31] Contrary here to Ryan-Collins et. al, *Rethinking*, 115, 131; Offer, 'Narrow banking', 162–163.
[32] Richardson and Aldcroft, *Building in the British economy*; Samy, *Building society promise*, ch. 3; Speight, 'Who bought the inter-war semi?'

onwards, down almost back to Victorian levels (Figure 6.2). But government did not withdraw from housing. In line with its preference for the private sector, it shifted the subsidy into a cash housing benefit for low earners which went to private landlords instead of local authorities. The imagined security of this revenue flow stimulated a revival of buy-to-let rental as a long-term investment for small savers, and reactivated some of its historical pathologies. With no historical memory, these petty landlords did not realise how vulnerable they were to the twists and turns of government policy, as proved to be the case when their allowances were cut and their taxes rose under austerity after 2010.

Commercial banks were allowed to enter housing finance after 1980, and most societies soon turned themselves into banks as well. Banks do not rely as much on deposits, and can create new money in response to credible borrower demand.[33] After credit controls were lifted in 1980, and especially after 1986, they expanded credit against what appeared to be the safe collateral of bricks and mortar.[34] With credit abundant, house prices soared. Banks lent ever more readily against rising house values, in a self-reinforcing cycle. Shelter is a necessity and people competed to buy, which pushed prices higher still. To meet the cost, more married women went out to work. With credit abundant interest rates fell, which inflated house prices further. The banks increased their leverage, i.e. lent out a higher multiple of their capital and reserves. Mortgage repayments were cycled by the banks into yet more lending. Eventually borrowers had to reduce consumption in order to service debt, and the fall in demand brought the boom to a halt.[35]

A high level of debt service appears to be the best predictor of financial crisis – it reached its peak in Britain shortly after the onset of the financial crisis of 2008.[36] First movers early on made a large property windfall. A social divide began to grow, between those already on the property ladder, and those unable to reach up to its first rung.[37] In 1996 banks began to finance buy-to-let landlords, mostly small investors who are re-creating the Victorian housing

[33] Goodhart, 'Determination of the money supply'.
[34] Offer, 'Market turn', 1060; Ryan-Collins et al., *Rethinking*, ch. 5.
[35] Offer, 'Market turn', 1065–1066; Clarke et al., *Housing headwind*.
[36] Drehmann and Juselius, 'Debt service costs', 26. [37] Corlett and Judge, 'Home affront'.

world of short and insecure tenancies.[38] A new 'generation rent' suffers insecure, expensive, and inadequate housing, without much hope of ownership except waiting decades for parental bequests.[39] Those who fail to buy may be driven into poverty when they retire, unable to pay the rent out of smaller retirement incomes.[40]

Subsidies continued, however, both overt and covert. As in Victorian times, private building alone, together with the relics of public housing, was not sufficient to provide adequate accommodation. Despite being more than four times wealthier than in 1914, Britain is again in the grip of a housing crisis, one of the most intractable of its social dilemmas.[41]

6.6 EUROPE

In the nineteenth century non-bank housing finance was the rule in advanced countries and the system was already in trouble by the first years of the twentieth.[42] For low earners, accommodation was overcrowded, insanitary, and in short supply. Governments only regulated public health and urban layout. In the autumn of 1914 construction stopped in the combatant countries. After several years of under-construction in peacetime, five more years were lost to the war. Most developed countries introduced rent controls and were slow to lift it afterwards.[43] Interest rates and inflation were high and volatile. Wartime governments had taken control of capital, labour, and land, and 'war socialism' continued into peacetime. In the aftermath of the war, most countries began to build public housing or to pay for it, some of them on a large scale (see table 6.2). In Austria government provided about three-quarters of new housing up to 1930 including the iconic Karl Marx Hof near Vienna. In Norway almost 50 per cent of new houses were built by government, and another quarter by housing associations. Governments preferred if possible not to act directly but by means of franchise arrangements, i.e. to provide a safety-net subsidy

[38] Ryan-Collins et al., *Rethinking*, 184. [39] Judge and Tomlinson, 'Home improvements'.
[40] Best and Martin, 'Rental housing'. [41] Corlett and Judge, 'Home affront'.
[42] Daunton, *Housing the workers*; Pooley, *Housing strategies in Europe*.
[43] Willis, 'Rent control laws', 67–77.

Table 6.2 *New building in Europe, 1914–1929, percentage by sector*

Countries and towns	Years covered	(1) Public	(2) Societies	(3) Private
England and Wales (whole country)	1919–1929	36	in col. 3	64
Netherlands (whole country)	1921–1929	11	18	71
Sweden (all towns)	1919–1928	10	13	77
Denmark (all towns)	1920–1929	16	31	53
Norway (5 most important towns)	1914–1928	47	29	24
Czechoslovakia (78 towns over 10,000)	1928–1929	10	16	74
Finland (all towns)	1924–1928	2	21	77
Austria (whole country)	1914–1928	73	9	18
Poland (Warsaw)	1922–1929	5	15	80
Germany (whole country)	1927–1929	11	31	58

Source: ILO, *Housing policy in Europe*, 45.

for private rental.[44] Much of this intervention took the form of grants and subsidies which are difficult to trace in detail.[45]

Unlike the United States and England, the typical housing form in Europe was not the suburban house on its plot, but an apartment in a housing bloc. The existing legacy of housing finance was designed for the construction and ownership of such structures. Germany had invented securitisation back in the eighteenth century. Housing investment there was financed by specialised banks which raised capital by issuing mortgage-backed bonds (*Pfandbriefe*). Each bond was secured on a particular mortgage, and also against the bank's whole loan book. Loan-to-value ratios did not exceed 60 per cent, and with many dwellings in every building, complete default was unlikely. Savers acquired a liquid, tradeable security, almost as good as government bonds. But if lenders were secure, builders and landlords were exposed: mortgages typically ran for less than a decade.

[44] International Labour Office (ILO), *Housing policy in Europe*, pt. 1; Pooley, *Housing strategies in Europe*.
[45] ILO, *Housing policy in Europe*, pt. 1.

The real constraint on housing quality was its affordability: the cost was too high for the earnings of manual workers. Like other European countries, Germany had an intractable 'housing question' that was already acute before the war.[46]

Between the wars in Germany the housing interface remained between landlord and tenant. Governments subsidised landlords, lenders, and tenants in different ways at different times. Lending was largely not-for-profit. Mortgage banks (some of them commercial) raised capital with mortgage bonds. Local government savings banks attracted middle-class savings. Co-operative banks did so on a mutual basis. The same system persisted into the post-war period.

6.7 THE UNITED STATES

The United States real estate boom of the 1920s can be compared to the British one of the 1890s. Before the war, personal lenders provided some 40 per cent of mortgage credit, with the rest coming from insurance companies and commercial banks. By the 1920s, as in Britain, housing credit came to be dominated by mutual societies (Building and Loan Associations). Somewhat like the railway mania in 1840s Britain, the real-estate boom of the 1920s was a financial frenzy which left behind a stock of solid assets after it collapsed. It was one of the causes of the Great Depression, which brought unrestricted private housing enterprise to an end, as the First World War did in Britain.[47]

The Great Depression caused widespread mortgage default. New Deal Washington responded with emergency credit for ailing institutions and borrowers. The second intervention was more drastic: a federal guarantee for mortgage lending. At a stroke this replaced the short time-boundary lender horizon constraint with an encompassing franchise, in which government took the risk, and lenders the benefit. As in Germany, risky private lending was replaced by tradeable bonds; as in Britain, mortgage lender lock-in was replaced by easy exit.

---

[46] Bullock and Read, *Movement for housing reform*, chs. 8–14; Bullock, 'Berlin'; Daunton, *Housing the workers*.

[47] White et al., *Housing and mortgage markets*, pt. 1.

The Federal Housing Administration (FHA, set up in 1935) provided a government guarantee for mortgage lending. It brought mortgages down to the same level of risk as government bonds, but with higher rates of return. Investors also obtained an easy exit option: another government agency (later known colloquially as 'Fannie Mae') created in 1938 to purchase mortgages and issue bonds against them, thus expanding the supply of housing credit. Existing mutual societies were reformed into 'Thrifts', tightly regulated local savings and loans associations that offered thirty-year mortgages with high loan-to-value ratios, somewhat similar to those available in Britain with twenty-five-year maturities. After 1945, similar guarantees were extended to veterans.[48]

For owner-occupying borrowers, housing offered a massive tax advantage over financial assets. Unlike financial investors, and like Britain after 1963, owner-occupiers were not liable for tax on their imputed rental income, nor on capital gains, and (unlike Britain most of the time) also received a tax deduction for interest payments. Housing also shielded against inflation. Most importantly, it achieved the main purpose of housing policy, which is to provide security of tenure and stable neighbourhoods.

It is something of a paradox that the United States, with a strong ideological commitment to 'free markets', adopted such a robust safety-net franchise regime for housing, effectively nationalising its long-term financial risk. With the break-even boundary thus removed, the way was open for an immense post-war building boom which eventually realised the 'American Dream' of home ownership for about two-thirds of households. The paradox, however, is only apparent if one accepts the rhetoric of free markets at face value. The American way is franchise, not markets; not risk taking but risk shifting. Competition benefits society, but not the competitors themselves, who strive to suppress it. Collusion of business and government at every level, from the individual household to the biggest banks, is consistent with the actual logic of capitalism, if not with its rhetoric.[49]

---

[48] Headey, *Housing policy*, ch. 8; Jackson, *Crabgrass frontier*, ch. 11; Schwartz, *Housing policy*, ch. 3; Rose, 'Prolonged resolution'.
[49] Mirowski, 'Postface: Defining neoliberalism', 433–446; Philippon, *Great Reversal*.

Those who benefited were owner-occupiers and their lenders, i.e. the top two-thirds of households by income. Another third did not earn enough. Housing was segregated informally and formally (by means of zoning). Black neighbourhoods were often 'red-lined', their residents unable to borrow. Mortgage guarantees had bipartisan support, but public housing or subsidies for renters encountered congressional resistance on the unstated grounds that they might benefit blacks.[50] The miseries of urban rental housing were left untreated, one reason for the devastating urban riots of the 1960s in which inner cities were gutted.

In Britain, housing policy worked for all classes, albeit in different ways for each. Owner-occupation allowed the middle classes to capture a share of rising land values in the form of housing equity, while the working classes achieved security of tenure in rent-controlled houses or in public housing. As society became wealthier, lower earners also migrated out of rental and into owner-occupation, driven by the dilapidation of pre-war housing, the stigma attached to public housing, and substantial tax benefits, including the exemption from tax on the imputed rent of owner-occupied houses in 1963, a tax allowance for mortgage interest in 1983 (MIRAS), and exemption from capital gains tax for the primary residence.[51]

Despite the success of the government interventions in both countries, or perhaps because of it, a hankering for 'free markets' persisted, not least from academic market advocates. The existing regime in the United States had a built-in defect. Maturities were longer than in Britain but interest rates were fixed, and in many states mortgages were 'no recourse', i.e. owners could walk away with no penalty if house price declines liquidated their equity. Selling off mortgage loans by Fannie Mae turned out to be safe and profitable for the same reasons that lending was secure in Britain, namely their alignment with long-term family horizons. In 1968 the agency was privatised and began to securitise more aggressively, relying on an implicit 'too big to fail' franchise government guarantee. Savings and loans societies suffered in the 1970s because of the mismatch between the low fixed interest paid by borrowers and the rising interest rates

[50] Headey, *Housing policy*, 205–218; Schwartz, *Housing policy*, ch. 11.
[51] Saunders, *Nation of home owners*.

available to depositors elsewhere. In the spirit of the times, they were deregulated, and soon plunged into an orgy of speculation and fraud. Between 1986 and 1995 more than a thousand savings and loans (S&L) associations failed (about a third of the total), with total assets of about $500bn (about 8 per cent of GDP in 1990). This failure overwhelmed the resources of deposit insurance and the federal government had to back up the commitment with a total loss of $153bn. Thousands of thrift managers and owners went to prison.[52]

Following the lead of Fannie Mae, in the late 1990s large banks began to buy up mortgages from their originators and to issue bonds secured against them. By 2000, less regulated, more risky mortgages had displaced Fannie Mae (and a similar agency known as Freddie Mac) as the main sources of mortgage securities. Risky mortgages were securitised and packaged into highly speculative bundles and sold off to investors. Credit surged and house prices soared. In 2008 the bubble exploded with devastating consequences which are still playing out. House prices collapsed, and millions found themselves either in default or owing more than their properties were worth. In contrast with New Deal priorities, this time round the American Treasury saved the creditors and left borrowers stranded. About 14 million Americans lost their homes. In contrast with the New Deal response, the government held back and did not rescue the borrowers in default.[53]

In the United States and Britain credit was deregulated in the 1970s and 1980s. Asset prices went up and the rising cost of debt service imposed a large deadweight cost. What survived of the franchise regime was not designed to prevent a crisis but to pick up the pieces afterwards. They were picked up after 2008 – by government, and not by the bankers who had taken the risks and inflicted the harms. The cost to society was enormous.

6.8 GERMAN-SPEAKING EUROPE

With a different housing legacy Germany, Austria, and Switzerland avoided the ravages of financialisation after 1980.

---

[52] Calavita, *Big money crime*, ch. 5; Curry and Shibut, 'Cost of the savings and loan crisis', 33.
[53] Glantz, *Homewreckers*; Immergluck, *Foreclosed*; McDonald, *Fannie Mae and Freddie Mac*; Martin and Niedt, *Foreclosed America*; Odinet, *Foreclosed*; Stout, *Dispossessed*.

Like the English-speaking countries, however, their governments also intervened to provide secure and adequate housing. In Germany, public housing was provided by private enterprise under government contracts and once paid off, reverted to private ownership. Rents were regulated and tenants had security of tenure. Low inflation reduced the allure of housing as an asset. In consequence, the three German-speaking countries, Austria, Switzerland, and Germany had the lowest levels of owner-occupation, and high levels of private rental. This elaborate system of regulation and public finance provided no handle for deregulated financialisation. German-speaking countries were not destabilised socially and economically by a house price surge after 1980, and remained largely immune to the housing disorders of the English-speaking countries. Their seventy-year regime of socialised housing franchise continued unbroken after the 1980s.[54]

6.9 IS PROSPERITY AN ILLUSION?

Between 1900 and 2000 real incomes have risen four to seven times in advanced countries.[55] Housing outlays, however, have kept up and have risen about the same and even more. The benefit of economic growth is that everything costs less, at least in relative terms. For example, food has fallen from around a third to less than 10 per cent of consumer spending over the twentieth century. But housing actually costs more as a share of income and, absolutely, a great deal more. Housing is now the most expensive component of the standard of living. Figure 6.4 shows the share of housing and food in consumer expenditure in the USA and the UK since 1900. Housing and transport costs are combined since they are substitutes for each other: housing in central locations commands higher rents but incurs lower transport costs and vice versa. Spending figures alone, however, underestimate the cost of housing and for two reasons. The time cost of transport is not included here, but when costs and benefits of economic growth are estimated, the cost of commuting is subtracted

[54] McCrone and Stephens, *Housing policy in Britain and Europe*, ch. 4; Schneider and Wagner, 'Housing markets'; Stephens, 'International models'.
[55] Maddison, *World economy*.

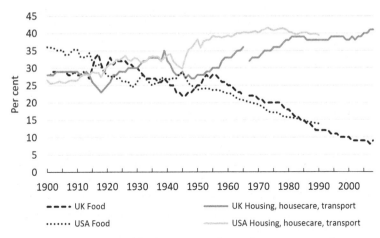

Figure 6.4 Housing and food: percentage shares of consumer expenditure,
UK and USA

Sources: United Kingdom: Feinstein, *National income, expenditure and output*, table 22, and GB Office of National Statistics, National accounts: household final expenditure at current prices, dataset natpe1, (electronic source, downloaded 30 June 2009), http://www.statistics.gov.uk/STATBAS E/tsdataset.asp?vlnk=630&More=N&All=Y;

United States: Lebergott, *Pursuing happiness: American consumers in the twentieth century*, Appendix A, Personal consumption table.

Note: US data are derived from constant 1987 prices, while the UK data are from current prices. Note the data break in the series in the UK in 1966, at the shift from Feinstein to Office of National Statistics estimates. Long-distance holiday and business travel is not included: 'travel' is measured separately.

from the benefits.[56] Those who could not afford to pay cash for housing could still pay for it in commuting time. Secondly, taxation does not count as a housing cost. House occupiers benefit from government support in many forms, but pay for it through taxes and not directly. In some countries, e.g. Sweden, this outlay can be very high: so if housing costs in Sweden are relatively low, some of the high taxes paid there are really housing costs.[57]

In both English-speaking countries the pattern is very similar (Figure 6.4). Housing and transport costs together did not exceed 30 per cent or so of consumer expenditure until the Second World

---

[56] E.g. Nordhaus and Tobin, 'Is growth obsolete?', 515.   [57] Headey, *Housing policy*, chs. 4–5.

War, rising to around 40 per cent from the 1950s onwards. Taking housing costs alone (excluding transport), in the USA, France, Sweden, and the UK, the share of housing costs has remained constant since the 1920s (at around 15 per cent), and in the UK it has increased sharply since the 1980s, to around 25 per cent.[58]

Housing and transport costs have risen more than incomes because the price of land has increased. Time and space are substitutes for each other. Land is in limited supply, and so is time. Time and good locations are intertwined: they both rise in value when the economy grows, with no input from the owner. When the cost of everything declines, 'everything' becomes more plentiful – except for time and for desirable locations, which then become more costly. Land is expensive in central (or otherwise attractive) sites because their locations economise on time use. For some places the attraction is not proximity but exclusion: a unique view from the house, or an agreeable neighbourhood, are not a matter of being close, but of social priority and privilege. Rising location values can be offset by time-saving technology: by rail, motor, air transport, telecommunications: if it takes half the time to get to work, we can live twice as far at the same cost in time, while the amount of land available is squared. Rising longevity also increases the supply of time. But countervailing effects have not sufficed to offset the shortage of time and good locations.

It would be good to check this on the ground. It is not easy to trace the price of single houses over time, but it has been done. In 1999 the *Guardian* newspaper obtained prices for six modest three-bedroom terraced houses which had been financed a hundred years earlier by the Co-operative Permanent building society (parent of the current Nationwide).[59] The newspaper estimated their current market value. The three London houses (all with below-average prices in 1999) had risen 500 times in value. The three other houses rose 118 (Dover), 200 (Wales), and 300 times (Hampshire) respectively. House price inflation exceeded retail price inflation over this period by almost ten-fold (Table 6.3).

[58] From spreadsheets kindly provided by Moritz Schularick.
[59] Justice, 'Bricks are worth their weight'; Samy, *Building society promise*, 73–131, esp. table 2.11, 118;

Table 6.3 *Increases in incomes, prices, and house prices, in multiples, UK 1899–2010*

	Multiples of initial values	
	1899 to 1999	1930 to 2010
Retail price index	65	49.3
Average earnings	236	149
Nominal GDP per head	363	257
	3 London houses	*Average UK house prices*
House prices	500	353

Sources: London house prices, Justice, 'Bricks are worth their weight in gold'; average house prices, ONS, 'Live tables on housing market and house prices', Table 502 (mix-adjusted price);[60] all other prices and incomes, www.measuringworth.com.

Over one hundred years from 1899 to 1999, the retail price index rose 65 times, average earnings rose 236 times, and nominal GDP income per head about 363 times (real income per head 400 times on the Maddison estimate).[61] This confirms the Figure 6.4 finding that housing costs rose more than income per head over a century.

Maybe housing costs rose because housing is better? This cannot bear very much on the three London houses, which were late-Victorian dwellings for people on high manual or low middle-class incomes. They now have modernised bathrooms and kitchens, electric wiring, central heating, and perhaps double glazing but the fabric is the same and they are a hundred years older. Rebuilding costs are usually much lower in the UK than market values. An insurance company reported recently that the rebuilding cost of houses (a measure of their quality) was only 31 per cent of the market value in London and 59 per cent overall in a recent large UK survey.[62] In the North-East, Britain's most deprived region, market prices and rebuilding costs were the same, implying no location premium at all.

---

[60] https://www.gov.uk/government/statistical-data-sets/live-tables-on-housing-market-and-house-prices.

[61] https://www.measuringworth.com/calculators/ukcompare/result.php?year_source=1899&amount=1000&year_result=1999. Income per head on this measure slightly lower than the Maddison estimate, see note 55.

[62] Direct Line Insurance, 'Bricks and mortar'.

Rising land values are cost for society but a windfall for the owners, who have the option of converting their windfall into other goods, whose cost is falling. This is the 'wealth effect' which is often observed in periods of rising house values, as when owner-occupiers borrow against the value of the house in order to finance consumption.[63]

When land values rise several stakeholders stand to benefit. (1) Landowners, either through development, or afterwards if they hold onto a stake. (2) Occupiers, e.g. rent-controlled tenants, who benefit from below-market rents; public housing tenants who likewise typically get cheap rents; and owner-occupiers, whose asset value continues to appreciate. (3) Lenders: as house prices rise, more credit comes on stream to bid house prices further up. In consequence, creditors capture a larger share of borrower income. (4) Society (mostly government) captures rising rents by means of taxation and ownership. Much of this taxation comes right back round to raise property values when it is spent on infrastructure, subsidies, and tax privileges.

Rising house prices benefit their owners but are they good for society? There are two possibilities. A benign one is that rising costs reflect rising benefits: that rents capture the payoffs of economic growth, and reflect the intensity of competition to enjoy its benefits. The implication is that the benefits of economic growth are distributed as unequally as housing wealth, and that a large part of society benefits very little, e.g. not at all in the North-East of England. A less happy possibility is that house prices rise (as in the late nineteenth century) due to competition for good employment in prosperous locations. They are a negative consequence ('externality') of economic growth, and arise from congestion and frictions, somewhat like (to use the metaphor again) fever in a patient. In other words, high land prices represent a failure by technology to keep up with the rising scarcity of land and time.

The social benefit of rising land values depends on who gets them. In the long nineteenth century, rising values were distributed among the elite, i.e. owners, lenders, and governments. They were paid for by the majority, by dwellers (most of them on short rentals), who got no share of the increment except indirectly through government spending on urban infrastructure. The classical economists Adam Smith and David Ricardo wrote that land rents do not incentivise

---

[63] Aron et al., 'Credit, housing collateral, and consumption'.

any useful economic activity, and were therefore appropriate revenues to tax. For more than a century before the First World War Radicals in Britain looked for ways to tax the increase in urban rent. In the 1870s and 1880s Henry George, an American reforming firebrand, asserted with much resonance that a 'single tax' on the 'unearned increment' could pay for everything that government spent on. David Lloyd George's 'People's Budget' of 1909–10 was designed to capture some of this unearned increment with several taxes.[64] The real intention was not to raise money (several leaders of his own Liberal party were landowners themselves), but mostly to provoke defiance in the House of Lords in order to end its upper-class veto on social policy.[65] Despite its parliamentary success, the cause failed and the Liberal party, its champion, fell into decline.

British voters chose not to tax the 'unearned increment' of land values but to appropriate it for themselves, by means of home ownership. Occupiers used their new voting power to capture rising land values. Owner-occupation, not-for-profit finance, public housing, rent control – all of these interwar innovations constituted housing windfalls. Dwelling-house landlords, the intermediaries between capital and occupier, suffered slow-motion expropriation in Britain. In Germany, in contrast, they were subsidised, and private rental remained the largest tenure until the end of the twentieth century while real house prices were stable between 1970 and 2000, and actually declined afterwards.[66]

Under financialisation, from 1980 onwards the benefits of rising house values were distributed between borrowers, especially early movers in the 1980s and early 1990s, and bankers. Other occupiers increasingly lost out. During the fixed exchange rate Bretton Woods regime, governments had regulated the amount of credit.[67] In the 1970s and 1980s these constraints were lifted gradually. It is now increasingly understood that bank lending is not constrained by the central bank, nor by the supply of savings. The main constraint on the banks' ability to lend and, hence, to make money is the supply of credible borrowers. Historically commercial banks avoided mortgage lending on account of long maturities and

---

[64] Offer, *Property and politics*, chs. 12, 16, 19.
[65] Dugdale, *Balfour*, vol. 2, 55; Thomson and Lloyd George, *Lloyd George*, 182.
[66] Muellbauer, 'When is a housing market overheated', fig. 1, 75.
[67] Monnet, 'Diversity in national monetary and credit policies'; idem, *Controlling credit*.

low liquidity. In the 1980s, however, banks discovered the lure of housing. Decades of building society lending had shown that lending for house purchase was safe. Ironically, this security arose out of enduring marital bonds and high levels of employment, both of which came under pressure with the rise of divorce and joblessness in the 1980s. Credit pumped up house prices, which made the loans look safer, and also intensified the competition for shelter. Loan-to-income ratios increased, and more wives went out to work to support debt service: which came first (the debt or employment) is not clear.[68] There is a view that credit expansion only accounted for about one-third of house price rises, with the rest being driven by rising household incomes.[69] But household incomes themselves rose in consequence of longer hours at work, largely a result of more women in the labour force.[70]

In the United States mortgages were guaranteed by government; in Britain the guarantee was only implicit. One aspect of credit liberalisation was a large increase of pay in finance, much higher than in legacy building societies.[71] For bank managers the maturity that counted was not that of loans, which was still twenty-five years, but the maturity of their jobs, which was typically much shorter.[72] In the great financial crisis of 2008 this wager paid off. No manager had to give up their past earnings and no lender was allowed to fail. Some of the lenders were nationalised for a while, but the only losers were shareholders, who turned out to be pension funds and other institutions, i.e. the loss was borne by society, not by capitalists.

Despite paying a higher share of their income to service mortgage debt, borrowers, especially those who bought their houses before 2000, collected a windfall of capital gains, driven by the lending surge. On average in the OECD in 2011, household housing assets were 2.5 times their financial debts.[73] Except for Switzerland, the majority of households were owner-occupiers, which inclined them to vote for neoliberal regimes, whether

[68] Offer, 'Narrow banking'; Offer, 'The market turn'.
[69] Muellbauer, 'Housing, debt and the economy', slide 9.
[70] Sources, Offer, 'British manual workers', 550–552.
[71] Shiwakoti et al., 'Conversion, performance and executive compensation'.
[72] Noe and Young, 'Limits to compensation'.
[73] Data kindly provided by Dr. Paul Lassenius Kramp, Danmarks Nationalbank. See Isaksen et al., 'Household balance sheets and debt', 49–51.

centre-right or centre-left.[74] The people who lost out were the poor and the young. In all countries public housing was run down. In Germany government subsidies shifted from public housing to home ownership.[75] The rise of house values widened inequality, with the house-owner 'haves' a long way ahead of the younger 'have-nots', who were destined never to own and could only aspire to parental bequests. If owner-occupation was the political bedrock of democratic consent, its withdrawal from younger cohorts is an element of the crisis which engulfs democracy today. But only in part: German-speaking countries, which avoided the extremes of financialisation and persisted with their somewhat different social-democratic housing regimes, have not avoided political crisis either.

CHAPTER 6, APPENDIX I

The sharp decline of mortgage credit flows 1894–1914 is investigated in the following OLS regression.

	MORTGAGES
INTEREST	−2.332***
	(0.765)
RATES	−2.239**
	(0.840)
YEAR	14.09**
	(5.445)
CONSTANT	−26,111**
	(10,224)
Observations	21

Standard errors in parentheses
*** $p<0.01$, ** $p<0.05$, * $p<0.1$

The dependent variable is MORTGAGES (annual flow of mortgages in England and Wales). The independent ones are INTEREST (the yield on consols (government perpetual bonds)) and RATES

---

[74] Offer, 'Market turn', fig. 5, 1064; Ansell, 'Politics of housing', 171–173.
[75] Mccrone and Stephens, *Housing policy*, ch. 4.

(the annual revenue from local taxation in England and Wales) – all converted to an index with base year 1895. Year is the year to March, with interest in calendar year of the previous year. The sources are indicated in Figure 6.1, which plots the variables in a slightly different form.

The regression has Newey-West standard errors robust to heteroskedasticity and autocorrelation. The lag is 1 and the variables remain significant at other lags. The variables are all stationary using the KPSS test (stationarity as the null). Non-stationarity is not rejected using a Dickey-Fuller test which has a unit root as the null. The latter test is biased against stationarity, and has low power with short time series like this one. The regressions are unlikely to be spurious as the cross-correlation coefficients are in the .50–.70 range.

Interpretation. The variables represent populations rather than samples, and the regression can be taken as describing the actual relation between the variables. Since this is an index, it shows the supply elasticity of mortgages on yield and rates at the base year. In that year (1895) the elasticity is larger than -2.2 for both independent variables. The elasticity was lower at the top of the cycle, and higher at the bottom, but always more (in a negative direction) than -1. The regression can also be considered as a sample from some larger undefined population, in which case it identifies a regularity.

In either case, the interpretation is that the supply of mortgages was highly responsive (in about equal measure) to a percentage increase/decrease in interest rates and in local taxation. Statistically, the strong contraction in the flow of mortgages after 1899 is substantially explained by rising interest rates and local taxes (Figure 6.1).

CHAPTER 7

Climate Change and Time Horizons

7.1 GLOBAL WARMING

Time horizons define the most fateful policy issue of our century so far, namely climate change. The climate challenge emerged at the same time as policy opinion embraced the virtues of markets and the futility of government. Business, finance, and privilege reordered society in their image by means of tax cuts, privatisations, and outsourcing. Government itself was remade. The long term was set aside. The future was captured by opportunists whose main concern was to get ahead here and now.

In the 1980s climate scientists sounded the alarm to a disaster in the making. The greenhouse gas emitted by burning fossil fuels (mostly CO_2) since the industrial revolution was raising global temperatures, which could eventually drive humans out of large parts of the planet. Governments turned to economists for advice.

In response economists rolled out their worldview model. This is the 'invisible hand' (as per Adam Smith) in which the pursuit of self-interest in market exchange scales up to the common good. In current invisible hand models ('general equilibrium') the individual pursues their well-being or 'welfare' by trading in competitive markets. Market exchange brings about an equilibrium which is 'optimal', i.e. resources are all utilised to maximise the total well-being of all and nothing is left on the shelf.

This is a deterministic piece of clockwork. Every person within it is an automaton which strives to satisfy a set of innate preferences by selling services out of their endowment (education, personality, skills, effort, inherited assets). They know the market price of everything. When preferences and endowments are confronted with market prices the device has no discretion: it can only maximise, by satisfying its preferences in rank order sequence. Markets add this up into the aggregate welfare of everybody, i.e. 'markets as maximization'.[1] Hence, when it came to global warming, a galaxy of Nobel-level economists told the discipline in 1997 that 'the most efficient approach to slowing climate change is through market-based policies'.[2]

Climate mitigation was straightforward: if consumers were made to pay for the harm of carbon emissions the market would take care of everything else:

Economic history and analysis indicate that it will be most effective to use market signals, primarily higher prices on carbon fuels, to give signals and provide incentives for consumers and firms to change their energy use and reduce their carbon emissions. In the longer run, higher carbon prices will also provide incentives for firms to develop new technologies to ease the transition to a low-carbon future.[3]

The means was a tax on carbon, or a tradeable carbon emission quota. What scale of tax? The carbon tax must be of the same order as the climate damages.[4] To work this out required estimates of anticipated harm from global warming, when it was going to occur, and the costs of reducing it. To obtain these data, the invisible hand mechanism was recast as a neoclassical growth model, which is used to predict the future course of an economy. In this model output is produced by a combination of capital and labour inputs. In the 1950s it was shown that the combined growth of capital and labour together could only account for about half of the total growth observed. The unexplained 'residual' was then attributed to technological change.

We cannot put our feet on the ground without land, we cannot live without water, we cannot breathe without air, but nature and her

---

[1] Nordhaus, 'Integrated economic and climate modeling', 1077, quoting Paul Samuelson.
[2] Kenneth Arrow, Robert Solow, Paul Krugman, Dale Jorgensen, William Nordhaus, 'Economists' statement on climate change' (1997), in DeCanio, *Limits of economic and social knowledge*, 165.
[3] Nordhaus, 'Integrated economic and climate modeling', 1073.
[4] Nordhaus, *Climate casino*, ch. 19.

services are not in the model. In this theory, natural resources, or their absence, do not impose any limit on economic growth. If nature falls short, ingenuity, labour, and capital will make up for it. With the stock of capital given (think of machinery), economic growth is assumed to depend on the growth of labour and its technologically driven productivity, both of them driven 'exogenously', i.e. from outside the model. Technical change was manna from heaven. The implication is that whatever happened to the climate, economic growth (and the consumption it fed) were bound to continue regardless, and consumers would continue to grow wealthier into the future at some constant historical rate.

Economists evaluate the challenge of climate change by means of integrated climate assessment models (IAMs). These are 'invisible hand' growth models ('computable general equilibrium') which strive to integrate models of the economy with geophysical climate models to estimate a level of carbon tax that will minimise future climate harm. In IAMs decisions are not assumed to be taken by individuals, but by national economies adding up to a global one maximising its output in the face of prospective climate change. 'In this approach, economies make investments in capital, education and technologies thereby reducing consumption today, in order to increase consumption in the future.' For climate change, these investments (financed perhaps by the carbon tax) are meant to reduce the harm caused by rising temperature. This model is seen 'as a means of simulating the behaviour of a system of competitive markets'. The purpose of policy is to find the level of investment that will minimise the combined cost of the anticipated harms and the mitigation efforts. Achieving that level is the most efficient, the 'optimal' climate policy.[5] Note that the result is arrived at by market exchange on its own, with no role for collective action apart from imposing the carbon tax.

How useful this is depends on the validity of the model. Elsewhere, I have called such models 'imaginary machines'.[6] One thing is for sure: they are a long way from the messy combination of

[5] Assumptions laid out in detail in Nordhaus, 'Integrated economic and climate modeling', quotes from pages 1,080, 1,081 respectively.
[6] Offer and Söderberg, *Nobel factor*, ch. 1.

households, markets, and governments described earlier in this book. Abstraction is required to make the models mathematically tractable, but how do they match to reality? Normally economics does not care too much. The model is the message. But when applied to climate change abstraction provides no protection: the model will confront the reality it imagines, and will be either right or not. Time will tell. Emissions build up in the atmosphere and stay there, so policy choices are irreversible. There is no second chance. It is a one-shot game.

Three model components are crucial: climate sensitivity, its economic impact, and discounting, i.e. how much to value future harms today. *Climate sensitivity* is the temperature response to a doubling of atmospheric CO_2 from pre-industrial levels. On current trends, with no mitigation and 'business as usual', this doubling is predicted to occur within the present century. The temperature increase range predicted by the consensus expert Intergovernmental Panel on Climate Change (IPCC) lies imprecisely between 1.5 and 4.5 degrees centigrade above the pre-industrial baseline. Other studies predict a climate sensitivity up to more than twice as high.[7]

The relation between temperature and economic damage can be expressed as a '*damage function*' which describes a trajectory of future climate economic harms. IAM damages are expressed as reductions in GDP, and some of them also (to a lesser extent) in non-market harms affecting mortality, health, and the environment. A narrow focus is useful because dollar losses can be converted into the dollar tax required. IAMs typically assume that climate harm still leaves the future better off than the present.

Discounting arises from the common-sense notion that a dollar fifty years hence is worth less than a dollar now. Carbon taxes and curtailed consumption (for the sake of lower emissions) are incurred now to avert greater losses in the future. Discounting is an estimate of the benefit of avoiding future harms as seen from the present. Future harms are perceived as lower than they actually are in proportion to their remoteness. When consumption is cut back to reduce emissions the savings can be diverted into investment in wind and solar power, and reducing emissions is a good on its own. Whose consumption are

---

[7] Stern, *Economics of climate change*, 11–12; Wadsell, 'Climate dynamics'.

we talking about? In the models, it is the present value of the aggregate consumption (or alternatively, the 'utility') of all present and future people, with a discount rate applied, which means (depending on the rate chosen) that the welfare of future people counts for less, possibly much less, than our own well-being. The discount rate does the same work as the interest rate in our time horizon model in Chapter 1 (1.3). The higher it is, the less the future counts, and the lower the sacrifice required.

Ever since 1979, scientists have been crying doom. More recently for example: 'A great change in our stewardship of the Earth and the life on it is required, if vast human misery is to be avoided.' Humanity is pushing the earth's ecosystems beyond their capacity to support life, towards an irreversible, uninhabitable 'hothouse earth'.[8] According to scientific forecasts, at 4 degrees of warming this century (within the predicted range of IPCC climate sensitivity) rising sea levels will inundate many of the world's coastal cities. Extreme heat will test the limits of human endurance, and will make some parts of the planet unsuitable for humans. Storms, wildfires, and floods will be more frequent and violent. Droughts will last longer, rivers will run dry, fresh water will run low, food will fall short. Hundreds of millions of people will seek refuge from habitats they can no longer endure.[9]

7.2 ECONOMICS AND CLIMATE SCIENCE

Economic models are seriously at odds with the climate science which they incorporate. We shall focus on DICE/RICE, one of the very first integrated assessment models (IAMs), developed by the economist William Nordhaus ever since 1991. Other IAMs share similar premises and produce similar results. Nordhaus estimates harmful impacts in terms of reductions of GDP from a future growth path. Neither technical change nor population, the two determinants of prosperity, are assumed to be affected by climate change, so growth

---

[8] Ripple et al., 'World scientists' warning to humanity', 9; Ripple et al., 'World scientists' warning of a climate emergency', signed by 15,634 and 11,258 scientists respectively; 'hothouse earth', Steffen et al., 'Trajectories of the Earth System', 8252.
[9] World Bank, 'Turn down the heat'; Richardson et al., *Climate change*, ch. 5.

is likely to continue at current levels, whatever happens. Climate change works to lower the level of future GDP.

For those accustomed to alarmist climate change discourse, its predicted economic effects are surprisingly small. For 3 degrees centigrade of warming above pre-industrial levels which is the IPCC best guess for climate sensitivity, the damage is assumed to be 2.1 per cent of global income. For 6 degrees, it is merely 8.5 per cent, not from current levels of GDP, but from much higher future ones.[10] But according to climate scientists 6 degrees, still possible this century, would represent a catastrophic failure with human life barely possible.[11]

A 2 per cent loss of GDP is difficult to distinguish from 'business as usual': it represents about one year's growth and loss mitigation is hardly worth the trouble. These reassuring estimates have been incorporated into the predictions of IPCC and form the agreed official view on climate change.[12] They have justified complacency and diminished urgency.

How to explain the gap between climate scientists and economists? It arises from a sequence of assumptions made by economists, all of them (on the face of it) biased to reduce expected harms.[13] The point of departure is 'business as usual'. Economic growth in the past, at around 2 per cent a year, is projected to continue into the future. Any harm from climate change is still likely to leave the world much better off than it is today. The task the modellers set themselves was to find a level of investment in emission reduction so as minimise the combined cost of the investment and the harms. At that level, temperatures would be economically 'optimal'.

In IAMs the future impact of temperature on the economy is mostly extrapolated from differences in economic performance at different latitudes today (i.e. from cross sections). The economic effects of north–south temperature gradients today are extrapolated into a warmer future. The current impact of temperature differences is shaped like an inverted U stretching from south to north.

[10] Nordhaus, 'Projections and uncertainties', 345.
[11] Lynas, *Our final warning*, 247; Lynas is endorsed by leading climate economists Wagner and Weitzman, *Climate shock*, passim.
[12] Arent and Tol, 'Key economic sectors', e.g. 663.
[13] Inspired and informed here by Keen, 'Appallingly bad'.

Economic performance is low in the south, low in the north, and highest (i.e. 'optimal') in the middle. If there is warming then the optimal latitude will simply move north, causing more harm to southern places and greater benefit to northern ones, but the difference will average out. Initial applications of this method suggested that there was going to be no future climate harm at all. The model is thin: Nordhaus populates it with the summary results of other studies, resulting in 27 instances providing just 38 data points, and the fit is poor.[14]

Nordhaus and his followers simply leave out much of the effect of the damage: 'Economic studies suggest that those parts of the economy that are insulated from climate, such as air-conditioned houses and most manufacturing operations, will be little affected directly by climate change over the next century or so.' That excludes some 87 per cent of economic activity in the United States.[15] Nordhaus focuses on the production side, so emissions generated in consumption, like those air-conditioned houses, or consumers driving around, appear to be neglected.

In contrast, recent empirical studies have shown strong temperature effects on productivity regardless of sector, including an international study of 7,684 municipalities.[16] Hot days reduce plant-level automobile output in the United States by 8 per cent. Output losses in manufacturing are about 2 per cent for every degree of increase over 25°C.[17] Rising temperatures have a strong adverse effect on farming, manufacturing, services, energy demand, labour productivity, health, conflict, political stability, and economic growth.[18]

When the results of cross-sectional comparisons were projected into the future, Nordhaus implicitly assumed that all other things remained equal. But this confuses weather with climate. The invulnerable sectors, and the small temperature effects on income, are embedded in today's cooler climate. Current latitude temperature gradients say little about the effect of raising temperature everywhere by an additional 3 or 4 or 5 degrees.[19]

---

[14] Nordhaus and Moffat, 'Survey of global impacts', table 5, 12.
[15] Arent and Tol, 'Key economic sectors', 688; Norhdaus, 'To slow or not to slow', 930–933; quote from Nordhaus, 'Integrated economic and climate modeling', 1,073–1,074.
[16] Dell et al., 'What do we learn from the weather?', 753. [17] Ibid., 761. [18] Ibid.
[19] Keen, 'Appallingly bad'.

A different, more credible approach is to extrapolate the economic effect of rising heat from the recent past. This is not an IAM – there is no economic model. It is purely empirical. Temperature data are rich and cover the whole planet. Historical trends are simply projected smoothly into the future, taking no account of any stepwise or threshold effects that might lie ahead. This omission imparts a downwards bias to damages but the results still diverge enormously from Nordhaus. Warming effects on the economy follow an inverse U shape, with some benefit during initial warming and severe losses afterwards. Nordhaus-type IAM damage trajectories are shallow curves. In contrast, the extrapolated longitudinal effects of temperature on GDP are deeply convex (i.e. non-linear, inverted U-shaped), with output rising initially, stabilising at around an annual average of 13°C to 15°C, then falling sharply when occasional daily temperatures begin to exceed about 30°C. The overall finding is that the average global economic damage by the end of the century is going to be an order of magnitude greater than that predicted by Nordhaus and other IAMs, at around 23 per cent of GDP (i.e. ten times more), with widening global inequalities. Canada, North America, and non-Mediterranean Europe were going to benefit, but most of the world will suffer considerable harm, with potential catastrophe in warmer countries.[20] The main IAMs and the longitudinal results are compared in Figures 7.1 and 7.2.

When damages are expressed in terms of losses to GDP that excludes some large non-market impacts, namely those on health and mortality, rising sea levels, food and water shortages, species extinction, displacement, migration, and social strife. The data that go into the IAMs have either wide variance if they are historical, or considerable uncertainty if they are yet in the future. Climate sensitivity estimates range widely too. Data for damage is sparse and uncertain. Nevertheless, Nordhaus reports his results as central measures ('best guesses') to one decimal point. Outcomes are assumed to be normally distributed, which implies that extreme outcomes have low probabilities. A more recent eclectic study by a large Swiss reinsurance company estimates economic damage taking into account differences in adaptive capacity, a broad range of harms,

---

[20] Burke et al., 'Global non-linear effect of temperature'.

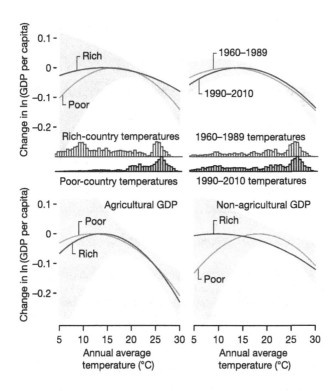

Figure 7.1 Global damage estimates arising from non-linear effects of temperature.
Source: Burke et al., 'Global non-linear effect of temperature on economic production', fig. 1, 236. Copyright: Springer Nature, *Nature*, 'Global non-linear effect of temperature on economic production', M. Burke, S. Hsiang, E. Miguel, Copyright @ 2015.

and the large uncertainties involved. Unlike previous studies, its focus is on the mid-twenty-first century, i.e. alarmingly close. The most striking prediction is how variable outcomes are likely to be. Wealthy northern countries (including the USA, Canada, the UK, Germany, and Scandinavia) are likely to suffer harms on the order of 3–12 per cent of GDP. In the worst-hit region, South-East Asia, harms could be on the order of 45 per cent of GDP.[21]

[21] Swiss Re Institute, 'Economics of climate change'.

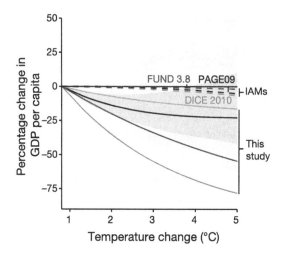

Figure 7.2 A comparison of IAMs and non-linear longitudinal estimates.
Source: Burke et al., 'Global non-linear effect of temperature on economic
production', fig. 2, 5, 236, 238. Copyright: Springer Nature, *Nature*, 'Global
non-linear effect of temperature on economic production', M. Burke,
S. Hsiang, E. Miguel, Copyright @ 2015.

The IAM future damage curves are smooth, shallow, and do not
take account of uncertain tipping points like the collapse of the
Antarctic and Greenland ice sheets, the retreat of glaciers, the changing course of warming ocean currents, permafrost melting and
methane emissions, and the burning down to savannah of the
Amazon rainforest. Especially worrisome are potential irreversible
climate tipping points and nature's reinforcing feedbacks (atmospheric, marine, and terrestrial) that could lead to a catastrophic
'hothouse Earth', well beyond human control.[22]

7.3 DISCOUNTING

After scientists raised the alarm in the 1980s, an international conference
in Kyoto in 1992 drafted a framework convention on climate change

---

[22] Steffen et al., 'Trajectories of the Earth System'.

which was signed by 192 countries. It finally came into effect in 2005 as a voluntary agreement to reduce emissions in accordance with agreed targets. To comply with this commitment, the New Labour government in Britain commissioned the economist Nicholas Stern to report. In 2006 his massive collaborative study proposed a sacrifice of 1 per cent of national income every year to avert a permanent loss of 5 per cent of GDP, possibly rising up to 20 per cent.[23]

Climate change politics is a fateful encounter between expertise and democracy of the type described in Chapter 3. Stern (an academic economist) was serving as a senior Treasury official and his report was the lucid voice of expert reasoning. But the message was not welcome. He was dismissed at short notice by the New Labour chancellor Gordon Brown.[24] Prime Minister Tony Blair, fresh from a family holiday in Miami, said that it was impractical to ask people to take holidays closer to home, 'it's like telling people you shouldn't drive anywhere', he said.[25] Even more so in the United States, where politicians did not want to know and voters did not want to hear. Republican Party leaders described climate change as a hoax, while President Trump dismantled mitigation polices and withdrew the country from the international Paris Climate Accord of 2015, the successor to Kyoto.[26]

In economics the question of whether an investment is worthwhile is determined by the technique of project appraisal. For public projects this takes the form of cost-benefit analysis. As described in Chapter 1 the hurdle often set is whether the project can return more than the prevailing interest or profit rate. Can it improve on the current market rate of return, or are there better alternatives for investment? In the UK and the United States in the 1970s and the 1980s public sector projects were set high rate-of-return hurdles derived explicitly from the private sector.[27]

[23] Stern, *Economics of climate change*.
[24] Hurst, 'Climate change author quits'; Rowell, 'Stern quits Treasury'.
[25] Watt, 'Carry on flying, says Blair'.
[26] Davenport and Lipton, 'How G.O.P. leaders came to view climate change as fake science'.
[27] Spackman, 'Discount rates', 1–3; idem, 'Time discounting', 472; Chapter 1 (1.3), and notes 23–26.

In contrast, Stern acknowledged that global warming was not a task for markets to handle on their own:

[it] involves a fundamental failure of markets: those who damage others by emitting greenhouse gases generally do not pay. Climate change is a result of the greatest market failure the world has seen. The evidence on the serious- ness of the risks from inaction or delayed action is now overwhelming. We risk damages on a scale larger than the two world wars of the last century. The problem is global and the response must be a collaboration on a global scale.[28]

Nordhaus in his IAM insisted on applying market discount rates, although this approach was rejected by many authorities and govern- ments for cost-benefit analysis.[29] Investment in climate change has to compete with alternative ones, says Nordhaus, and the interest rate in the model is set to reflect market rates of return. He suggested a rate of around 6 per cent a year.[30] At that discount rate, the future ceases to matter beyond seventeen years. It was another way to play down future harms.

In his report of 2006 Stern proposed a much lower discount rate. The argument was ethical: future generations deserve no less than those alive today and a high discount rate would leave them out of consideration.[31] Even later lives of those young today would unfold beyond a high discount rate time horizon, and to ignore that part of their lives was to discriminate among the living by age. The discount rate was social not commercial, and should make no distinction between present and future lives, rising above zero only to reflect the small possibility of total extinction (i.e. no future), and to avoid making a sacrifice today for the sake of wealthier descendants. On that basis Stern proposed a low composite discount rate of 1.4 per cent, which indicated that action was called for, and would not be too onerous.[32] At a 1.4 per cent discount rate, investing £1 for a £10 return in fifty years is worth £4.14 today – definitely worthwhile. At Nordhaus's 6 per cent discount rate (derived from the market rate),

[28] Stern, 'Climate change, ethics'.
[29] European Commission, *Guide to cost-benefit analysis*, 299–303.
[30] Nordhaus, 'Integrated economic and climate modeling', 1,112–1,114.
[31] This simplification of a more complicated argument preserves the essence. Stern, *Economics of climate change*, ch. 2; idem, *Why are we waiting*, ch. 5.
[32] Stern, *Economics of climate change*, 185–186.

investing £1 today for a £10 return in fifty years is worth only £0.33 today – a waste of money. Stern embodied the egalitarian social planner, Nordhaus the tough-minded neoliberal, for whom 'there is no ethical presumption that these are the correct prices or interest rates, but they should reflect market realities'.[33]

In terms of our own time-horizon model Nordhaus is simply wrong. As argued in Chapter 1, market interest rates restrict what business can do on its own to a distinct break-even horizon. At 6 per cent this is approximately seventeen years. What happens afterwards is beyond the reach of business on its own. Climate change is not a challenge for markets but for governments. Nordhaus himself admits this: his imaginary enlightened free-marketeer is made to say that 'we definitely cannot rely on free-market solutions'.[34] The high return on private capital which he invokes (otherwise known as the 'equity premium') is not an opportunity forgone by going public, but an extra cost, to compensate for business risk.[35]

Governments cannot default on their own currency and, unlike business, they do not pay taxes. When governments borrowed at 1.5 per cent (before the great financial crisis of 2008) their time horizon was sixty-seven years. Today governments can borrow at close to zero interest, which gives them almost infinite horizons. The problem is not the loss of more attractive investments, but a choice between short-term profits and escape from extinction. If our descendants are wiped out, that we have gratified our urgent appetites will not do them any good. Better lose money than lose everything. In the face of wipe-out, even financial markets apply very low or even negative discount rates.[36]

By selecting a commercial interest rate, Nordhaus explicitly endorses existing global inequalities. But fairness is not an academic indulgence, it is a practical necessity. Climate change requires global co-operation. Less-developed countries argue that they are late-comers to economic growth, with no responsibility for prior emissions, and disproportionately affected by climate change. A large prior stock of carbon emissions was already hanging in the atmosphere. These arguments have moral weight. In pursuit of its market

[33] Nordhaus, 'Integrated economic and climate modeling', 1114. [34] Nordhaus, *Climate casino*, 313. [35] Spackman, 'Time discounting', 479–483. [36] Wagner and Weitzman, *Climate shock*, 73.

fixation the United States insisted that Kyoto Protocol emissions be managed by means of tradeable emission quotas. It could then buy off developing countries with dollars, and continue with its own emissions as usual. When this was rejected, the United States withdrew from the Kyoto Protocol of 1997, and has done so again, from the Paris Agreement of 2015.[37]

But the discount rate may be a red herring. The problem is the model and its assumptions. Nordhaus runs a simulation which compares harm values using his own discount rate with those of Stern, and with another option of a world restricted to 2.5 degrees of warming. The absolute outcomes are very different, but total GDP is not very sensitive to them, the differences amounting to about 2 per cent of GDP.[38] This would fall within measurement error and amounts to less than two years of growth at his predicted rate. In another publication, his discount rate converged sharply downwards on to Stern's.[39] An expert critic has written, 'because reasonable arguments can be made for a low discount rate or a high rate, the modeler simply has too much flexibility in the choice of discount rate. If the modeler is at all biased towards a more or less stringent abatement policy, he/she can choose a discount rate accordingly.'[40] A British Treasury discounting expert has written separately that 'for policies dominated by the very long term, such as global warming, it is hard to see a case today for calculating present values of very long-term impacts'.[41]

Cost-benefit analysis is rational. If the benefits of action exceed the cost, then action should follow. IAMs like those of Nordhaus are supposed to be the voice of reason, guiding policymakers towards the 'optimum', the most efficient balance between present and future needs. They do this by means of the standard neoclassical microeconomic model in which the world economy is imagined as a competitive market. The premise (as stated above by a galaxy of Nobel Prize winners) is that government can place a price on carbon, and then go away. The market will solve the problem by itself. The result may not be fair to everybody, but it is economically optimal,

---

[37] DeCanio, *Economic models*, 154–155. [38] Nordhaus, 'Projections and uncertainties', table 2, 349.
[39] Nordhaus, 'Revisiting the social cost', fig. 3, 1520. [40] Pindyck, 'Use and misuse of models', 107.
[41] Spackman, 'Time discounting', 500.

even 'Pareto efficient', in the sense that all resources are fully utilised with minimum waste, so that nobody can be made better off without depriving somebody else.[42] Nordhaus forgets that Pareto efficiency is only achieved if there is a set of complete markets for everything, with complete information and perfect competition. None of these conditions obtain. This kind of modelling is populated by entities which are postulated but cannot be observed: preferences, marginal utilities, discount rates, elasticities, price indices, mathematical functions, GDP, representative agents. Intentionality is attributed to whole economies. Parameters are not observed but are 'calibrated' into the model to fit loosely with reality.

The 'optimal' result itself is not transparent: it comes out of a black-box curve-fitting algorithm which may or may not be computable and which frequently fails. As Nordhaus candidly reports, 'in some circumstances, solver simply stops and cannot find a solution, and sometimes it finds a wildly incorrect solution'.[43] Our expert critic (Pindyck) has written elsewhere that, 'the models are so deeply flawed as to be close to useless as tools for policy analysis. Worse yet, their use suggests a level of knowledge and precision that is simply illusory, and can be highly misleading.'[44] Other players are more polite but equally scathing.[45]

IAM publications are marvels of internal rigour, clarity, and candour. They are scrupulous about their own failings and respectful to critics. The formal skills displayed are of a high order. Maybe nothing less will do: it takes a rare creative talent to take spurious assumptions and derive meaningful results. What is lacking is judgement: the models have no external validity. The assumption of a perfectly competitive global market is at odds with reality. Masterly application, unsuitable approach?

Economist critics are careful not to dismiss the method altogether, to say that there is something there to be saved. But a model that is wrongly specified can instil a harmful complacency. The alternative damage estimates by Burke and his colleagues (Figures 7.1 and 7.2)

---

[42] Nordhaus, 'Integrated economic and climate modeling', 1091.
[43] Ibid., 1092. A sketch of computability in economics, Offer and Söderberg, *Nobel factor*, 263–268.
[44] Pindyck, 'Climate change policy', 861–862.
[45] Stern, *Why are we waiting?*, ch. 4; Weitzman, 'Review of William Nordhaus', 147–148.

required no economic modelling apart from standard statistical inference. What matters there are the measurable concepts of climate sensitivity and economic harm, both of them calculated directly from observation. The IAM economic modelling used to calculate a social cost of carbon is hypothetical, arbitrary, and has produced estimates that differ from each other by an order of magnitude. It has failed in its own terms. Despite pervasive awareness of the carbon tax concept and a few isolated applications, carbon taxes are not $197 per ton as proposed by Stern, and not $31 as proposed by Nordhaus, but around $3 per ton.[46] It is impossible to calculate the correct carbon tax merely on the basis of market prices and damage functions, even assuming the latter were correct.[47] The world is far from the benign equilibrium it is supposed to find by itself. After decades of advocacy, the real tax on carbon is barely above zero. The premise that actions will follow from self-interest is so deeply embedded in the collective mind that its failure is hardly noticed. If IAMs were meant to guide policymakers, they have failed.

7.4 THE PURPOSE OF FLAWED ECONOMICS

How then to understand the IAM project? In the face of a remote threat, there is a bias for inaction. When it comes to climate change, rationality and science are under pressure. Denial is widespread in climate change discourse.[48] One gambit is called 'agnotology' – the term was originally coined for public denial of causal links between smoking and cancer, as well as carbon emissions and climate change. It denotes the pretence of good faith, without credible evidence, intended to sow confusion and doubt.[49] Agnotology invokes dissenting, opportunistic, and maverick scientists to support denial. Nordhaus accepts that climate change is harmful. He is unlikely to be in anybody's pay. But he regards the risks as manageable and insists on market solutions. Market efficiency for him is an article of

---

[46] Nordhaus, 'Revisiting the social cost', 1, 520; idem, 'Climate change', slide 8; World Bank, *State and trends*.

[47] Millner and Heal, 'Choosing the future', 28.

[48] Leonard, 'David Koch was the ultimate climate change denier'; Nordhaus, *Climate casino*, chs. 25–26.

[49] Proctor and Schiebinger, *Agnotology*.

faith. Technology can solve any problem. Nordhaus is the co-author of later editions of Paul Samuelson's *Economics*, a textbook of the post-war neoclassical consensus of erstwhile bible-like standing, and with a stake in its continuing success.[50]

Economics bears some responsibility for the predicament it would like to solve. Its vision of market efficiency has justified the neoliberal thrust of the last forty years, the argument that business pursuing its own unfettered interest delivers the best outcome for all, as manifested in a growing economy. The mathematical proofs of this notion are tenuous and irrelevant.[51] In practice the dealmaker pursues their self-interest on the assumption that other things will remain equal, with no regard for externalities, i.e. for the effect of their actions on the system as a whole. The result is the greatest market failure ever and the prospect of a scorched earth.

Nordhaus's orthodoxy was celebrated by its custodians with the award of the prize in economics in memory of Alfred Nobel in December 2018. The original Nobel prizes were intended for individuals who in the previous year had conferred 'the greatest benefit on mankind'. That was not the justification given by the Swedish Academy for Nordhaus's award. The prize was awarded for 'integrating climate change into long-run macroeconomic analysis', i.e. for his IAM model. The academic citation document dwelt at great length on how Nordhaus (and his co-winner Paul Romer) had extended the neoclassical growth theory initially developed by Robert Solow in the 1950s.[52]

The classical economics of Smith, Ricardo, and Marx assumed three factors of production: labour, capital, and land. Capital and labour could grow, but the supply of natural resources ('land') was fixed, and their growing scarcity was likely to stifle economic growth. Solow's growth theory embodied the techno-optimism of the roaring 1950s – nature was left out of the model altogether. Human ingenuity could make up for any shortfall of natural resources. Hence, in all

---

[50] The price of the nineteenth edition (2009) of this undergraduate text was reported as $307 in 2016 (Komlos, *Principles of economics*, vi). The hardback was $219 on the publisher's website in December 2020.

[51] Offer and Söderberg, *Nobel factor*, ch. 1.

[52] Nobel Committee, 'Economic growth, technological change'. Solow had received the prize in 1987.

neoclassical IAMs the historical rate of economic growth is extrapolated into the future, ignoring the potential impact of climate havoc on the drivers of growth. Higher temperatures are still assumed to leave future generations better off than people today, thus greatly reducing the perceived urgency of the problem.[53]

But the 'technology' driving economic growth was not an empirical variable, it was an accounting artefact, a residual invoked airily as self-evident to explain the excess of economic growth over the growth of labour and capital. Nature is absent from this model, but it is the impact of nature that the model has to deal with. 'How can models that assume energy has no role in economic growth explain the economic impact of a new energy system? They don't. And they can't.'[54] The cost of energy inputs is less than 10 per cent of GDP but that does not measure its importance: nothing can replace it. Without energy, everything stops. In recent decades new heterodox growth models have substituted the measured value of energy input, or, more precisely, of the physical work done, for the intangible concept of 'technology'. 'Measurable work' combines the quantity of energy used and the efficiency with which it is applied, thus incorporating measurable concepts of technical change and the efficiency of energy use. When physical work done replaces technology in the model, the result follows observed economic growth very closely.[55] The implication for climate change policy is that we cannot count on technology to drive the economy upwards. Climate change requires a shift from energy-rich fossil fuels to less energetic renewables. Without fossil fuel energy to drive it there is no guarantee of cheap energy for technological progress in the future.

All this was known for more than a decade when the prize was awarded. It was ignored by neoclassical economists. The long Nobel document says nothing about the validity of growth theory. Faith is affirmed even as the house is literally burning down; humanity can go to the stake for the Swedish committee's beliefs. Sectarian purity trumped prudential caution, the prize committee thus setting the seal on its own irrelevance. The prize in economics was endowed in 1968

[53] Stern, *Why are we waiting?*, 144–145; Dietz and Stern, 'Endogenous growth'.
[54] King, *Economic superorganism*, 285.
[55] Ibid., ch. 6, esp. 272–285; Ayres and Warr, *Economic growth engine*.

by the Swedish central bank in order to shore up academic resistance to the country's social-democratic orientation. It has mostly celebrated the orthodox economics of the American mainstream of the discipline.[56] In selecting the complacent Nordhaus over the more wary Stern and Weitzman (discussed further below) the committee weighed on the side of denial, aligning itself with the priority for immediate gratification promoted by tobacco, opioid, and energy companies in the neoliberal era. The most recent manifestation of these preferences was President Trump and his tens of millions of supporters, climate deniers most of them.[57] Politicians have to rely on experts without being able to master or even understand the procedures that produced the result. Nordhaus and his acolytes provided false comfort and the Nobel endorsement reinforced their authority.[58] For the Nobel committee, its alliance with sectarian neoclassical orthodoxy is literally a test to destruction of the 'free market' paradigm.

7.5 HOW TO DO BETTER

To remove harm takes an effort, and economics has come up with the concept of an 'optimal bad'. For example, 'optimal crime' minimises the combined cost of crime and law enforcement, so that some crime might be better than none. Likewise, Nordhaus's concept of the 'optimal' level of global warming strives to minimise the combined cost of climate harm and its mitigation. Nordhaus is content for temperature to rise up to this 'optimum' level which he calculates is around 4 degrees above pre-industrial temperatures, a level not experienced by humanity since the dawn of civilisation, and one at which climate scientists predict devastation.

With so much uncertainty a more prudent approach is not to maximise efficiency but to avoid harm. A discount rate implies that the cost of future payoffs is evaluated and borne now. It implies continuous process of change expressed in mathematical functions which trace the increment in harm caused by smoothly rising temperatures. But change may also be stepwise, and some developments,

[56] Offer and Söderberg, *Nobel factor*. [57] Favelle, 'How Trump tried'.
[58] Linden, 'The economics Nobel went to a guy who enabled climate change denial'.

expected or not, might tip the climate into a bad state. The northern ice cap is melting rapidly. If the Greenland ice sheet collapses sea levels will rise and flood coastal cities. Ocean currents might change their course and alter terrestrial temperatures. Nordhaus initially dismissed such 'tipping point' events by misrepresenting a single survey article, which actually reached the opposite conclusions. He then added an arbitrary 25 per cent to his damage estimates to take account of possible tipping points.[59]

Tipping point events are not unlikely. The IPCC's 'best guess' of climate sensitivity is 3 degrees of warming with a two-thirds chance of falling between 1.5 and 4.5 degrees. The remaining one-third of probability was likely to concentrate at the high end, leading Martin Weitzman (another important protagonist) to estimate the chance of global temperature exceeding 6 degrees this century at 10 per cent. With that skewed shape, the distribution had an asymmetric 'fat tail'.[60]

The magnitude of a risk is the probability of an adverse event multiplied by its impact. A world-destroying event with low probability cannot be set aside. With a probability as high as 10 per cent, the global effort should be motivated primarily by striving to avert catastrophic events, not by a quest for efficiency and 'best guess' averages. To prevent disaster will require large sacrifices. The implication is that there is no market solution for the climate crisis. As in other long-term ventures only societies collectively can take on the uncertainty involved. The cost of mitigation can be seen as an insurance policy which a prudent humanity needs to take out. Blaise Pascal famously wrote in the seventeenth century that if there is even a remote possibility of eternal damnation, it is prudent to dismiss any doubt and believe in God. Weitzman's climate investment is Pascal's wager with much more daunting odds, a 'roughly 10 percent chance of near-certain disaster'.[61]

Climate economists have another blind spot. Global warming is not an investment appraisal problem but a psychological one.

---

[59] Keen, 'Appallingly bad', 12–13: repeated three times, see Nordhaus and Moffat, 'Survey of global impacts', 35; the survey in question by Lenton et al., 'Tipping elements', is not even listed among Nordhaus's references in these publications.

[60] Wagner and Weitzman, *Climate shock*, ch. 3, esp. 51–54. [61] Ibid., 54, 78.

Rationality implies that people will act for their own good once they know what it is. But they are no more keen to acknowledge the extinction of humanity then to face the certainty of their own death. Comfort now counts for more than future survival. Procrastination resists the disruption of a settled life. Even gradual changes are only tolerated if there is no hardship involved. Perhaps our emotional and social brains cannot rise to cope with a challenge of this order. Nordhaus is not immune to it. That makes the problem 'wicked'. Even if a few societies can make the prudential choice, effective international action is unlikely.[62]

In standard economic theory, consumers are the best judges of their own welfare. They are consistent, informed, and far-sighted. They optimise consumption over the life cycle by buying, borrowing, and saving in appropriate markets. In contrast, behavioural economics has found that consumers are myopic. In their 'hyperbolic discounting' model, value declines sharply with delay, the discount rate changes over time, and the objective ranking of preferences by desirability and price can be inverted, so that smaller-sooner dominates larger-later.[63] Taken literally, a 'myopic trap' keeps the delayed reward forever out of reach. Overcoming myopia is difficult and costly, and individual choice cannot be relied on as a measure of welfare.

Greenhouse gas emissions are driven by the pursuit of affluence. Stern, Nordhaus, Weitzman, all restrict their analysis to rational policy choices. If they take account of denial, it is only to argue that business and right-wing politicians have conspired to distort the truth in support of sectional interests.[64] There is scant consideration of how keen people are to deceive themselves.

For Martin Weitzman, the point of departure was uncertainty. We don't know how global warming is going to unfold. No single discount rate is likely to be correct. Different people are likely to have different discount rates. It was more reasonable to assign a probability distribution over the range of discount rates. The average of two exponential discount rates produces a variable discount rate, which (unlike a constant one) is hyperbolic and does not converge on zero for a long time. Such

[62] Marshall, *Don't even think about it.* [63] Offer, *Challenge of affluence*, esp. chs. 3–4.
[64] Nordhaus, *Climate casino*, Pt. V.

a discount rate, which remains elevated in the distant future, justifies earlier and more intense mitigation.[65] Variable discount rates have been adopted officially in Britain and France. Long-term markets in real estate also apply a variable discount rate.[66] Viewed from this aspect, collective provision serves as a 'commitment device' for individuals to help them escape from 'myopic traps' and to allocate resources better over time.

With a constant discount rate, the ranking of choices is invariant over time. Our current priority is a diagnostic for what we are likely to do in the future. If we were going to act later, we would be acting now as well. Alternatively, inaction now indicates that our motivation is not consistent but myopic. Our challenge is not whether it is worth acting now but whether we are ever going to act, how to overcome myopia and motivate action.

Rationality alone does not guarantee prudence. Economists differ in their moral premises. For Stern, ethics assigns future lives an equal value with our own. Nordhaus's premise is possessive individualism, the imperative to maximise the present value of our own lives, and the confidence that markets will provide. Weitzman modifies Nordhaus by giving priority to the more extreme disasters that may affect those already alive, or their immediate offspring.

Economist climate modellers all fail to ask how to implement the policies they recommend. Although behavioural economics has acknowledged myopia for decades now, it required a climate activist to spell out the mental hurdles that have to be scaled.[67] When Nordhaus ventures into politics and public opinion only two classes of problem are identified, pushback by vested interests like coal and oil companies, and ignorance of science by public and politicians.[68] Denial (as in his own case) is motivated by rational calculation. But economic orthodoxy knows better, and has expected politicians to act myopically in order to please their voters since the 1980s.[69]

---

[65] Weitzman, 'Gamma discounting'; Wagner and Weitzman, *Climate shock*, 68–69, 187; Arrow et al., 'Should governments use a declining discount rate'.

[66] Millner and Heal, 'Choosing the future', 13–14. [67] Marshall, *Don't even think about it*.

[68] Nordhaus, *Climate casino*, pt. V.

[69] Phelps and Pollak, 'Second best national-savings'; that is the main reason why central banks have been granted independence; Blanchard and Fischer, *Lectures on macroeconomics*.

7.6 THREE FORMS OF DENIAL

Denial comes in three forms: rational ('it's not really happening'), emotional ('I don't want to know'), and optimism ('something will turn up'). Some controversies are inconclusive but not this one. Predictions are either true or not. We shall find out for sure.

Rational deniers reject evidence which is inconsistent with their interests. They are free riders who expect their current benefit to exceed their future harm. Emotional denial is myopic: it prefers peace of mind. In alliance with emotional deniers, rational ones created the movement for climate denial. Optimists expect rising carbon prices to induce technological solutions. Such breakthroughs cannot be ruled out. There is energy enough in the sun. Fusion or geo-engineering might come to the rescue. But technology has failed to solve other enduring challenges, like cancer and the common cold, or indeed every person's certain extinction. Past doomsters have often been wrong, but many were right. The prospects are not symmetrical. If you prepare for the worst and nothing happens, the effort will not have been in vain though we won't know what made the difference. Economic growth will drop a fraction but its levels will eventually recover. If nothing is done and the worst happens, there is no recovery.

When the interests of the future are sufficiently compelling there is, however, a method to motivate action. To overcome the compelling grip of consumer desire, e.g. Tony Blair's imperative of holiday flights, a long-term commitment only applies to the future. That is how actual climate policy is made. Not carbon taxes, whose application has been fitful, scattered, and ineffective. Rather, a growing number of countries have committed themselves with 'legally binding' legislation or otherwise to net zero emissions a generation hence. The United States and China have joined recently, although few countries are on track to fulfil such obligations.[70] This pragmatic approach takes account of myopia. It may be difficult to impose restrictions now, but once the future arrives previous commitments will have become a *fait accompli* which is difficult to reverse. This technique is popular with politicians. For example, a higher age of

---

[70] Darby and Gerretsen, 'Which countries have a net zero carbon goal?'

retirement is never introduced immediately, but always applies only some years hence.

A target is identified and a commitment made. As in other long-term enterprises, little is known for certain except that something must be done. It is not a problem that markets can handle. Climate change is like an enemy in wartime who is likely to surprise. Nothing is certain except the imperative to act. Staying the course requires endurance and commitment. Commitment is a public good, not a private one. Compare it to the Cold War of yore: a portent of disaster even more extreme than climate change and likewise unformed, uncertain, and indefinite. Vast capabilities were built up with bipartisan support and broad social consent. International co-operation was sought and paid for. Climate change likewise is already high on the agenda of national security.[71] In the past, mobilisation required external enemies. The enemy now is ourselves, our own resource-hungry lifestyles.

---

[71] Holland and Vagg, 'Global security defense index'; Verbeek, 'Planetary security'.

Conclusion

In free markets only individuals count. But society has needs which it is nobody's interest to satisfy. After war and justice,

> the third and last duty of the sovereign or commonwealth is that of erecting and maintaining those public institutions and those public works, which, though they may be in the highest degree advantageous to a great society, are, however, of such a nature, that the profit could never repay the expense to any individual or small number of individuals.[1]

Such ventures, like society itself, live longer than any person. To create them is fraught with uncertainty. Without security of a franchise (or a windfall profit) no prudent banker will finance a project that only pays off beyond the limit embodied in the current interest rate. Entrepreneurs are lauded as risk-takers but do so only for themselves. Government is the risk-taker of last resort.

Victorian societies were energised by coal-driven windfall gains, by trade and by plunder overseas, and came to believe in commercial freedom. By the end of the century their growing wealth required a longer vision than that of any single capitalist. Governments can be foolish too. In 1914 they plunged into a world war. After that frightful experience, developed societies set about to safeguard domestic security by means of housing, education, old-age pensions, health-care, every country at its own pace and in its own way. Network infrastructures undergirded societies, waterworks, paved roads and highways, railways, urban transport, electricity, broadcasting, overseen by law-abiding and competent administrations.

Governments had to decide how much to manage themselves and what to hand over to business. How to do without the checks and

---

[1] Smith, *Wealth of nations*, Bk. V. ch. I, pt. iii, 723.

enterprise of market competition? Governments themselves were kept in check imperfectly by means of electoral democracy. Staff were kept in line by a committed system of expert administration, embodied in Weberian bureaucracy. Only one country, the Soviet Union, relied on government alone. All others were dominated, for much of the time, by the male elites of business, the professions, and finance. To mobilise commercial capacity for long-term development required shielding from competition, uncertainty, and risk. That kind of freedom was the true aspiration of business.

Whether undertaken by governments' own staff or by means of commercial concessions, long-term activities undisciplined by competition gave rise to conflicts of interest and opportunities for corruption. The peculation of public servants facilitated massive enrichment in business and sometimes in government. Contracts and financial incentives might discourage embezzlement but the only enduring protection was integrity in politics and administration, an honest institutional culture, internalised by individuals and underpinned by regulation. Only a few countries in north-western Europe have managed to instil such norms enduringly, and they do not include the main English-speaking countries.

From the 1960s onwards the advanced economies of Western Europe and North America gradually lost their industrial prowess and moved into services. Voters turned away from collective provision towards private consumption and accumulation. They voted for neoliberal governments (and oppositions as well) to satisfy these aspirations, home ownership foremost, with its motorised lifestyle and financial underpinning.

Advocates of privilege beguiled the voters and captured governments with the rhetoric of markets. Official authority made way for private-sector energy and drive. Economists proliferated in government and licensed the market turn from the academy as well. They wrote the playbooks in finance ministries, central banks, the IMF, and the World Bank. Neoclassical market models had no role for government or virtue, and nor did their Hayekian neoliberal variants. The primacy of self-interest influenced political science and philosophy, and undermined the commitment to integrity and collective action. An opportunistic new class took over politics and embraced finance and business. Government, money, and business intertwined in a single self-serving entity, a new version of eighteenth-century 'Old Corruption'. The public good is sidelined, household insecurity is rife, the public domain neglected and sad.

In the meantime, a new social challenge is rising, unlike any in the past, in the form of global warming. Business and consumers have done what they could to ignore this distant threat. Neoclassical economists waved their hands to make it go away. Covid-19 emerged suddenly to inflict another, more immediate challenge beyond the capacity of business to solve, while most governments have also fallen short.

The role of government is to act as a commitment agent for society. It endures in a hostile climate because government performs this role more efficiently than private contracts can ever do. Consumers find it difficult to overcome myopic cravings, and turn, as voters, to government for help. The welfare state is not primarily a remedy for indigence or inequality. Controlling the future by means of a private contract is uncertain and costly. Uncertainty grows exponentially with time. Government is the solution that society has evolved. In most countries, it provides education, healthcare, and social insurance, as well as physical infrastructures. Forms of private provision that operate tolerably well, like mortgages, life insurance and private pensions, and energy and water infrastructures, depend on government regulation to resolve inherent conflicts of interests between providers and the public.

IMPLICATIONS

What is there for readers to take away, as students or teachers, consumers, parents, citizens, activists, business people, civil servants, politicians, and media commentators? Here it is in brief.

- 'Free markets' in developed societies have a circumscribed role. Competitive firms provide brilliantly for items with product cycles shorter than that of a bank loan, in food, retail, personal services, holidays, some forms of entertainment and recreation, mobile phones, computers, cars. The list is not exhaustive because it is always being refreshed. Competition is the source of innovation and 'creative destruction'. But the market for many of these products is often dominated by a few suppliers, and production by national champions.

- The test is the length of the product cycle. If the product is made and paid for over hours, days, weeks, a few years, then competition is good. If it requires many years, or even decades, to create, sustain, and deliver it will not work because the market alone cannot give long-term security to investors and creditors. Finance, whose task is to prioritise private investment and provide insurance, operates under a protective government tutelage. Much of its activity serves no productive social function.
- There is no warrant for extending market norms to the rest of social activity, to the family, government, infrastructure, education, healthcare, science and arts, social insurance, old age, defence, protecting the environment and the climate. Together these are the source of most economic welfare. When housing supply is driven exclusively by market priorities its provision is unfair and inadequate.
- Governments that issue their own currency (e.g. not in the Eurozone) can finance any worthwhile project at the lowest possible rates, and have no need to pay over the odds to borrow in financial markets. No less than central banks, commercial bank finance also creates money out of nothing for secure creditors.[2] Hence there is no financial requirement to placate the bond markets or mobilise private–public partnerships. Quantitative easing since 2008 has shown how elastic public credit can be.
- The problem for government is rather whether to manage by itself, or to delegate to not-for-profits or to business by means of a franchise. This provides non-government entities with security for long-term commitment, at a cost in regulation and oversight.
- To what extent can government trust its servants and those entrusted with its franchise? And can society trust its governments? What is best for government to self-manage or to outsource depends on its competence and capacity, and the capabilities of the private sector.
- The exercise of authority is a temptation for corruption. Historically corruption was defeated in the nineteenth century by means of 'Weberian' bureaucracies, small bodies of expert officials insulated from politics, appointed by competitive selection, beholden to hierarchy, motivated by peer norms and monitoring, written codes, promotion by merit, and incentives for continuity and long service.

---

[2] Deutsche Bundesbank, 'The role of banks'; McLeay et al., 'Money creation'.

• Such competence is undermined by the intermingling of government and business norms and personnel, and by the ideology of market perfection. At the time of writing, this is the foremost lesson. Government needs to re-establish its capacity to look after the public interest.

Today government is like the wanderer in Caspar David Friedrich's painting (Figure 8.1). He stands atop a rocky crag, his

Figure 8.1 The wanderer above the sea of fog. Caspar David Friedrich (1818)
Location: Kunsthalle, Hamburg.[3]

---

[3] https://commons.wikimedia.org/wiki/File:Caspar_David_Friedrich_-_Wanderer_above_the_sea_of_fog.jpg.

dignity a frock coat, his authority a cane, looking out into a landscape shrouded in mist. Space is like time: distant horizons stand for promise. The outcrops visible ahead stand for market time horizons. The distance is hidden in fog. Remote peaks are lit by the sun. We want to get there but how? The market delusion draws a veil on things that matter most: security, equity, compassion, knowledge, art, and science. As a response to climate change it is a threat to our very existence.

References

Aaron, H. J., 'Social security: Tune it up, don't trade it in', in Freidman, B. M., ed., *Should the United States privatize social security?* (Cambridge, MA, 1999), 55–112.

Abed, G. T. and S. Gupta, eds., *Governance, corruption and economic performance* (Washington DC, 2002).

Abelson, R., 'Many with insurance still bankrupted by health crises', *New York Times*, 1 Jul. 2009.

Abramitzky, R., *The mystery of the kibbutz: Egalitarian principles in a capitalist world* (Princeton, NJ, 2019).

Abrams, F., 'Kings science academy scandal raises questions over free school policy', *The Guardian*, 1 Apr. 2014.

Adams, R., 'Lauded academy chain to be stripped of schools after finances inquiry', *The Guardian*, 28 Mar. 2016.

Akers, B., and M. M. Chingos, *Game of loans: The rhetoric and reality of student debt* (Princeton, NJ, 2016).

Alexander, M., *The new Jim Crow: Mass incarceration in the age of color-blindness*, rev. edn. (London, 2019).

Ally, M., 'Understanding financial wrongdoing, c.1970–2010', University of Oxford D. Phil. thesis (Oxford, 2019).

American Medical Association and Center for Health Policy, 'Competition in health insurance: A comprehensive study of US markets, 2009 update', American Medical Association (Chicago, IL, 2009).

Angell, M., 'Opioid nation', *New York Review of Books* (6 Dec. 2018).

Angrisano, C., D. Farrell, B. Kocher, M. Laboissiere, and S. Parker, 'Accounting for the cost of health care in the United States', McKinsey Global Institute (2007).

Anonymous, *The great estates: Sustainable development over the centuries* (London, 2006).

Anonymous, and T. Harper, *License to steal: The secret world of Wall Street and the systematic plundering of the American investor* (New York, 1999).

Ansell, B. W., 'The "nest egg" effect? Housing, the welfare state, and political incentives', University of Minnesota, conference paper (Apr. 2009).

Ansell, B. W., 'The politics of housing', *Annual Review of Political Science*, 22 (2019), 165–185.

Arent, D. J., and R. S. J. Tol, 'Key economic sectors and services', in Field, C. B. and V. R. Barros, eds., *Climate change 2014 impacts, adaptation, and vulnerability part A: Global and sectoral aspects working group II contribution to the fifth assessment report of the Intergovernmental Panel on Climate Change* (New York, 2014).

Armona, L., R. Chakrabarti, and M. F. Lovenheim, 'How does for-profit college attendance affect student loans, defaults and labor market outcomes?' *NBER working paper series*, 25042 (2018).

Arnold, A. J., and S. McCartney, 'Rates of return, concentration levels and strategic change: British railways from 1830 to 1912', *Journal of Transport History*, 26 (2005), 41–60.

Aron, J., J. V. Duca, J. Muellbauer, K. Murata, and A. Murphy, 'Credit, housing collateral, and consumption: Evidence from Japan, the U.K. and the U.S.', *Review of Income and Wealth*, 58, 3 (2012), 397–423.

Arrow, K. J., 'The economic implications of learning by doing', *Review of Economic Studies*, 29 (1962), 155–173.

Arrow, K. J., 'Uncertainty and the welfare economics of medical care', *American Economic Review*, 53 (1963), 941–973.

Arrow, K. J., and R. C. Lind, 'Uncertainty and the evaluation of public investment decisions', *American Economic Review*, 60 (1970), 364–368.

Arrow, K. J. et al., 'Should governments use a declining discount rate in project analysis?' *Review of Environmental Economics and Policy*, 8 (2014), 145–163.

Arthur, T. and C. Taylor, 'The UK pensions crisis', The TaxPayers' Alliance Research Note 38, 3 Nov. 2008 (London, 2008).

Arza, C., 'Basic old-age protection in Latin America: Noncontributory pensions, coverage expansion strategies, and aging patterns across countries', *Population and Development Review*, 45 (2019), 23–45.

Associated Press, 'Supreme Court tells judges not to rule on major backers', *New York Times*, 8 Jun. 2009.

Atkins, G., N. Davies, and T. K. Bishop, 'Public versus private: How to pick the best infrastructure finance option', Institute for Government, (London, Nov. 2017).

Atkinson, R., 'Project management: Cost, time and quality, two best guesses and a phenomenon, its time to accept other success criteria', *International Journal of Project Management*, 17, 6 (1999), 337–342.

Authers, J., 'Is it back to the fifties', *Financial Times*, 29 Mar. 2009.

Ayres, I., and Q. Curtis, 'Beyond diversification: The pervasive problem of excessive fees and "dominated funds" in 401(k) plans', *Yale Law Journal*, 124 (2015), 1,476–1,552.

Ayres, R. U., and B. Warr, *The economic growth engine: How energy and work drive material prosperity* (Cheltenham, 2009).

Baker, B. D., 'Exploring the consequences of charter school expansion in U.S. Cities', Economic Policy Institute (Washington DC, 30 Nov. 2016).

Baker, D., 'Saving social security with stocks: The promises don't add up', Twentieth Century Fund/Economic Policy Institute (New York, 1997).

Baker, D., 'Insurance fraud: The lack of transparency in the US healthcare industry means insurance companies can abuse patients by denying their claims', *The Guardian*, 1 Mar. 2008.

Bamford, T. W., *Rise of the public schools: A study of boys' public boarding schools in England and Wales from 1837 to the present day* (London, 1967).

Bar-Eli, A., 'It is time to tell the truth about those who manage 2 trillion shekels of our money – and live on another planet', *The Marker [Haaretz]*, 8 May 2020 (in Hebrew).

Barfort, S., N. A. Harmon, F. Hjorth, and A. L. Olsen, 'Sustaining honesty in public service: The role of selection', *American Economic Journal: Economic Policy*, 11 (2019), 96–123.

Barker, A., and N. Timmins, 'Taxpayers' cash to be used for PFI projects', *Financial Times*, 13 Feb. 2009.

Barker, T. C., and M. Robbins, *A history of London transport: Passenger travel and the development of the metropolis*, rev. edn. (London, 1976).

Barlow, J., J. Roehrich, and S. Wright, 'Europe sees mixed results from public-private partnerships for building and managing health care facilities and services', *Health Affairs*, 32 (2013), 146–154.

Barr, N. A., *The welfare state as piggy bank: Information, risk, uncertainty, and the role of the state* (Oxford, 2001).

Barret, E. D., 'Fixing the revolving door between government and business', Transparency International, Policy Paper 2, (London, Apr. 2012).

Baumann, N., 'Permission to encroach the bench', *Mother Jones*, 25 Aug. 2010.

Baumol, W. J., 'On the social rate of discount', *American Economic Review* 58 (1968), 788–802.

Bayliss, K., and E. Van Waeyenberge, 'Unpacking the public private partnership revival', *Journal of Development Studies*, 54 (2018), 577–593.

BBC, 'Tube maintenance back "in house" as new deal is signed' (2010), in http://news.bbc.co.uk/1/hi/england/london/8669823.stm.

BBC Question Time, 'The chairman of RBS, Howard Davies, says that PFI "has been a fraud on the people"', #bbcqt, 18 Jan. 2018.

Beck, T., A. Demirgüç-Kunt, and R. Levine, 'Financial institutions and markets across countries and over time – data and analysis', World Bank Policy Research Working Paper 4943 (Washington DC, May 2009).

Beetsma, R., Z. Lekbuite, and E. Ponds, 'Reforming American public-sector pension plans: Truths and consequences', *Rotman International Journal of Pension Management*, 7 (2014), 66–74.

Benn, M., and J. Downs, 'Who runs our schools?' *London Review of Books* (18 Jun. 2015), 4.

Bent, P. H., and R. Esteves, 'Government-supported industries and financial crises in developing economies, 1880–1913' (Unpublished draft paper 2021).

Berberich, C., *The image of the English gentleman in twentieth-century literature: Englishness and nostalgia* (Aldershot, 2007).

Berry, C., 'Austerity, ageing and the financialisation of pensions policy in the UK', *British Politics*, 11 (2016), 2–25.

Best, J., and E. Best, *The student loan mess: How good intentions created a trillion-dollar problem* (Berkeley, CA, 2014).

Best, R., and A. Martin, 'Rental housing for an ageing population', All Party Parliamentary Group for Housing and Care for Older People (London, Jul. 2019).

Better Finance, 'Pension savings: The real return 2019 edition', The European Federation of Investors and Financial Services Users, 2019 (Brussels, 2019).

Bignon, V., R. Esteves, and A. Herranz-Loncn, 'Big push or big grab? Railways, government activism, and export growth in Latin America, 1865–1913', *Economic History Review*, 68, 4 (2015), 1,277–1,305.

Black, J., and R. Nobles, 'Personal pensions misselling: The causes and lessons of regulatory failure', *Modern Law Review*, 61 (1998), 789–820.

Blanc-Brude, F., and R. Strange, 'How banks price loans to public-private partnerships: Evidence from the European markets', *Journal of Applied Corporate Finance*, 19, 4 (2007), 94–106.

Blanchard, O., and S. Fischer, *Lectures on macroeconomics* (Cambridge, MA, 1989).

Blatt, J. M., *Dynamic economic systems: A post-Keynesian approach* (Armonk, NY, 1983).

Blum, B., 'Here's the case for impeaching Clarence Thomas – the most corrupt Supreme Court Justice', *Raw Story*, 27 Oct. 2020.

Boardman, A., and M. Hellowell, 'A comparative analysis and evaluation of specialist PPP units' methodologies for conducting value for money appraisals', *Journal of Comparative Policy Analysis*, 19, 3 (2016), 191–206.

Boardman, A., M. Siemiatycki, and A. R. Vining, 'The theory and evidence concerning public-private partnerships in Canada and elsewhere', University of Calgary School of Public Policy SPP Research Papers (Calgary, Mar. 2016).

Bodie, Z., 'On the risk of stocks in the long run', *Financial Analysts Journal*, 51, 3 (1995), 18.

Bodie, Z., 'Letter: Are stocks the best investment for the long run?' *The Economist's Voice*, 6 (2009), 1–2.

Boffey, D., 'Public sector workers need "discipline and fear", says Oliver Letwin', *The Guardian*, 30 Jul. 2011.

Boffey, D., 'Academy chain under fire following revelation of payments made to bosses', *Observer*, 20 Jul. 2013.

Bogart, D., 'Nationalizations and the development of transport systems: Cross-country evidence from railroad networks, 1860-1912', *Journal of Economic History*, 69 (2009), 202–237.

Bogart, D., 'Engines of development? Cross-country evidence on the interconnection between private and state railroad construction and GDP, 1870–1912', *Journal of Economic History*, 69 (2009), 585.

Bogart, D., 'A global perspective on railway inefficiency and the rise of state ownership, 1880–1912', *Explorations in Economic History*, 47 (2010), 158–178.

Bogart, D., and L. Chaudhary, 'Off the rails: Is state ownership bad for productivity?' *Journal of Comparative Economics*, 43 (2015), 997–1,013.

Bogle, J. C., *The battle for the soul of capitalism* (New Haven, CT, 2005).

Borenstein, S., 'The trouble with electricity markets: Understanding California's restructuring disaster', *Journal of Economic Perspectives*, 16 (2002), 191–211.

Borzutzky, S., and M. Hyde, 'Chile's private pension system at 35: Impact and lessons', *Journal of International and Comparative Social Policy*, 32, 1 (2016), 57–73.

Boswell, J., and J. Peters, *Capitalism in contention: Business leaders and political economy in modern Britain* (Cambridge, 1997).

Boughton, J., *Municipal dreams: The rise and fall of council housing* (London, 2019).

Bourquin, P., C. Emmerson, and J. Cribb, 'Who leaves their pension after being automatically enrolled?' Institute of Fiscal Studies, IFS Briefing Notes, BN272 (London, Mar. 2020).

Bowcott, O., 'Lawyers call for apology from Johnson and Patel for endangering colleagues', *The Guardian*, 25 Oct. 2020.

Bower, T., *The Paymaster: Geoffrey Robinson, Maxwell and New Labour* (London, 2001).

Bradley, J., S. Gerekidan, and A. McCann, 'Waste, negligence and cronyism: Inside Britain's pandemic spending', *New York Times*, 20 Dec. 2020.

Brealey, R. A., S. C. Myers, and F. Allen, *Principles of corporate finance*, 10th edn, global edn. (New York, 2011).

Brewer, M., *Poverty and inequality in Britain: 2006* (London, 2006).

Broeders, D., and E. H. M. Pounds, 'Dutch pension system reform – a step closer to the ideal system?' *DICE Report: Journal for Institutional Comparisons* (2012), 65–76.

Brooks, R., 'The Bourn complicity', *Private Eye* (5–18 Sep. 2008), 17–23.

Brooks, R., 'Tax, lies and videotape: Britain's shadow tax system revealed', *Private Eye* (20 Sep. 2013).

Brooks, R., *The great tax robbery: How Britain became a tax haven for fat cats and big business* (Richmond, 2013).

Brooks, R., *Bean counters: The triumph of the accountants and how they broke capitalism* (London, 2018).

Brooks, R., and S. Hughes, 'Public servants, private paydays … Revolving doors special report', *Private Eye* (2–15 Sep. 2016), 19–24.

Brown, G., J. Prescott, and R. F. Cook, 'Financing infrastructure investment: Promoting a partnership between public and private finance' Labour Finance and Industry Group Symposium on Public-Private Finance (London, 1994).

Brown, G., E. Balls, and G. O'Donnell, *Reforming Britain's economic and financial policy: Towards greater economic stability* (Basingstoke, 2002).

Brummer, A., *The great pensions robbery: How New Labour betrayed retirement* (London, 2011).

Buchanan, J. M., 'Public choice: The origins and development of a research program', Center for Study of Public Choice, George Mason University (Fairfax, VA, 2003).

Buchanan, J. M., and R. A. Musgrave, *Public finance and public choice: Two contrasting visions of the state* (Cambridge, MA, 1999).

Buffet, W. R., 'Chairman's letter, Berkshire Hathaway Inc. 2003 annual report', Berkshire Hathaway Inc. (n.p., 27 Feb. 2004).

Bullock, N., 'Berlin', in Daunton, M. J., ed., *Housing the workers: A comparative history, 1850–1914* (Leicester, 1990), 182–248.

Bullock, N., and J. Read, *The movement for housing reform in Germany and France, 1840–1914* (Cambridge, 1985).

Bureau of Investigative Journalism, 'Insurance lobby weakens pension plan for low paid' (2012), in https://www.thebureauinvestigates.com/stories/2012-07-09/insurance-lobby-weakens-pension-plan-for-low-paid.

Burke, E., *Speech of Edmund Burke, Esq., member of Parliament for the city of Bristol, on presenting to the House of Commons (on the 11th of Feb., 1780) a plan for the better security of the independence of Parliament, and the oeconomical reformation of the civil and other establishments* (London, 1780).

Burke, E., *Thoughts and details on scarcity, originally presented to the right hon. William Pitt, in the month of November, 1795* (London, 1800).

Burke, M., S. Hsiang, and E. Miguel, 'Global non-linear effect of temperature on economic production', *Nature*, 527 (2015), 235–239.

Burtless, G., 'Social security privatisation and financial market risk: Lessons from US financial history', in Ihori, T. and Toshiaki T., eds., *Social security reform in advanced countries: Evaluating pension finance* (London, 2002), 52–80.

Burton, J., 'Antonin Scalia's death during secret junket points to new ethical violations' (2016), in https://www.wsws.org/en/articles/2016/02/20/scalf2o.html?view=print.

Butler, S., and P. Germanis, 'Achieving a "Leninist" strategy', *Cato Journal*, 3 (1983), 547–561.

Butzbach, O., 'British building societies 1970–2010 the changing conditions for a viable not-for-profit alternative in a financialised economy', in Cantaluppi, A., ed., *Social aims of finance: Rediscovering varieties of credit in financial archives* (Frankfurt, 2019), 133–154.

Calavita, K., H. N. Pontell, and R. Tillman, *Big money crime: Fraud and politics in the savings and loan crisis* (Berkeley, CA, 1997).

Caldwell, B., *Hayek's challenge: An intellectual biography of F.A. Hayek* (Chicago, IL, 2004).

Caldwell, B., and L. Montes, 'Friedrich Hayek and his visits to Chile', CHOPE (Center for the history of political economy), Discussion paper 2014–12 (Durham, NC, 2014).

Camdessus, M., and M. Naím, 'A talk with Michel Camdessus about God, globalization, and his years running the IMF', *Foreign Policy*, Sept.–Oct. (2000), 32–45.

Carr-Brown, J., and M. Gould, 'Series of blunders lead to the billion-pound hospital', *Sunday Times*, 3 Aug. 2003.

Carter, S. B., et al., eds., 'Historical statistics of the United States millennial edition online' (2006).

Carvel, J., 'Flagship PFI hospital "technically bankrupt"', *The Guardian*, 16 Dec. 2005.

Case, A., and A. Deaton, *Deaths of despair and the future of capitalism* (Princeton, NJ, 2020).

Cassis, Y., G. De Luca, and M. Florio, *Infrastructure finance in Europe: Insights into the history of water, transport, and telecommunications* (Oxford, 2016).

Casson, M., *The world's first railway system: Enterprise, competition, and regulation on the railway network in Victorian Britain* (Oxford, 2009).

Celarier, M., 'Privatization: A case study in corruption', *Journal of International Affairs*, 50 (1970), 531–543.

Chait, J., *The big con: The true story of how Washington got hoodwinked and hijacked by crackpot economics* (Boston, MA, 2007).

Chakrabortty, A., 'Now the Tories are allowing big business to design their own tax loopholes', *The Guardian*, 13 Oct. 2015.

Chandler, A. D., *The visible hand: The managerial revolution in American business* (Cambridge, MA, 1977).

Charron, N., G. De Luca, and M. Florio, 'Careers, connections, and corruption risks: Investigating the impact of bureaucratic meritocracy on public procurement processes', *Journal of Politics*, 79 (2017), 89–104.

Chaudhary, L., and D. Bogart, 'Public-private partnerships and efficiency: A historical perspective from Indian railways', *Journal of Economic History*, 70 (2010), 486–486.

Chayes, S., *Everybody knows: Corruption in America* (London, 2020).

Chick, M., *Electricity and energy policy in Britain, France and the United States since 1945* (Cheltenham, 2007).

Chłoń-Domińczak, A., et al., 'The first wave of NDC reforms: The experiences of Italy, Latvia, Poland, and Sweden', in Holzmann, R., E. Palmer, and D. Robalino, eds., *Nonfinancial defined contribution pension schemes in a changing pension world*, vol. 1. Progress, lessons, and implementation (Washington DC, 2013), 31–84.

Chorley, M., 'Yes Minister creator Jonathan Lynn says show gave rise to cult of Cummings', *The Times*, 30 Mar. 2021.

Ciepley, D., 'Beyond public and private: Toward a political theory of the corporation', *American Political Science Review*, 107 (2013), 139–158.

Christensen, T., and P. Lægreid, eds., *The Ashgate research companion to new public management* (Farnham, 2011).

Clarke, S., A. Corlett, and L. Judge, 'The housing headwind: The impact of rising housing costs on UK living standards', Resolution Foundation (London, 2017).

Cockett, R., *Thinking the unthinkable: Think-tanks and the economic counter-revolution, 1931–1983* (London, 1994).

Coffee, J. C., *Corporate crime and punishment: The crisis of underenforcement* (Oakland, CA, 2020).

Cohen, G. B., 'The Austrian bureaucracy at the nexus of state and society', in Aldgasser, F. and F. Lindstrom, eds., *The Habsburg civil service and beyond: Bureaucracy and civil servants from the Vormarz to the inter-war years* (Vienna, 2019), 49–65.

Collini, S., *What are universities for?* (London, 2012).

Confessore, N. et al., 'The swamp that Trump built', *New York Times*, 10 Oct. 2020.

Cordelli, C., *The privatized state* (Princeton, NJ, 2020).

Corlett, A., and L. Judge, 'Home affront: Housing across the generations', Resolution Foundation (London, 2017).

Craig, D., and R. Brooks, *Plundering the public sector: How New Labour are letting consultants run off with 70 billion of our money* (London, 2006).

Craig, S., W. K. Rashbaum, and T. Kaplan, 'Cuomo's office hobbled ethics inquiries by Moreland commission', *New York Times*, 23 Jul. 2014.

Crawford, M., 'The big pension lie: Contrary to fashion, "pay as you go" is affordable', *Progressive Review*, 4 (1997), 38–44.

Cumbo, J., 'FSA steps up campaign on PPI products', *Financial Times*, 24 Feb. 2009.

Cummins, N., 'Hidden wealth', London School of Economics, Unpublished paper (London, 1 Jul. 2020).

Cunningham, H., 'The decline of child labour: Labour markets and family economies in Europe and North America since 1830', *Economic History Review*, 53, 3 (2000), 409–428.

Curry, T., and L. Shibut, 'The cost of the savings and loan crisis', *FDIC Banking Review*, 13 (2000), 26–35.

Dahlstedt, M., and A. Fejes, eds., *Neoliberalism and market forces in education: Lessons from Sweden* (Abingdon, 2019).

Daily News, *No room to live: papers on the housing question in town and country* (London, 1900).

Daily Telegraph, 'The complete expenses files' (London, 2009).

Darby, M., and I. Gerretsen, 'Which countries have a net zero carbon goal?' (2020), in https://www.climatechangenews.com/2019/06/14/countries-net-zero-climate-goal/.

Dartmouth Atlas Working Group, 'The Dartmouth atlas of healthcare' (2011), in http://www.dartmouthatlas.org/.

Daunton, M. J., *House and home in the Victorian city: Working-class housing 1850–1914* (London, 1983).

Daunton, M. J., ed., *Housing the workers, 1850–1914: A comparative perspective* (Leicester, 1990).

Davenport, C., and E. Lipton, 'How G.O.P. Leaders came to view climate change as fake science', *New York Times*, 3 Jun. 2017.

Davey, M., and N. Confessore, 'South Dakota legislators seek hasty repeal of ethics law voters passed', *New York Times*, 25 Jan. 2017.

Davis, A., *Reckless opportunists: Elites at the end of the establishment* (Manchester, 2018).

Dayen, D., 'Wall Street pays bankers to work in government and it doesn't want anyone to know', *The New Republic*, 4 Feb. 2015.

DeCanio, S. J., *Economic models of climate change: A critique* (New York, 2003).

DeCanio, S. J., *Limits of economic and social knowledge* (London, 2014).

Dell, M., B. F. Jones, and B. A. Olken, 'What do we learn from the weather? The new climate–economy literature', *Journal of Economic Literature*, 52 (2014), 740–798.

DeLong, J. B., and K. Magin, 'The U.S. Equity return premium: Past, present, and future', *Journal of Economic Perspectives*, 23, 1 (2009), 193–208.

Deutsche Bundesbank, 'The role of banks, non-banks and the central bank in the money creation process', *Deutsche Bundesbank Monthly Report*, April (2017), pp. 13–33.

Di Matteo, L., and F. Summerfield, 'The shifting Scully curve: International evidence from 1870 to 2016', *Applied Economics*, 52 (2020), 4263–4283.

Dickinson, T., 'Inside the Koch brothers' toxic empire', *Rolling Stone*, 24 Sep. 2014.

Dietz, S., and N. Stern, 'Endogenous growth, convexity of damage and climate risk: How Nordhaus's framework supports deep cuts in carbon emissions', *Economic Journal*, 125 (2015), 574–620.

Dimson, E., P. Marsh, and M. Staunton, *Triumph of the optimists: 101 years of global investment returns* (Princeton, NJ, 2002).

Direct Line Insurance 'Bricks and mortar account for only 59 percent of a property's market value' (2018), in https://www.directlinegroup.co.UK/e n/news/brand-news/2018/bricks-and-mortar-account-for-only-59-percent-of-a-property-s-ma.html.

Dixit, A. K., and R. S. Pindyck, *Investment under uncertainty* (Princeton, NJ, 1994).

Dixon, N. F., *On the psychology of military incompetence* (London, 1976).

Doig, A., 'Politics and public sector ethics: The impact of change in the United Kingdom', in Little, W. and E. Posada-Carbo, eds., *Political corruption in Europe and Latin America* (Basingstoke, 1996), 173–192.

Drehmann, M., and M. Juselius, 'Do debt service costs affect macroeconomic and financial stability?' *BIS Quarterly Review* (2012), 21–35.

Duckworth, T., 'Isn't honesty the best policy?' *New York Times*, 10 Jun. 2016.

Dudkin, G., and T. Välilä, 'Transaction costs in public-private partnerships: A first look at the evidence', European Investment Banks, Economic and Financial Report 2005/03 (Luxembourg, 2005).

Duffy, C., *The army of Frederick the Great* (Newton Abbot, 1974).

Dugdale, B. E. C., *Arthur James Balfour: First earl of Balfour, K.G., O.M., F. R.S., etc* (London, 1936).

Dujovne, N., 'G20 economies must push to invest more in infrastructure', *Financial Times*, 19 Mar. 2018.

Dunhill, L., and R. Syal, 'Whitehall "infantilised" by reliance on consultants, minister claims', *The Guardian*, 29 Sep. 2020.

Dunleavy, P., and C. Hood, 'From old public administration to new public management', *Public Money & Management* (July–Sep. 1994), 9–16.

Dutch Association of Industry-wide Pension Funds, 'The Dutch pension system: An overview of the key aspects' (n.d.).

The Economist, 'Mind the money gap: Taxpayers pick up the bill for another corporate meltdown', 7 Feb. 2008.

The Economist, 'A losing bet', 7 May 2016.

The Economist, 'Remodelling the model. Can Chile reinvent itself?', 12 Mar. 2020.

Edelman Intellectual Property, 'Edelman trust barometer 2020' (n.pl., 2020).

Edsall, T. B., 'After Citizens United, a vicious cycle of corruption', *New York Times*, 6 Dec. 2018.

Edwards, C., 'The private finance initiative (PFI) and value for money? A case study of the Norfolk and Norwich university hospital (NNUH)', University of East Anglia (Norwich, 15 Nov. 2005).

Edwards, P., J. Shaoul, A. Stafford, and L. Arblaster, *Evaluating the operation of PFI in roads and hospitals* (London, 2004).

Eeckhout, J., *The profit paradox : How thriving firms threaten the future of work* (Princeton, NJ, 2021).

Eichelberger, E., 'Lobbyist secretly wrote house Dems' letter urging weaker investor protections' (2013), in https://www.motherjones.com/politics/20 13/08/congressional-black-caucus-fiduciary-duty-rule-financial-services-institute/.

Eisinger, J., *The Chickenshit Club: Why the Justice Department fails to prosecute executives* (New York, 2017).

Eley, J., 'Debenhams liquidation compounds crisis in UK high street', *Financial Times*, 1 Dec. 2020.

Elster, J., 'The Valmont effect: The warm-glow theory of philanthropy', in Illingworth, Patricia M. L., T. Pogge, and L. Wenar, eds., *Giving well: The ethics of philanthropy* (New York, 2011), 67–83.

English, B., and J. Saville, *Strict settlement: A guide for historians* (Hull, 1983).

European Commission. Directorate-General for Regional and Urban Policy, Sartori, D. et al., *Guide to cost-benefit analysis of investment projects: Economic appraisal tool for cohesion policy 2014–2020* (Brussels, 2019).

Evans, P., and J. E. Rauch, 'Bureaucracy and growth: A cross-national analysis of the effects of "Weberian" state structures on economic growth', *American Sociological Review*, 64 (1999), 748–765.

Express & Star, 'Row reignited over appointment to Whitehall jobs amid Hancock kiss with aide', *Express & Star*, 26 June 2021.

Farnsworth, K., 'The British corporate welfare state: Public provision for private businesses', Sheffield Political Economy Research Institute, SEPRI Paper 24 (Sheffield, Jul. 2015).

Favelle, C., 'How Trump tried, but largely failed, to derail America's top climate report', *New York Times*, 2 Jan. 2021.

Feinman, J. M., *Delay, deny, defend: Why insurance companies don't pay claims and what you can do about it* (New York, 2010).

Feinstein, C. H., *National income, expenditure and output of the United Kingdom, 1855–1965* (Cambridge, 1972).

Feldstein, M., 'Social security, induced retirement, and aggregate capital accumulation', *Journal of Political Economy*, 82 (1974), 905–926.

Feldstein, M., 'Privatizing social security: The $10 trillion opportunity', Cato Institute, Social Security Paper 7 (Washington DC, 31 Jan. 1997).

Feldstein, M., *Privatizing social security* (Chicago, IL,1998).

Feldstein, M., 'Structural reform of social security', *Journal of Economic Perspectives*, 19, 2 (2005), 33–56.

Feldstein, M., 'A double dip is a price worth paying', *Financial Times*, 22 Jul. 2010.

Ferguson, T., P. Jorgensen, and J. Chen, 'How much can the U.S. Congress resist political money? A quantitative assessment', Institute for New Economic Thinking, INET working paper 109 (New York, Jan. 2020).

Ferlie, E., L. E. Lynn, and C. Pollitt, *The Oxford handbook of public management* (2005).

Ferrara, P. J., *Social security: The inherent contradiction* (San Francisco, CA, 1980).

Financial Times, 'UK's ailing infrastructure can no longer be ignored', *Financial Times*, 22 Aug. 2017.

Finlayson, A. *Making sense of New Labour* (London, 2003).

Finnerty, J. D., *Project financing: Asset-based financial engineering*, 3rd edn. (New York, 2013).

Florio, M., *The great divestiture: Evaluating the welfare impact of the British privatizations, 1979–1997* (Cambridge, MA, 2004).

Florio, M., ed., *Network industries and social welfare: The experiment that reshuffled European utilities* (Cambridge, 2013).

Flyvbjerg, B., 'Introduction: The iron law of megaproject management', in Flyvbjerg, Bent, ed., *The Oxford handbook of megaproject management* (Oxford, 2017), 1–21.

Flyvbjerg, B., *The Oxford handbook of megaproject management* (Oxford, 2017).

Flyvbjerg, B., M. S. Holm, and S. Buhl, 'Underestimating costs in public works projects: Error or lie?' *Journal of the American Planning Association*, 68, 3 (2002), 279–296.

Flyvbjerg, B., N. Bruzelius, and W. Rothengatter, *Megaprojects and risk: An anatomy of ambition* (Cambridge, 2003).

Foot, P., 'P.F. Eye: An idiot's guide to the private finance initiative', *Private Eye*, (1 Apr. 2004).

Forden, S., 'Why Medicare can't catch the fraudsters', *Bloomberg Business Week*, 10–16 Jan. 2011.

Foreman-Peck, J., and R. Millward, *Public and private ownership of British industry, 1820–1990* (Oxford, 1994).

Foster, J., 'The US consumption function: A new perspective', University of Queensland, discussion paper (Brisbane, AU, 2019).

Frank, T., *The wrecking crew: The American right and the lust for power* (London, 2008).

Frank, T., *Listen, liberal: Or, what ever happened to the party of the people?* (New York, 2016).

Frean, A., 'Accountancy watchdog should be scrapped, says pensions body', *The Times*, 19 Mar. 2018.

Friedman, M., and R. D. Friedman, *Capitalism and freedom* (Chicago, IL, 1962).

Friedman, M., and R. D. Friedman, *Free to choose: A personal statement* (New York, 1980).

FT View, 'Selling off student loans makes next to no sense', *Financial Times*, 9 Feb. 2017.

Fulton, Lord, ed., 'The civil service', vol. 1. Report of the Committee 1966–68, Cmnd. 3638 (London, 1968).

Fukui, Y., and K. Oda, 'Discussion paper: Who should take responsibility for unexpected interest changes? Lesson from the privatization of Japanese railroad system', *New Spatial Economics*, 12 (2012), 263–278.

Furman, J., 'Would private accounts provide a higher rate of return than social security?' Center on Budget and Policy Priorities (Washington DC, 2005).

Gaffney, D., A. M. Pollock, D. Price, and J. Shaoul, 'NHS capital expenditure and the private finance initiative–expansion or contraction?' *British Medical Journal*, 319 (1999), 48–51.

Gaffney, D., A. M. Pollock, D. Price, and J. Shaoul, 'PFI in the NHS – is there an economic case?' *British Medical Journal*, 319 (1999), 116–119.

Gaffney, M., and F. Harrison, 'Neo-classical economics as a stratagem against Henry George', in Gaffney M., ed., *Corruption of economics* (London, 1994), 29–122.

Galbraith, J. K., 'Cold truth: The Texas freeze is a catastrophe of the free market' (2021), in https://www.ineteconomics.org/perspectives/blog/cold-truth-the-texas-freeze-is-a-catastrophe-of-the-free-market.

Garber, A. M., and J. Skinner, 'Is American health care uniquely inefficient?' *Journal of Economic Perspectives*, 22 (2008), 27–50.

Garrett, B., *Too big to jail: How prosecutors compromise with corporations* (Cambridge, MA, 2014).

Garrigues, C. H., *You're paying for it! A guide to graft* (New York, 1936).

Gawande, A., 'The cost conundrum: What a Texas town can teach US about health care', *The New Yorker*, 1 June 2009, 36–44.

Gawande, A., 'Letting go: What should medicine do when it can't save your life?' *New Yorker*, 2 Aug. 2010, 36–49.

Geoghegan, P., *Democracy for sale: Dark money and dirty politics* (London, 2020).

Gilens, M., and B. I. Page, 'Testing theories of American politics: Elites, interest groups, and average citizens', *Perspectives on Politics*, 12 (2014), 564–581.

Giridharadas, A., *Winners take all: The elite charade of changing the world* (London, 2018).

Girouard, M., *The return to Camelot: Chivalry and the English gentleman* (New Haven, CT, 1981).

Glaeser, E., and J. Scheinkman, 'Neither a borrower nor a lender be: An economic analysis of interest restrictions and usury laws', *Journal of Law and Economics*, 41,1 (1998), 1–36.

Glaeser, E., 'Public ownership in the American city', National Bureau of Economic Research, NBER Working paper 8613 (Cambridge, MA, 2001).

Glaeser, E. L., 'Introduction', in Glaeser, E. L., ed., *The governance of not-for-profit organizations* (Chicago, IL, 2003), 1–35.

Glaeser, E. L., and C. D. Goldin, 'Corruption and reform: Introduction', in Glaeser E. L. and C. D. Goldin, eds. *Corruption and reform: Lessons from America's economic history* (Chicago, IL, 2006), 3–22.

Glantz, A. A., *Homewreckers: How a gang of Wall Street kingpins, hedge fund magnates, crooked banks, and vulture capitalists suckered millions out of their homes and demolished the American dream* (New York, 2019).

Glynn, P., S. J. Kobrin, and M. Naím 'The globalization of corruption', in Elliott, K. A., ed., *Corruption and the global economy* (Washington DC, 1997), 7–27.

Goff, S., 'Public sector staff set for wealthier retirement', *Financial Times*, 15 Nov. 2008.

Goldberg, M., 'The MAGA revolution devours its own', *New York Times*, 4 Dec. 2020.

Goldthorpe, J. H., 'On the service class, its formation and future', in Giddens, A. and G. Mackenzie, eds., *Social class and the division of labour* (Cambridge, 1982), 162–185.

Gollier, C., 'Intergenerational risk-sharing and risk-taking of a pension fund', *Journal of Public Economics*, 92, 5–6 (2008), 1,463–1,485.

Gollier, C., *Pricing the planet's future: The economics of discounting in an uncertain world* (Princeton, NJ, 2013).

Goodhart, C. A. E., 'The determination of the money supply: Flexibility versus control' *Manchester School*, 85, sup. 1 (2017), 33–56.

Goolsbee, A., 'In retirement planning, there is nothing certain about death and taxes', *New York Times*, 9 Nov. 2006.

Gordon, R. J., and I. Dew-Becker, 'Controversies about the rise of American inequality: A survey', NBER Working Papers 13982 (Cambridge, MA, 2008).

Graham, J. R., and C. R. Harvey, 'The theory and practice of corporate finance: Evidence from the field', *Journal of Financial Economics*, 60, 2–3 (2001), 187–243.

Great Britain 'Inland revenue annual reports', Parliamentary Papers (London, 1894–1914).

Great Britain, All Party Parliamentary Group on Responsible Tax, 'A more responsible global tax system or a "sticking plaster"? An examination of the OECD's base erosion and profit shifting (BEPS) process and recommendations' (London, 2016).

Great Britain, Financial Conduct Authority, 'Asset management market study final report' Market Study MS15/2.3 (London, Jun. 2017).

Great Britain, Financial Services Authority, 'FSA update on payment protection insurance (PPI)' (London, 4 Nov. 2005).

Great Britain, Financial Services Authority, '11.8 billion compensation for pensions and FSAVC reviews' (London, 2006).

Great Britain, HM Treasury, 'Public private partnerships: The government's approach' (London, 2000).

Great Britain, HM Treasury, 'PFI: Meeting the investment challenge', (London, Jul. 2003).

Great Britain, House of Commons, Committee of Public Accounts, 'Update on PFI debt refinancing and the PFI equity market' (London, 15 May 2007).

Great Britain, House of Commons, Committee of Public Accounts, 'PFI in housing and hospitals' (London, 18 Jan. 2011).

Great Britain, House of Commons, Committee of Public Accounts, 'Private finance initiatives' [HC 894] (London, 20 Jun. 2018).

Great Britain, House of Commons, Committee of Public Accounts, 'Sale of student loans' [HC 1527] (London, 22 Nov. 2018).

Great Britain, House of Commons [Lord Penrose, Chair], 'Report of the Equitable Life inquiry' (London, 8 Mar. 2004).

Great Britain, House of Commons, Public Administration Select Committee, 'Goats and tsars: Ministerial and other appointments from outside parliament' [HC 330] (London, 2010).

Great Britain, House of Commons, Select Committee on Treasury, 'Ninth report: The mis-selling of personal pensions' (London, 17 Nov. 1998).

Great Britain, House of Commons, Treasury Committee, 'Private finance initiative', [HC 1146] (London, 18 Jul. 2011).

Great Britain, House of Commons, Treasury Committee, 'Private finance initiative seventeenth report of session 2010–12' [HC 1146] (London, 18 Jul. 2011).

Great Britain, National Audit Office, 'Performance of PFI construction' (London, Oct. 2009).

Great Britain, National Audit Office, 'Lessons from PFI and other projects', [HC 920] (London, 28 Apr. 2011).

Great Britain, National Audit Office, 'Review of the VfM assessment process for PFI briefing' (London, Oct. 2013).

Great Britain, National Audit Office, 'The choice of finance for capital investment' (London, Mar. 2015).

Great Britain, National Audit Office, Comptroller and Auditor General, 'PFI and PF2' (London, 18 Jan. 2018).

Great Britain, National Audit Office, 'Investigation into government procurement during the covid-19 pandemic', [HC 959] (London, 18 Nov. 2020).

Great Britain, National Audit Office, 'The government's approach to test and trace in England – interim report', [HC 1070] (London, 11 Dec. 2020).

Great Britain, Office of National Statistics, 'United Kingdom national accounts 2003' (London, 2003).

Great Britain, Office of National Statistics., 'Pension wealth in Great Britain: Apr. 2016 to Mar. 2018', Statistical bulletin (London, 5 Dec. 2019).

Great Britain, Office of National Statistics, 'Employee workplace pensions in the UK: 2019 provisional and 2018 final results' (London, 4 Mar. 2020).

Great Britain, Parliamentary and Health Service Ombudsman, 'Equitable Life: A decade of regulatory failure: Fourth report', [HC 815-I] (London, 16 Jul. 2008).

Great Britain, Pensions Commission [Turner Report], 'Pensions: Challenges and choices the first report of the pensions commission' (London, 2004).

Great Britain, Pensions Commission [Turner Report], 'A new pension settlement for the twenty-first century the second report of the pensions commission' (London, 2005).

Great Britain, Pensions Commission [Turner Report], 'Implementing an integrated package of pension reforms: The final report of the pensions commission' (London, 2006).

Green, E. L., 'Devos ends Obama-era safeguards aimed at abuses by for-profit colleges', *New York Times*, 10 Aug. 2018.

Greenwood, G., and D. Kennedy, 'Management consultancy firms reap the rewards of Brexit bonanza', *The Times*, 28 Oct. 2020.

Grimsey, D., and M. Lewis, *Public private partnerships: The worldwide revolution in infrastructure provision and project finance* (Cheltenham, 2004).

Grimsey, D., and M. K. Lewis, 'Are public private partnerships value for money?' *Accounting Forum*, 29, 4 (2005), 345–378.

Grossmann, M., *Red state blues: How the conservative revolution stalled in the states* (Cambridge, 2019).

Grow, B., R. Berner, and J. Silver-Greenberg, 'Fresh pain for the uninsured: As doctors and hospitals turn to GE, Citi, and smaller rivals to finance patient care, the sick pay much more', *Business* Week, 3 Dec. 2007.

Grylls, G., and O. Wright, 'Tories make donors and friends directors of civil service boards', *The Times*, 5 Aug. 2020.

Gudmundsson, M., 'The Icelandic pension system', *Central Bank of Iceland Monetary Bulletin* 1 (2001), 42–59.

Hacker, J. S., *The Great Risk Shift: The new economic insecurity and the decline of the American dream*, rev. edn. (New York, 2019).

Haddon, C., 'Reforming the civil service: The efficiency unit in the early 1980s and the 1987 next steps report' (London, 2012).

Hagen, J., 'A history of the Swedish pension system', Uppsala University, Working paper/Uppsala Centre for Fiscal Studies 2013:7 (Uppsala, 2013).

Hakim, R., *The kibbutzim in Israel as a public good: The financing of their establishment, recurring crises, their end? An economic history study* (Ramat-Gan, Israel, 2005) (in Hebrew).

Haldane, A., 'Andrew Haldane: Patience and finance', Oxford China Business Forum (Beijing, 9 Sept. 2010).

Halevy, E., *The growth of philosophic radicalism* (London, 1972).

Halperin, D., *Stealing America's future: How for-profit colleges scam taxpayers and ruin students' lives*, Kindle edn. (Washington DC, 2014).

Hamilton, C., and J. Vielkind, 'Bharara ends probe of Cuomo's Moreland Commission shutdown' (2016), in https://www.politico.com/states/new-york/albany/story/2016/01/bharara-ends-probe-of-cuomos-moreland-commission-shutdown-029847.

Hamm, P., et al., 'Mass privatization, state capacity, and economic growth in post-communist countries', *American Sociological Review*, 77 (2012), 295–324.

Hannah, L., *Occupational pension funds: Getting the long-run answers right* (London, 1986).

Hare, P., 'PPP and PFI: The political economy of building public infrastructure and delivering services', *Oxford Review of Economic Policy*, 29, 1 (2013), 95–112.

Harling, P., 'Rethinking "Old Corruption"', *Past & Present*, 147(1995), 127–158.

Harling, P., *The waning of "Old Corruption": The politics of economical reform in Britain, 1779–1846* (Oxford, 1996).

Harris, R., and C. Hamnett, 'The myth of the promised land: The social diffusion of home ownership in Britain and North America', *Annals of the Association of American Geographers*, 77 (1987), 173–190.

Hart, O. D., *Firms, contracts, and financial structure* (Oxford, 1995).

Hart, O. D., 'Incomplete contracts and public ownership: Remarks, and an application to public-private partnerships', *Economic Journal*, 113 (2003), C69-C76.

Hastings, M., 'The sofa government of Blairism has been an unmitigated disaster', *The Guardian*, 16 May 2006.

Hausman, D. M., *The inexact and separate science of economics* (Cambridge, 1992).

Hawthorne, F., *Pension dumping: The reasons, the wreckage, the stakes for Wall Street* (New York, 2008).

Hayek, F. A., 'The use of knowledge in society', *American Economic Review*, 35 (1945), 519–530.

Hazen, D., E. Hines, S. Rosenfeld, and S. Salett, *Who controls our schools? The privatization of American public education* (New York, 2016).

Headey, B. W., *Housing policy in the developed economy: The United Kingdom, Sweden and the United States* (London, 1978).

Heald, D., 'Value for money tests and accounting treatment in PFI schemes', *Accounting Auditing and Accountability Journal*, 16, 3 (2003), 342–371.

Healy, D., *Pharmageddon* (Berkeley, CA, 2012).

Heath, J., 'The structure of intergenerational cooperation', *Philosophy & Public Affairs*, 41 (2013), 31–66.

Hedberg, P., and L. Karlsson, 'Den internationella och nationella börshandelns omvandling och tillväxt 1963–2013', in Larsson M., ed., *Stockholmsbörsen på en förändrad finansmarknad* (Stockholm, 2016), 191–263.

Hellowell, M., 'The UK's private finance initiative: History, evaluation, prospects', in Hodge, G. A. et al., eds., *International handbook on public-private partnerships* (Cheltenham, 2010), 307–332.

Helm, T., and R. Syal, 'Storm over Blunkett role with private jobs firm', *The Observer*, 1 Feb. 2009.

Hennessy, P., *Whitehall* (London, 1989).

Hennessy, P., 'The British civil service: The condition of Mr Gladstone's legacy as the century turns', *The Stakeholder* (1999), Special supplement.

Henry, J. B., 'Fortune 500: The total cost of litigation estimated at one-third profits', *Corporate Counsel Business Journal* (1 Feb. 2008).

Heywood, P. M., 'Integrity management and the public service ethos in the UK: Patchwork quilt or threadbare blanket?' *International Review of Administrative Sciences*, 78 (2012).

Hills, J., 'Ends and means: The future roles of social housing in England', Centre for Social Exclusion (London, 2007).

Hills, J., *Good times, bad times: The welfare myth of them and us* (Bristol, 2014).

Hochschild, A. R., *Strangers in their own land: Anger and mourning on the American right* (New York, 2016).

Hodge, G., 'Reviewing public–private partnerships: Some thoughts on evaluation', in Hodge, G. A., C. Greve, and A. Boardman, eds., *International Handbook on Public-Private Partnerships* (Cheltenham, 2010), 81–112.

Hodge, G. A., C. Greve, and A. Boardman, eds., *International handbook on public-private partnerships* (Cheltenham, 2010).

Holland, A., and X. Vagg, 'The global security defense index on climate change: Preliminary results', American Security Project (New York, 21 Mar. 2013).

Holm, A.-S., and L. Lundahl, 'A stimulating competition at the Swedish upper secondary school market?' in Dahlstedt M. and A. Fejes, eds., *Neoliberalism and market forces in education: Lessons from Sweden* (Abingdon, 2019), 141–155.

Holmberg, S., B. Rothstein, and N. Nasiritousi, 'Quality of government: What you get', *Annual Review of Political Science*, 12 (2009), 135–161.

Hood, C., and R. Dixon, *A government that worked better and cost less?: Evaluating three decades of reform and change in UK central government* (Oxford, 2015).

Hopkins N., R. Evans, and R. Norton-Taylor, 'MoD staff and thousands of military officers join arms firms', *The Guardian*, 15 Oct. 2012.

Horioka, C. Y., 'The life and work of Martin Stuart ("Marty") Feldstein', University of the Philippines School of Economics, Discussion Paper 2014–10 (Quezon City, Philippines, Jul. 2014).

Hough, D., *Corruption, anti-corruption and governance* (London, 2013).

Houlder, V., 'Did light touch tax become soft touch?' *Financial Times*, 31 May 2012.

Houlder, V., and G. Parker, 'Osborne appoints former bank lobbyist to untangle tax code', *Financial Times*, 9 Dec. 2015.

Hume, D., *A treatise of human nature* (Oxford, 2000).

Humphries, J., 'Child labor: Lessons from the historical experience of today's industrial economies', *World Bank Economic Review*, 17, 2 (2003), 175–196.

Hurst, G., 'Climate change author quits Treasury after Brown freezes him out', *The Times*, 8 Dec. 2006.

Hutton, W., *How good we can be: Ending the mercenary society and building a great country* (London, 2015).

Hyde, M., and S. Borzutzky, 'Chile's neoliberal retirement system? Concentration, competition, and economic predation in private pensions', *Poverty & Public Policy*, 7 (2015), 123–157.

International Monetary Fund, 'Public-private partnerships' (Washington DC, 12 Mar. 2004).

Immergluck, D., *Foreclosed: High-risk lending, deregulation, and the undermining of America's mortgage market* (Ithaca, NY, 2009).

Immergluck, D., *Preventing the next mortgage crisis: The meltdown, the federal response, and the future of housing in America* (New York, 2015).

International Labour Office., *Housing policy in Europe: Cheap home building* (Geneva; [London], 1930).

Iordanoglou, C. H., *Public enterprise revisited: A closer look at the 1954–79 UK labour productivity record* (Cheltenham, 2001).

Irwin, T. C., 'Accounting devices and fiscal illusions', International Monetary Fund SDN/12/02 (Washington DC, 28 Mar. 2012).

Isaksen, J., P. L. Kramp, L. F. Sørensen, and S. V. Sørensen, 'Household balance sheets and debt – an international country study', *Danmarks Nationalbank Monetary Review* 4th Qtr, pt. 1 (2011), 47–58.

Ivashina, V., and J. Lerner, *Patient capital: The challenges and promises of long-term investing* (Princeton, NJ, 2019).

Jackson, K. T., *Crabgrass frontier: The suburbanization of the United States* (New York, 1985).

Jacobson, M., 'Forest finance 8: To cut or not cut – tree value and deciding when to harvest timber' (2008), in https://extension.psu.edu/forest-finance-8-to-cut-or-not-cut-deciding-when-to-harvest-timber.

James, K. R., 'The price of retail investing in the UK', Financial Services Authority, Occasional Paper 6 (London, Feb. 2000).

Janeway, W. H., *Doing capitalism in the innovation economy: Reconfiguring the three-player game between markets, speculators and the state*, 2nd edn. (Cambridge, 2018).

Jenkins, K., K. Caines, A. Jackson, R. Ibbs, and Great Britain, Office of Public Service and Science, Efficiency Unit, 'Improving management in government: The next steps: Report to the prime minister' (London, 1988).

Jenkins, S., 'No man is an island except maybe Tony Blair', *The Times*, 2 Oct. 2002.

Johnston, M., *Corruption, contention and reform: The power of deep democratization* (Cambridge, 2014).

Jolly, J., and R. Syal, 'Consultants' fees "up to £6,250 a day" for work on Covid test system', *The Guardian*, 14 Oct. 2020.

Jomo, K. S., 'A critical review of the evolving privatization debate', in Roland, G., ed., *Privatization: Successes and failures* (New York, 2008), 199–212.

Jones, C., and J. Hurley, 'Financial ombudsman "sided with banks" to meet targets', *The Times*, 19 Mar. 2018.

Jones, G. Stedman, *Outcast London: A study in the relationship between classes in Victorian society* (Oxford, 1971).

Jubilee Debt Campaign, 'The UK's PPPs disaster: Lessons on private finance for the rest of the world' (London, Feb. 2017).

Judge, L., and D. Tomlinson, 'Home improvements: Action to address the housing challenges faced by young people', Resolution Foundation (London, n.d. 2018?).

Judson, P. M., *The Habsburg empire: A new history* (Cambridge, MA, 2016).

Justice, J., 'Bricks are worth their weight in gold: A century of house prices', *The Guardian*, 18 Dec. 1999.

Kantor, A., 'The $1.6tn US student debt nightmare', *Financial Times*, 27 Dec. 2019.

Kaplan, S. N., 'Are U.S. Companies too short-term oriented? Some thoughts', *Journal of Applied Corporate Finance*, 30 (2018), 8–18.

Kaplow, L., and S. Shavell, *Fairness versus welfare* (Cambridge, MA, 2002).

Kassirer, J. P., *On the take: How medicine's complicity with big business can endanger your health* (New York, 2005).

Keefe, P. R., 'Why corrupt bankers avoid jail', *The New Yorker*, 31 Jul. 2017.

Keen, S., 'The appallingly bad neoclassical economics of climate change', *Globalizations* (1 Sept. 2020), at https://doi.org/10.1080/14747731.2020.1807856.

Kelly, T., 'Bosses at Fraud Office used secret emails to cover up £1 m payoffs', *Daily Mail*, 2 Aug. 2013.

Kerstenetzky, C. L., and G. P. Guedes, 'Great recession, great regression? The welfare state in the twenty-first century', *Cambridge Journal of Economics*, 45 (2021).

Kilbourne, R. H., *Debt, investment, slaves: Credit relations in East Feliciana parish, Louisiana, 1825–1885* (Tuscaloosa, AL, 1995).

Kimes, M., and M. Smith, 'Laureate, a for-profit education firm, finds international success (with a Clinton's help)', *Washington Post*, 18 Jan. 2014.

Kinder, T., G. Plimmer, and J. Pickard, 'Watchdog criticises government over awarding of £17bn Covid contracts', *Financial Times*, 18 Nov. 2020.

Kindleberger, C. P., and R. Z. Aliber *Manias, panics and crashes: A history of financial crises*, 5th. edn. (Basingstoke, 2005).

King, A., and I. Crewe, *The blunders of our governments* (London, 2014).

King, C. W., *The economic superorganism: Beyond the competing narratives on energy, growth, and policy* (Cham, Switzerland, 2021).

Klein, N., *The shock doctrine: Rise of disaster capitalism* (London, 2007).

Knights, M., 'Old Corruption: What British history can tell us about corruption today', University of Warwick (Coventry, Nov. 2016).

Komlos, J., *Principles of economics for a post-meltdown world* (n.pl., 2016).

Kondor, J., 'The relative efficiency of enterprises in public ownership: World experience and findings on industry in Israel', Sapir Institute for Development, Discussion Paper 4–91 (Tel-Aviv, Oct.1991) (in Hebrew).

Kornai, J., E. Maskin, and G. Roland, 'Understanding the soft budget constraint', *Journal of Economic Literature*, 41 (2003), 1,095–1,136.

Kotlikoff, L. J., and S. Burns, *The coming generational storm: What you need to know about America's economic future* (Cambridge, MA, 2004).

Koyama, M., 'Evading the "taint of usury": The usury prohibition as a barrier to entry', *Explorations in Economic History*, 47, 4 (2010), 420–442.

Krastev, I., *Shifting obsessions: Three essays on the politics of anticorruption* (Budapest, 2004).

Krauss, C., M. Fernandez, I. Penn, and R. Rojas, 'How Texas's drive for energy independence set it up for disaster', *New York Times*, 21 Feb. 2021.

Krugman, P. R., *Peddling prosperity: Economic sense and nonsense in the age of diminished expectations* (London, 1994).

Kwoka, J. E., 'Privatization, deregulation, and competition: A survey of effects on economic performance', World Bank (Washington DC, 1996).

Kwoka, J. E., 'The comparative advantage of public ownership: Evidence from U.S. Electric utilities', *Canadian Journal of Economics*, 38, 2 (2005), 622–640.

Lain, D., *Reconstructing retirement: Work and welfare in the UK and USA* (Oxford, 2016).

Langley, P., 'The making of investor subjects in Anglo-American pensions', *Environment and Planning D-Society & Space*, 24 (2006), 919–934.

Laugesen, M. J., and S. A. Glied, 'Higher fees paid to US physicians drive higher spending for physician services compared to other countries', *Health Affairs*, 30 (2011), 1,647–1,656.

Laursen, E., *The people's pension: The struggle to defend social security since Reagan* (Oakland, CA, 2012).

Lea, R., 'Carillion rivals warn MPs on the risks of using contractors', *The Times*, 10 May 2018.

Lea, R., 'Bumps and dents in all the operators', *The Times*, 29 Jun. 2018.

Leap, T. L., *Phantom billing, fake prescriptions, and the high cost of medicine: Health care fraud and what to do about it* (Ithaca, NY, 2011).

Lebergott, S., *Pursuing happiness: American consumers in the twentieth century* (Princeton, NJ, 1993).

Lefcourt, D., 'A corporate "culture of fraud"' (2011), in http://www.opednews.com/articles/A-Corporate-Culture-of-Fr-by-Dave-Lefcourt-1 10913-182.html.

Lenton, T. M., et al., 'Tipping elements in the earth's climate system', *Proceedings of the National Academy of Sciences*, 105 (2008), 1,786–1,793.

Leonard, C., 'David Koch was the ultimate climate change denier', *New York Times*, 23 Aug. 2019.

Lesnoy, S. D., and D. R. Leimer, 'Social-security and private saving – theory and historical evidence', *Social Security Bulletin*, 48 (1985), 14–30.

Levell, P., B. Roantree, and J. Shaw, 'Redistribution from a lifetime perspective', Institute of Fiscal Studies, IFS Working Paper W15/27 (London, 2015).

Levitt, M., 'Rightwinger who saw risks of PFI', *Financial Times*, 26 Mar. 2012.

Levy, P., and P. Temin, 'Inequality and institutions in 20th century America', NBER Working Papers 13106 (Cambridge MA, 2007).

Lewin, H. G., *The railway mania and its aftermath, 1845–1852: (being a sequel to 'early British railways')* (London, 1936).

Lewis, M., *Liar's poker: Rising through the wreckage on Wall Street* (New York, 1989).

Lewis, M., *Flash boys: Cracking the money code* (London, 2014).

Lewis, M., 'Martin Lewis accuses student loan company of misleading graduates', *The Guardian*, 20 Jul. 2020.

Lewis, O., and A. Offer, 'Railways as patient capital', *Oxford Review of Economic Policy*, 38 (2022), np.

Lind, R. C., 'Introduction', in Lind, R. C. et al., eds., *Discounting for time and risk in energy policy* (Washington DC, 1982), 1–19.

Lind, R. C. et al., eds., *Discounting for time and risk in energy policy* (Washington DC, 1982).

Linden, E., 'Op-ed: The economics Nobel went to a guy who enabled climate change denial and delay', *Los Angeles Times*, 25 Oct. 2018.

Lindorff, D., 'Supreme Court junket king Scalia dies while vacationing with wealthy patrons at private West Texas getaway' (2016), in https://thiscantbe happening.net/supreme-court-junket-king-scalia-dies-while-vacationing-with-wealthy-patrons-at-private-west-texas-getaway.

Lipsey, R. G., and K. Lancaster, 'The general theory of second best', *Review of Economic Studies*, 24 (1956), 11–32.

Liptak, A., 'Supreme court vacates ex-Virginia governor's graft conviction', *New York Times*, 27 Jun. 2016.

Lipton, E., and B. Williams, 'Researchers or corporate allies? Think tanks blur the line', *New York Times*, 7 Aug. 2016.

Lipton, E., N. Confessore, and B. Williams, 'Think tank scholar or corporate consultant? It depends on the day', *New York Times*, 8 Aug. 2016.

Lowe, R., *The official history of the British civil service: Reforming the civil service* (London, 2011), vol. 1.

Lowe, R., and H. Pemberton, *The official history of the British civil service: Reforming the civil service* (London, 2020), vol. 2.

Lubienski, C., 'NEPC review: 12 myths and realities about private educational choice programs (Institute for Justice, Aug. 2017)', National Education Policy Center (Boulder, CO, 2019).

Lubienski, C., and S. T. Lubienski, *The public school advantage: Why public schools outperform private schools* (Chicago, IL, 2009).

Lynas, M., *Our final warning: Six degrees of climate emergency* (London, 2020).

Lynch, D. J., 'Clinton's accumulation of wealth invites campaign attacks', 13 Oct. 2016.

Lynn, L. E., 'The myth of the bureaucratic paradigm: What traditional public administration really stood for', *Public Administration Review*, 61 (2001), 144–160.

Macaulay, T. B., Lord Ashburton, B. Jowett, H. Melvill, and J. G. Shaw Lefevre, 'Report on the Indian civil service', in

Fulton, Lord, ed., 'The civil service', vol. 1, Report of the Committee 1966–68 (London, 1845/1968), 119–128.

MacLean, N., *Democracy in chains: The deep history of the radical right's stealth plan for America* (London, 2017).

Maddison, A., *The world economy: A millennial perspective* (Paris, 2001).

Maddison, A., *The world economy: Historical statistics* (Paris, 2001).

Malik, O., *Broadbandits: Inside the $750 billion telecom heist* (Hoboken, NJ, 2003).

Malnick, E., L. Heighton, L. Telford, and C. Newell, 'Revealed: The true scale of Tony Blair's global business empire', *Daily Telegraph*, 11 June 2015.

Mance, H., 'Britain has had enough of experts, says Gove', *Financial Times*, 3 June 2016.

Mankiw, N. G., M. Weinzierl, and D. Yagan, 'Optimal taxation in theory and practice', *Journal of Economic Perspectives*, 23, 4 (2009), 147–174.

Mansell, W., and M. Savage, 'Top academy schools sound alarm as cash crisis looms', *The Guardian*, 27 Jan. 2018.

Marriage, M., 'UK accounting regulator rejected 90% of FOI requests', *Financial Times*, 12 Apr. 2018.

Marshall, A., *Principles of economics: An introductory volume*, 6th edn. (London, 1910).

Marshall, G., *Don't even think about it: Why our brains are wired to ignore climate change* (London, 2015).

Marshall, L., S. Pellerin, and J. Walter, 'Bailout barometer: 2016 estimate', Federal Reserve Bank of Richmond (Richmond, VA, Sep. 2017).

Martens, P., 'Insiders tell all: Both the stock market and the SEC are rigged', Wall Street on Parade (14 April 2014) http://wallstreetonparade.com/20 14/04/insiders-tell-all-both-the-stock-market-and-the-sec-are-rigged/.

Martin, B., 'Slavery's invisible engine: Mortgaging human property', *Journal of Southern History*, 76 (2010), 817–866.

Martin, D., 'Snouts in trough! 52 ex-ministers land plum private jobs', *Daily Mail*, 27 Jul. 2017.

Martin, I. W., and C. Niedt, *Foreclosed America* (Stanford, CA, 2015).

Martin, R. L., 'Yes, short-termism really is a problem' (2015), in https://hbr .org/2015/10/yes-short-termism-really-is-a-problem.

Mason, P., *The men who ruled India* (London, 1953).

Mason, P., *The English gentleman: The rise and fall of an ideal* (London, 1982).

Maude, F., 'Francis Maude speech to Civil Service live' (2011), in https://www .gov.UK/government/speeches/francis-maude-speech-to-civil-service-live.

Mayer, C. P., *Firm commitment: Why the corporation is failing us and how to restore trust in it* (Oxford, 2013).

Mayer, J., *Dark money: The hidden history of the billionaires behind the rise of the radical right* (London, 2016).

McCartney, S., and J. Stittle, '"A very costly industry": The cost of Britain's privatised railway', *Critical perspectives on accounting*, 49 (2017), 1–17.

McCrone, G., and M. Stephens, *Housing policy in Britain and Europe* (London, 1995).

McDonald, O., *Fannie Mae and Freddie Mac: Turning the American dream into a nightmare*, revised, updated edn. (London, 2013).

McGuire, S. K., and C. B. Delahunt, 'Predicting United States policy outcomes with random forests', Institute for New Economic Thinking, INET Working Papers 138 (New York, 27 Oct. 2020).

McInerney, L., 'The academy dream is in freefall. Schools should not have to pick up the pieces', *The Guardian*, 19 Jun. 2018.

McKay, J. P., *Tramways and trolleys: The rise of urban mass transport in Europe* (Princeton, NJ, 1976).

McLeay, M., et al., 'Money creation in the modern economy', *Bank of England Quarterly Bulletin*, Q1 (2014), 1–14.

Megginson, W. L., *The financial economics of privatization* (New York, 2005).

Mercer, 'Melbourne Mercer pension index', Monash Centre for Financial Studies (Melbourne, 2019).

Mesa-Lago, C., 'Reversing pension privatization: The experience of Argentina, Bolivia, Chile and Hungary', International Labor Office, ESS Working Paper 44 (Geneva, 2014).

Michels, R., *Political parties: A sociological study of the oligarchical tendencies of modern democracy* (London, 1915).

Miles, A., 'We can't go on paying gold-plated pensions', *The Times*, 17 Dec. 2008.

Miller, J., 'Walker and the Kochs make Wisconsin corruption-friendly', *New York Times*, 26 Oct. 2015.

Millner, A., and G. Heal, 'Choosing the future: Markets, ethics, and rapprochement in social discounting', NBER Working Paper 28653 (Cambridge, MA, 2021).

Millward, R., 'The political economy of urban utilities in Britain 1840-1950', in Palliser, D. M., P. Clark, and M. Daunton, eds., *Cambridge urban history of Britain*, vol. 3 (Cambridge, 2000), 315–349

Millward, R., 'State enterprise in 20th century Britain', in Toninelli, P. M., *The rise and fall of state enterprises in western countries* (Cambridge, 2000).

Millward, R., *Private and public enterprise in Europe: Energy, telecommunications and transport, 1830–1990* (Cambridge, 2005).

Millward, R., 'Privatisation: Successes and failures', *Business History*, 51 (2009), 138–139.

Millward, R., 'Public enterprise in the modern western world: An historical analysis', *Annals of Public and Cooperative Economics*, 82 (2011), 378–398.

Minns, R., *The Cold War in welfare: Stock markets versus pensions* (London, 2001).

Minns, R. and S. Sexton, 'Too many grannies?: Private pensions, corporate welfare and growing insecurity' (Sturminster Newton, 2006).

Mirowski, P., 'Naturalizing the market on the road to revisionism: Bruce Caldwell's Hayek's challenge and the challenge of Hayek interpretation', *Journal of Institutional Economics*, 3 (2007), 351–372.

Mirowski, P., 'Postface: Defining neoliberalism', in Mirowski, P. and D. Plehwe, eds., *The road from Mont Pelerin* (Cambridge, MA, 2009), 417–458.

Mirowski, P., *Science-mart: Privatizing American science* (Cambridge, MA, 2011).

Mitchell, B., D. Chambers, and N. Crafts, 'How good was the profitability of British railways, 1870–1912?' *Economic History Review*, 64 (2011), 798–831.

Mitchell, B. R., *British historical statistics* (Cambridge, 1988).

Mitchell, O., 'Administrative costs in public and private retirement systems', in Feldstein M., ed., *Privatising social security* (Chicago, IL, 1998), 403–452.

Mitchell, B., 'Martin Feldstein should be ignored' (2011), http://bilbo .economicoutlook.net/blog/?p=14356.

Mokyr, J., *The enlightened economy: Britain and the Industrial Revolution 1700–1850* (London, 2011).

Monbiot, G., *Captive state: The corporate takeover of Britain* (Basingstoke, 2000).

Monnet, E., 'The diversity in national monetary and credit policies in western Europe under the Bretton Woods system', in Feiertag, O. and M. Margairaz, eds., *Les banques centrales et l'etat-nation* (Paris, 2016), 451–487.

Monnet, E, *Controlling credit: Central banking and the planned economy in postwar France, 1948–1973* (Cambridge, 2019).

Morris, N. *Management and regulation of pension schemes: Australia – a cautionary tale* (London, 2018).

Morris, S., 'Market solutions for social problems: Working-class housing in nineteenth-century London', *Economic History Review*, 54, Part 3 (2001), 525–545.

Mosutrous, A., and B. Kenber, 'Consultants take billions from foreign aid budget', *The Times*, 1 Apr. 2018.

Mowery, D. C., and N. Rosenberg, *Technology and the pursuit of economic growth* (Cambridge, 1989).

Muellbauer, J., 'When is a housing market overheated enough to threaten stability?' in Heath, A., F. Packer, and C. Windsor, eds., *Property markets and financial stability* (Sydney, Australia, 2012), 73–105.

Muellbauer, J., 'Housing, debt and the economy: A tale of two countries' (Berlin, 2017) (Powerpoint presentation).

Munnell, A. H., 'Employer-sponsored plans: The shift from defined benefit to defined contribution', in Clark, G. L., A. H. Munnell, and J. M. Orszag, eds., *The Oxford handbook of pensions and retirement income* (Oxford, 2006), 359–383.

Munnell, A. H., and A. E. Sunden, *Coming up short: The challenge of 401(k) plans* (Washington DC, 2004).

Munnell, A. H., and S. A. Sass, *Social security and the stock market: How the pursuit of market magic shapes the system* (Kalamazoo, MI, 2006).

Munnell, A. H., R. C. Fraenkel, and J. Hurwitz, 'The pension coverage problem in the private sector', Center for Retirement Research at Boston College 12–16 (Boston, 2012).

Munshi, N., and N. Cohen, 'US public finance: Day of reckoning', *Financial Times*, 29 Dec. 2013.

Murphy, S., 'Robert Jenrick says he regrets dining with donor before planning decision', *The Guardian*, 22 Jul. 2020.

Murray, C. K., and P. Frijters, *Game of mates: How favours bleed the nation* (n.pl., Australia, 2017).

Murthi, J., P. Orszag, and M. Orszag, 'The charge ratio on individual accounts: Lessons from the UK experience', Birkbeck College, Birkbeck College Working Paper 99–2 (London, 1999).

Murthi, J., P. Orszag, and M. Orszag, 'Administrative costs under a decentralised approach to individual accounts: Lessons from the United Kingdom', in Holzmann, R., J. E. Stiglitz, M. L. Fox, E. James, and P. Orszag, eds., *New ideas about old age security: Towards sustainable pension systems in the 21st century* (Washington DC, 2001), 308–335.

Musgrave, R. A., 'Leviathan cometh – or does he?' in Ladd, H. and E. Tideman, eds., *Tax and expenditure limits* (Washington DC, 1981), 77–120.

Naím, M., 'Latin America: post-adjustment blues', *Foreign Policy*, 92 (1993), 133–150.

Naím, M., 'Corruption eruption' (1995), in http://carnegieendowment.org /1995/06/01/corruption-eruption/3248.

National Bureau of Economic Research, 'NBER aging program' (2020), in https://www.nber.org/programs/ag/.

National Civic Federation. Commission on Public Ownership and Operation, *Municipal and private operation of public utilities: Report to the National Civic Federation Commission on public ownership and operation* (New York, 1907), 3 vols.

National Employment Savings Trust [NEST], 'All the facts' (London, 2012).

Needleman, L., *The economics of housing* (London, 1965).

Neild, R. R., *Public corruption: The dark side of social evolution* (London, 2002).

Nelson, F., and P. Hoskin, 'The great debt deceit: How Gordon Brown cooked the nation's books', *Spectator*, 17 Sept. 2008.

Nelson, L., 'Bill Clinton's $18 million job as "honorary chancellor" of a for-profit college chain, explained' (2016), in https://www.vox.com/2016/9/7/12817676/laureate-education-bill-clinton-university.

Neville, S., 'Deloitte appoints official criticised over 'sweetheart' tax deals', *The Guardian*, 27 May 2013.

New York Times, 'The road to retirement', *New York Times*, 15 Sept. 2012.

New York Times editorial board., 'Justice and junkets', *New York Times*, 27 Jan. 2006.

New York Times editorial board, 'Gov. Cuomo's broken promises', *New York Times*, 23 Jul. 2014.

New York Times editorial board, 'Judges and Justice for sale', *New York Times*, 18 May 2014.

New York Times editorial board, 'Rules to make retirement investing safer', *New York Times*, 17 Apr. 2015.

New York Times editorial board, 'Democrats undermine efforts to protect retirement savers', *New York Times*, 5 Nov. 2015.

New York Times editorial board, 'Predatory colleges, freed to fleece students', *New York Times*, 22 May 2018.

New York Times editorial board, 'The republican party's Supreme Court', *New York Times*, 26 Oct. 2020.

Newell, C., E. Malnick, L. Heighton, and T. Lyndsey, 'Jack Straw and Sir Malcolm Rifkind in latest "cash for access" scandal', *Daily Telegraph*, 22 Feb. 2015.

Newfield, C., *The great mistake: How we wrecked public universities and how we can fix them* (Baltimore, MD, 2016).

Nguyen, D., C. Ornstein, T. Weber, and Propublica, 'Dollars for docs: How industry dollars reach your doctors' (2011), in http://www.propublica.org/.

Nicholls, A., et al., eds., *Social finance* (Oxford, 2015).

Nicoletti, C., and J. F. Ermisch, 'Intergenerational earnings mobility: Changes across cohorts in Britain', *The British Journal of Economic Analysis & Policy*, 7 (2007), 777–826.

Nobel, Alfred, Committee for the Prize in Economic Sciences in memory of, 'Scientific background on the Sveriges Riksbank prize in economic sciences in memory of Alfred Nobel 2018: Economic growth, technological change, and climate change' (Stockholm, 2018).

Noe, T., and H. P. Young, 'The limits to compensation in the financial sector', in Morris, N. and D. Vines, eds. *Capital failure: Rebuilding trust in financial services* (Oxford, 2014), 65–78.

Nordhaus, W., 'To slow or not to slow?', *Economic Journal*, 101 (1991), 920–937.

Nordhaus, W. D., 'Expert opinion on climatic change', *American Scientist*, 82 (1994), 45–51.

Nordhaus, W. D., 'A review of the "Stern review on the economics of climate change"', *Journal of Economic Literature*, 45 (2007), 686–702.

Nordhaus, W. D., 'Integrated economic and climate modeling', in Dixon, P. B. and D. W. Jorgensen, eds., *Handbook of computer general equilibrium modelling* (Amsterdam, 2013), 1,069–1,131.

Nordhaus, W. D., *The climate casino: Risk, uncertainty, and economics for a warming world* (New Haven, CT, 2013).

Nordhaus, W. D., 'Revisiting the social cost of carbon', *Proceedings of the National Academy of Sciences*, 114 (2017), 1518–1523.

Nordhaus, W. D., 'Projections and uncertainties about climate change in an era of minimal climate policies', *American Economic Journal: Economic Policy*, 10 (2018), 333–360.

Nordhaus, W. D., 'Climate change: The ultimate challenge for economics' (2018), in https://www.nobelprize.org/uploads/2018/10/nordhaus-slides.pdf.

Nordhaus, W. D. and Moffat, A., 'A survey of global impacts of climate change: Replication, survey methods, and a statistical analysis', NBER working paper 23646 (Cambridge, MA, 2017).

Nordhaus, W. and J. Tobin, 'Is growth obsolete?' in Moss, M., ed., *The measurement of economic and social performance* (New York, 1973), 509–564.

Norris, P., R. W. Frank, and F. Martinez i Coma, 'The year in elections, 2013: The world's flawed and failed contests', Electoral Integrity Project, University of Sydney (Sydney, Feb. 2014).

Norris, P., and M. Grömping, 'Electoral integrity worldwide', Electoral Integrity Project, University of Sydney (Sydney, May 2019).

Northcote, S. H., and C. E. Trevelyan, 'Report on the organisation of the permanent civil service', House of Commons (London, 1854).

Norton-Taylor, R., 'Ministry of defence cuts programme criticised by commons watchdog', *Financial Times*, 25 May 2012.

Noubma-Um, P., 'Empirical evidence of infrastructure public-private partnerships: Lessons from the World Bank experience', in Hodge, G. A., G. Carsten, and A. E. Boardman, eds., *International Handbook on Public-Private Partnerships* (Cheltenham, 2010), 456–478.

Oborne, P., *The rise of political lying* (London, 2005).

Oborne, P., *The triumph of the political class* (London, 2007).

Odinet, C. K., *Foreclosed: Mortgage servicing and the hidden architecture of homeownership in America* (Cambridge, 2019).

Odlyzko, A., 'Collective hallucinations and inefficient markets: The British railway mania of the 1840s', University of Minnesota (Minneapolis, 15 Jan. 2010).

Odlyzko, A., 'The early British railway system, the Casson counterfactual, and the effectiveness of central planning', *Essays in Economic & Business History*, 34 (2016), 60–94.

OECD, *Public-private partnerships in pursuit of risk sharing and value for money* (Paris, 2008).

OECD, 'Improving schools in Sweden: An OECD perspective' (Paris, 2015).

OECD, 'Pensions at a glance 2019: OECD and G20 indicators' (Paris, 2019).

OECD, 'General government spending (indicator)' (2021), in https://data.oecd.org/gga/general-government-spending.htm.

Offer, A., 'Ricardo's paradox and the movement of rents in England, c. 1870–1910', *Economic History Review*, 33, 2 (1981), 236–252.

Offer, A., *Property and politics, 1870–1914: Landownership, law, ideology and urban development in England* (Cambridge, 1981).

Offer, A., 'Between the gift and the market: The economy of regard', *Economic History Review*, 50, 3 (1997), 450–476.

Offer, A., 'Why has the public sector grown so large in market societies? The political economy of prudence in the UK, c. 1870-2000' (Oxford, 2003).

Offer, A., *The challenge of affluence: Self-control and well-being in the United States and Britain since 1950* (Oxford, 2006).

Offer, A., 'British manual workers: From producers to consumers, c. 1950–2000', *Contemporary British History*, 22 (2008), 537–571.

Offer, A., 'The economy of obligation: Incomplete contracts and the cost of the welfare state', University of Oxford Discussion Papers in Economic and Social History 103 (Oxford, 2012).

Offer, A., 'A warrant for pain: Caveat emptor vs. the duty of care in American medicine, c.1970–2010', *Real World Economics Review*, issue 61 (2012), 85–99.

Offer, A., 'Narrow banking, real estate, and financial stability in the UK, c.1870–2010', in Dimsdale, N. and A. Hotson, eds., *British financial crises since 1825* (Oxford, 2014), 158–173.

Offer, A., 'The market turn: From social democracy to market liberalism', *Economic History Review*, 70, 4 (2017), 1,051–1,071.

Offer, A., 'Patient and impatient capital: Time horizons as market boundaries', University of Oxford Discussion Papers in Economic and Social History, rev. version, 165 (Oxford, Nov. 2019).

Offer, A., and G. Söderberg, *The Nobel factor: The prize in economics, social democracy, and the market turn* (Princeton, NJ, 2016).

Olen, H., *Pound foolish: Exposing the dark side of the personal finance industry* (New York, 2019).

Olsen, D. J., *Town planning in London: The eighteenth & nineteenth centuries* (New Haven, CT, 1964).

Ornaghi, A., 'Civil service reforms: Evidence from U.S. Police departments' unpublished paper, University of Warwick (Coventry UK, 2018).

Ornstein, C. and K. Thomas, 'Memorial Sloan Kettering leaders violated conflict-of-interest rules, report finds', *New York Times*, 4 Apr. 2019.

Orszag, P. R., 'Administrative costs in individual accounts in the United Kingdom', Center on Budget and Policy Priorities (Washington DC, 1999).

Osborne, D., and T. Gaebler, *Reinventing government: How the entrepreneurial spirit is transforming the public sector* (New York, 1992).

Ostrogorski, M., *Democracy and the organization of political parties* (London, 1902).

Owen, B. M., 'What would Madison say? Calling strikes in the political ballpark', Stanford University, Stanford Institute for Economic Policy Research Discussion Paper 15–006 (Stanford, CA, 18 May 2015).

Owen, J., and B. Brady, 'This is like paying for schools by credit card', *Independent on Sunday*, 24 Jan. 2010, 30.

Oxfam America, 'Broken at the top: How America's dysfunctional tax system costs billions in corporate tax dodging' (New York, 2016).

Packard, J., and G. Plimmer, 'Labour party threatens to nationalise PFI contracts', *Financial Times*, 25 Sept. 2017.

Panchamia, N., and P. Thomas, 'The next steps initiative', Institute for Government (London, 2019).

Parker, D., *The official history of privatisation* (Abingdon, 2009).

Parris, M., 'Smirking ministers don't care what we think', *The Times*, 26 Oct. 2020.

Pear, R., 'Report on Medicare cites prescription drug abuse', *New York Times*, 3 Oct. 2011.

Pear, R., 'U.S. To force drug firms to report money paid to doctors', *New York Times*, 16 Jan. 2012.

Pegg, D., 'Fifth of UK covid contracts "raised red flags for possible corruption"', *The Guardian*, 22 Apr. 2021.

Pemberton, H., P. Thane, and N. Whiteside, eds., *Britain's pensions crisis: History and policy* (Oxford, 2006).

Perez, C., *Technological revolutions and financial capital: The dynamics of bubbles and golden ages* (Cheltenham, 2002).

Perraudin, F., '40,000 children trapped in "zombie" academy schools', *The Guardian*, 3 Dec. 2017.

Perraudin, F., 'Collapsing academy trust "asset-stripped" its schools of millions', *The Guardian*, 21 Oct. 2017.

Peterson, P. G., *Gray dawn: How the coming age wave will transform America – and the world* (New York, 1999).

Pew Charitable Trust, 'The trillion dollar gap: Underfunded state retirement systems and the roads to reform', The Pew Center on the States (Washington DC, 2011).

Phelps, E. S., and R. A. Pollak, 'On second-best national saving and game-equilibrium growth', *Review of Economic Studies*, 35 (1968), 185–199.

Philippon, T., *The great reversal: How America gave up on free markets* (Cambridge, MA, 2019).

Pickard, J., 'Former foreign secretaries caught in undercover payments sting', *Financial Times*, 22 Feb. 2015.

Picot, A., M. Florio, N. Grove, and J. J. Kranz, *The economics of infrastructure provisioning: The changing role of the state* (Cambridge, MA, 2016).

Pierre, J. and B. Rothstein, 'Reinventing Weber: the role of institutions in creating social trust' in Christensen, T. and P. Lægreid, eds., *The Ashgate research companion to new public management* (Farnham, 2011), 405–416.

Pim, F. W., *The railways and the state* (London, 1912).

Pindyck, R. S., 'Climate change policy: What do the models tell US?' *Journal of Economic Literature*, 51 (2013), 860–872.

Pindyck, R. S., 'The use and misuse of models for climate policy', *Review of Environmental Economics and Policy*, 11 (2017), 100–114.

Plimmer, G., and G. Parker, 'Theresa May sticks by private sector, picking up pace of PFI deals', *Financial Times*, 28 Sep. 2017.

Plimmer, G., and J. Pickard, 'PWC's role in advising OFWAT on prices scrutinised', *Financial Times*, 17 Sept. 2017.

Plimmer, G., M. Arnold, G. Parker, and J. Cumbo, 'Cable warns taxpayers must not bear brunt of Carillion bailout', *Financial Times*, 13 Jan. 2018.

Plunkitt, G. W., and W. L. Riordon, *Plunkitt of Tammany Hall: A series of very plain talks on very practical politics* (New York, 1924/1963).

Pogrund, G., and J. Collingridge, 'David Cameron and the toxic banker: The exclusive inside story', *The Sunday Times*, 28 March 2021.

Pogrund, G., and J. Collingridge, 'David Cameron, Jeremy Heywood, Lex Greensill and all that "free money"' *The Sunday Times*, 4 April 2021.

Pollock, A. M. J., Shaoul, and N. Vickers, 'Private finance and "value for money" in NHS hospitals: A policy in search of a rationale?' *British Medical Journal*, 324 (2002), 1205–1209.

Pollock, A. M., D. Price, and S. Player, 'The private finance initiative: A policy built on sand' (London, 2005).

Pooley, C. G., *Housing strategies in Europe, 1880–1930* (Leicester, 1992).

Pope, R. and R. Selten, 'Public debt tipping point studies ignore how exchange rate changes may create a financial meltdown', *Real-World Economics*, 59 (2012), 2–38.

Powell, L. F., 'Confidential memorandum: Attack of American free enterprise system' (1971), in https://reclaimdemocracy.org/powell_memo_le wis/.

Prasad, M., *The politics of free markets: The rise of neoliberal economic policies in Britain, France, Germany, and the United States* (Chicago, IL, 2006).

Price, C., *Time, discounting and value* (Oxford, 1993).

Private Eye, 'Tubular balls-up' (3–16 Aug. 2007), 26.

Proctor, R., and L. L. Schiebinger, *Agnotology: The making and unmaking of ignorance* (Stanford, CA, 2008).

Project on Government Oversight, 'Dangerous liaisons: Revolving door at SEC creates risk of regulatory capture' (Washington DC, 11 Feb. 2013).

Protess, B., and P. Lattman, 'A legal bane of Wall Street switches sides', *New York Times*, 22 Jul. 2013.

Quinn, B., 'Dozens of arms firm employees on MoD secondments', *The Guardian*, 16 Feb. 2015.

Quinn, W., and J. D. Turner, *Boom and bust: A global history of financial bubbles* (Cambridge, 2020).

Rakoff, J. S., 'The financial crisis: Why have no high-level executives been prosecuted?', *New York Review of Books*, 9 Jan. 2014.

Ramsay, R., *The rise of New Labour: The pocket essential* (Harpenden, 2002).

Rappeport, A., 'Under Trump, an already depleted I.R.S. Could face deep cuts', *New York Times*, 2 Mar. 2017.

Rauch, J. E., and P. B. Evans, 'Bureaucratic structure and bureaucratic performance in less developed countries', *Journal of Public Economics*, 75 (2000), 49–71.

Ravitch, D., *Slaying Goliath: The passionate resistance to privatization and the fight to save America's public schools* (New York, 2020).

Rawnsley, A., *Servants of the people: The inside story of New Labour*, new edn. (London, 2001).

Rawnsley, A., *The end of the party*, rev. edn. (London, 2010).

Razi, A., and P. L. Loke, 'Fan chart: The art and science of communicating uncertainty', Bank of International Settlements (Basel, Sep. 2016).

Reinert, E., 'Austrian economics and 'the other canon': The Austrians between the activistic-idealistic and the passivistic-materialistic traditions of economics', in Backhaus, J. G., ed., *Evolutionary economic thought: European contributions and concepts* (Cheltenham, 2003), 160–207.

Reinert, E. S., *How rich countries got rich – and why poor countries stay poor* (London, 2007).

Reisenberg, B., T. Stubbs, A. Kentiklenis, and L. King, 'Bad governance: How privatization increases corruption in the developing world', *Regulation and governance*, 14 (2020), 698–717.

Relman, A. S., 'What market values are doing to medicine', *Atlantic Monthly*, 269 (1992), 99–106.

Relman, A. S., *A second opinion: Rescuing America's healthcare: A plan for universal coverage serving patients over profit* (New York, 2007).

Richardson, H. W., and D. H. Aldcroft, *Building in the British economy between the wars* (London, 1968).

Richardson, K., et al., *Climate change: Global risks, challenges and decisions* (Cambridge, 2011).

Rider, D., *Ten years' adventures among landlords and tenants: The story of the rent acts* (London, 1927).

Ripple, W. J. et al., 'World scientists' warning to humanity: A second notice', *Bioscience*, 67 (2017), 1,026–1,028.

Ripple, W. J. et al., 'World scientists' warning of a climate emergency', *Bioscience*, 70 (2020), 8–12.

Roberts, K., *Cromwell's war machine: The new model army, 1645–1660* (Barnsley, 2005).

Robinson, G., *The unconventional minister: My life inside New Labour* (London, 2001).

Robson, W. A., 'The public utility services', in Laski, H. J., I. Jennings, and W. A. Robson, eds., *A century of municipal progress, 1835–1935* (London, 1932) 99–331.

Roland, G., ed., *Privatisation: Successes and failures* (New York, 2008).

Roland, G., 'Private and public ownership in economic theory', in Roland, G., ed., *Privatization: Successes and failures* (New York, 2008), 9–31.

Rose, J. D., 'The prolonged resolution of troubled real estate lenders during the 1930s', in White, E. N., K. A. Snowden, and P. V. M. Fishback, eds., *Housing and mortgage markets in historical perspective* (Chicago, IL, 2012), 245–285.

Rose, R., and C. Peiffer, *Paying bribes for public services: A global guide to grass roots corruption* (Basingstoke, 2015).

Rose, R., and C. Peiffer, *Bad governance and corruption* (Basingstoke, 2019).

Rose-Ackerman, S., 'Democracy and "grand" corruption', *International Social Science Journal*, 49 (1996), 365–380.

Roser, M., 'Link between health spending and life expectancy: The US is an outlier' (May 26, 2017), in https://ourworldindata.org/the-link-between-life-expectancy-and-health-spending-us-focus.

Rotberg, R. I., *The corruption cure: How citizens and leaders can combat graft* (Princeton, NJ, 2017).

Rothstein, B., *The quality of government: Corruption, social trust, and inequality in international perspective* (Chicago, IL, 2011).

Rothstein, B., 'What is the opposite of corruption?' *Third World Quarterly*, 35 (2014), 737–752.

Rothstein, B., and A. Varraich, *Making sense of corruption* (Cambridge, 2018).

Rowell, A., 'Stern quits treasury after Brown freezes him out', *Oilchange International*, 8 Dec. 2006.

Russell, J. W., 'How the Koch brothers, Wall Street and politicians conspire to drain social security' (2014), in https://readersupportednews.org/opi nion2/277-75/23614-how-the-koch-brothers-wall-street-and-politicians-conspire-to-drain-social-security.

Ryan-Collins, J., T. Lloyd, and L. MacFarlane, *Rethinking the economics of land and housing* (London, 2017).

Saad-Lessler, J., and T. Ghilarducci, 'Near retirees' defined contribution account balances', New School: Schwartz Center for Economic Policy Analysis (New York, 2012).

Sabadish, N., and M. Morrissey, 'Retirement inequality chartbook: How the 401(k) revolution created a few big winners and many losers', Economic Policy Institute, Report (Washington DC, 6 Sep. 2013).

Sabbagh, D., 'KPMG abandons controversial lending of researchers to MPs', *The Guardian*, 28 May 2018.

Saez, E., and G. Zucman, *The triumph of injustice: How the rich dodge taxes and how to make them pay* (New York, 2019).

Samuelson, P. A., 'An exact consumption-loan model of interest with or without the social contrivance of money', *Journal of Political Economy*, 66 (1958), 467–482.

Samy, A., *The building society promise: Access, risk, and efficiency 1880–1939* (Oxford, 2016).

Samy, L., 'Indices of house prices and rent prices of residential property in London, 1895–1939', University of Oxford Discussion Papers in Economic and Social History 134 (Oxford, Apr. 2015).

Sangster, A., 'Capital investment appraisal techniques: A survey of current usage', *Journal of Business Finance and Accounting*, 20, 3 (1993), 307.

Sass, S. A., 'The U.K.'s ambitious new retirement savings initiative', Center for Retirement Research at Boston College 14–5 (Boston, MA, Mar. 2014).

Sasse, T., and E. Norris, 'Moving on: The costs of high staff turnover in the civil service', Institute of Government (London, Jan. 2019).

Saunders, P., *A nation of home owners* (London, 1990).

Sayer, D., *Rank hypocrisies: The insult of the REF* (London, 2015).

Schleef, H. J., 'The joint determination of marginal rate of return and interest adjusted cost for whole life-insurance' *Management Science*, 29 (1983), 610–621.

Schneider, M., and K. Wagner, 'Housing markets in Austria, Germany and Switzerland', in *The Narodowy Bank Polski workshop: Recent trends in the real estate market and its analysis* (Warsaw, 2016), 144–162.

Schneider, M. K., *School choice: The end of public education?* (New York, 2016).

Schultz, E., *Retirement heist: How companies plunder and profit from the nest eggs of American workers* (New York, 2011).

Schumpeter, J. A., *The theory of economic development: An inquiry into profits, capital, credit, interest, and the business cycle* (Cambridge, MA, 1911/1934).

Schwartz, A. F., *Housing policy in the United States*, 3rd edn. (New York, 2010).

Schwartz, B., *The paradox of choice: Why more is less*, (New York, 2004).

Schwartz, N., *The velvet rope economy: How inequality became big business* (New York, 2020).

Schwartz, N. D., 'When it's this easy at the top, it's harder for everyone else', *New York Times*, 28 Feb. 2020.

Segal, P., 'Inequality as entitlements over labour', London School of Economics, Working Paper 43 (London, 2020).

Seyd, M., 'Our economy is increasingly sick, and any doctor can tell you why', *The Times*, 7 Feb. 2021.

Shaoul, J., 'Corporations reached secret deals with Luxembourg to avoid tax payments' (2014), in https://www.wsws.org/en/articles/2014/12/22/avoid-d22.html.

Shaxson, N., *Treasure islands: Tax havens and the men who stole the world*, Post-Brexit edition with a new Panama Papers chapter (London, 2012).

Shear, M. D., and K. Kelly, 'Obama balances civic-minded side with the lure of a $400,000 speech', *New York Times*, 26 Apr. 2016.

Shepherd, J., and M. S. Kang, 'Skewed Justice: Citizens United, television advertising and state Supreme Court Justices' decisions in criminal cases', American Constitution Society for Law and Policy (Washington DC, Oct. 2014).

Shiller, R., 'Stock market data used in "irrational exuberance"' (2006), in http://www.irrationalexuberance.com/.

Shiwakoti, R. K., et al., 'Conversion, performance and executive compensation in UK building societies', *Corporate Governance*, 12, 3 (2004), 361–370.

Shoji, K., 'Lessons from Japanese experiences of roles of public and private sectors in urban transport', *Japan Railway & Transport Review* (2001), 12–18.

Siegel, J. J., *Stocks for the long run: The definitive guide to financial market returns and long-term investment strategies*, 4th edn. (New York, 2008).

Siemiatycki, M., and N. Farooqi, 'Value for money and risk in public-private partnerships', *Journal of the American Planning Association*, 78 (2012), 286–299.

Sirota, D., 'The plot against pensions: The Pew–Arnold campaign to undermine America's retirement security – and leave taxpayers with the bill', Institute for America's Future (Washington DC, 2013).

Slack, J., 'Enemies of the people: Fury over "out of touch" judges who have "declared war on democracy" by defying 17.4m Brexit voters and who could trigger constitutional crisis', *Daily Mail*, 3 Nov. 2016.

Smith, A., *An inquiry into the nature and causes of the wealth of nations* (Oxford, 1976). 2 vols.

Smith, G. B., 'Are cheating doctors running bill scams to insurance companies? Charging huge "out of network" fees', *New York Daily News*, 18 Feb. 2012.

Smith, Y., 'The continued stealth takeover of the courts,' Naked Capitalism blog, 27 Aug. 2010.

Smith, Y., 'William Black: Theoclassical law and economics makes the law an ass', Naked Capitalism blog, 31 Aug. 2010.

Spackman, M., 'Discount rates and rates of return in the public sector: Economic issues', HM Treasury, Government economic working paper no. 113; Treasury working paper no. 58 (London, 1992).

Spackman, M., 'Time discounting and of the cost of capital in government', *Fiscal studies*, 25 (2004), 467–518.

Speight, G., 'Who bought the inter-war semi? The socio-economic characteristics of new-house buyers in the 1930s', University of Oxford Discussion Paper in Economic and Social History 38 (Oxford, Dec. 2000).

Spiro, M. E., *Children of the kibbutz* (Cambridge, MA, 1958).

Spivak, A., 'Pensions in Israel and abroad: Major developments, approaches and ideological influences', Van Leer Jerusalem Institute, Program for Economy and Society, Disputes in Economics, 2nd series 4 (Jerusalem, 2013) (in Hebrew).

Stacey, K., and J. Pickard, 'Critics attack job moves between Big Four and government', *Financial Times*, 28 May 2013.

Stafford, B., and J. Doling, 'Rent control and rent regulation in England and Wales: 1915-1980', Centre for Urban and Regional Studies University of Birmingham, Occasional paper 2 (Birmingham, Jun. 1981).

Stamp, J., *British incomes and property: The application of official statistics to economic problems* (London, 1916).

Starr, P., *The social transformation of American medicine* (New York, 1982).

Steffen, W., et al., 'Trajectories of the Earth System in the Anthropocene', *Proceedings of the National Academy of Sciences*, 115 (2018), 8,252–8,259.

Steffens, L., *The shame of the cities* (New York, 1904).

Stein, B., 'When you fly in first class, it's easy to forget the dots', *New York Times*, 29 Jan. 2006.

Steinhauer, J., 'Bob McDonnell, ex-governor of Virginia, is sentenced to 2 years for corruption', *New York Times*, 6 Jan. 2015.

Stephens, M., 'International models of housing finance: Housing systems in western and transition economies', in OECD, ed., *Housing finance markets in transition economies* (Paris, 2002), 175–182.

Stern, N., 'Climate change, ethics and the economics of the global deal' (2007), in https://voxeu.org/article/climate-change-ethics-and-economics.

Stern, N. H., *The economics of climate change: The Stern review* (Cambridge, 2007).

Stern, N. H., *Why are we waiting? The logic, urgency, and promise of tackling climate change* (Cambridge, MA, 2015).

Stiglitz, J., 'Foreword', in Roland, G., ed., *Privatization: Successes and failures* (New York, 2008), xi–xix.

Stockfisch, J. A., 'Measuring the social rate of return on private investment', in Lind, R. C. et al., ed., *Discounting for time and risk in energy policy* (Washington DC, 1982), 257–271.

Stout, N. M., *Dispossessed: How predatory bureaucracy foreclosed on the American middle class* (Berkeley, CA, 2019).

Stover, J. F., *American railroads*, 2nd edn. (Chicago,1997).

Street, P., 'The shell game of the economic elite's Hamilton project' (2016), in https://www.truthdig.com/articles/the-shell-game-of-the-economic-elites-hamilton-project-2/page/1/.

Summers, L. H., 'Investment incentives and the discounting of depreciation allowances', in Feldstein M., ed., *The effects of taxation on capital accumulation* (Chicago, IL, 1987), 295–304.

Swiss Re Institute, 'The economics of climate change: No action not an option', Swiss Re Institute (Zurich, Apr. 2021).

Syal, R., 'Pension management firms warned over excessive charges', *The Guardian*, 16 Sep. 2013.

Syal, R., 'UK's super rich appear to get special deal from HMRC, says watchdog', *The Guardian*, 27 Jan. 2017.

Syal, R., 'Brexit drives government consultancy fees to £450 m in three years', *The Guardian*, 6 Oct. 2020.

Syal, R., and P. Walker, 'Cameron's "insurgents" under scrutiny amid row over lobbyist influence', *The Guardian*, 17 Apr. 2021.

Syal, R., et al., '"Big Four" accountants "use knowledge of Treasury to help rich avoid tax"', *The Guardian*, 26 Apr. 2013.

Tanzi, V., 'Corruption around the world: Causes, consequences, scope, and cures', in Abed, G. T. and S. Gupta, eds., *Governance, corruption and economic performance* (Washington DC, 2003), 19–58.

Tarbuck, E. L., *Handbook of house property: A popular and practical guide to the purchase, mortgage, tenancy & compulsory sale of houses and land, including dilapidations and fixtures: With examples of all kinds of valuations, information on building, and on the right use of decorative art*, 7th edn. (London, 1904).

Teachout, Z., *Corruption in America: From Benjamin Franklin's snuff box to Citizens United* (Cambridge, MA, 2014).

Teachout, Z., 'There's no such thing as a free Rolex', *New York Times*, 29 Apr. 2016.

Terhune, C., 'Wrangling over "reasonable" fees', *Business Week*, 1 Mar. 2008.

Terhune, C., 'Many hospitals, doctors offer cash discount for medical bills', *Los Angeles Times*, 27 May 2012.

Thibierge, C., and A. Beresford, *A practical guide to corporate finance: Breaking the financial ice* (London, 2015).

Thompson, D. F., 'Bureaucracy and democracy', in Graeme, D., ed., *Democratic theory and practice* (Cambridge, 1983), 235–250.

Thompson, F. M. L., *English landed society in the nineteenth century* (London, 1963).

Thomson, M., and F. Lloyd George, *David Lloyd George: The official biography* (London, 1948).

Thomson, P., *School scandals: Blowing the whistle on the corruption of our education system* (Bristol, 2020).

Timmins, N., 'NHS trust buys back PFI hospital', *Financial Times*, 2 Feb. 2011.

Timmins, N., 'PFI projects switched to tax havens, report claims', *Financial Times*, 19 Jun. 2011 2011.

Toobin, J., 'The Supreme Court gets ready to legalize corruption', *New Yorker*, 4 Jun. 2016.

Torrance, J., 'Social class and bureaucratic innovation: The commissioners for examining the public accounts 1780-1787', *Past & Present* 78 (1978), 56–81.

Toynbee, A., 'Are Radicals socialists?' in Toynbee, A., *Lectures on the industrial revolution of the eighteenth century in England, popular addresses, notes, and other fragments* (London, 1884/1908), 219–238.

Transparency International, 'Cabs for hire? Fixing the revolving door between government and business' (London, 2011).

Trawinski, L. A., 'Nightmare on main street: Older Americans and the mortgage market crisis', AARP Public Policy Institute 2012–08 (Washington DC, Aug. 2012).

Treynor, J. L., and F. Black, 'Corporate investment decisions', in Myers, S. C., ed., *Modern developments in financial management* (New York, 1976), 310–327.

Trumberg, A., 'Market reforms in Sweden and the OECD', in Dahlstedt M. and A. Fejes, eds., *Neoliberalism and market forces in education: Lessons from Sweden* (Abingdon UK, 2019), 65–77.

Turner, A. et al., 'Implementing an integrated package of pension reforms: The final report of the pensions commission', Powerpoint presentation at the launch press conference, London, 4 April 2006.

United States Census Bureau, 'Voting and registration', in http://www.census.gov/population/www/socdemo/voting.html, accessed 3 Jul. 2009.

United States Social Security Administration, 'Annual statistical supplement, 2000 to the social security bulletin' (Washington DC, 2000).

Urbina, I., 'Suit names 2 judges accused in a kickback case', *New York Times*, 13 Feb. 2009.

Van Riper, P. P., *History of the United States civil service* (Evanston IL, 1958).

Verbeek, A., 'Planetary security: The security implications of climate change' (2019), in https://www.nato.int/docu/review/articles/2019/12/10/planetary-security-the-security-implications-of-climate-change/index.html.

Vickers, J., and G. Yarrow, 'Economic perspectives on privatization', *Journal of Economic Perspectives*, 5 (1991), 111–132.

Wade, J., *The extraordinary black book: An exposition of the united church of England and Ireland; civil list and crown revenues; incomes, privileges, and power, of the aristocracy; privy council, diplomatic, and consular establishments; law and judicial administration; representation and prospects of reform under the new ministry; profits, influence, and monopoly of the bank of England and East-India company, with strictures on the renewal of their charters; debt and funding system; salaries, fees and emoluments in courts of Justice, public offices, and colonies; lists of pluralists, placemen, pensioners, and sinecurists: The whole corrected from the latest official returns, and presenting a complete view of the expenditure, patronage, influence, and abuses of the government, in church, state, law, and representation* (London, 1831).

Wadsell, D., 'Climate dynamics: Facing the harsh realities of now' (2015), in http://www.apollo-gaia.org/Harsh%20Realities.pdf.

Wagner, G., and M. L. Weitzman, *Climate shock: The economic consequences of a hotter planet* (Princeton, NJ, 2015).

Walford, G., *Life in public schools* (London, 1986).

Wall, A., and C. Connolly, 'The private finance initiative', *Public Management Review*, 11 (2009), 707–724.

Ward, S., 'Personal pensions in the UK, the mis-selling scandal and the lessons to be learnt', in Hughes, G. and J. Stewart, eds., *Pensions in the European Union: Adapting to economic and social change* (Boston, MA, 2000), 139–146.

Warrell, H., 'MPs say loopholes in regulation of academies must be closed', *Financial Times*, 17 Sept. 2014.

Warren, E., Letter to Mary Jo White, 2 Jun. 2015. https://www
.warren.senate.gov/files/documents/2015-6-2_Warren_letter_to_SEC.pdf.
Wasserman, J., *The marginal revolutionaries: How Austrian economists fought
the war of ideas* (New Haven, CT, 2019).
Watt, N., 'Carry on flying, says Blair – science will save the planet', *The
Guardian*, 9 Jan. 2007.
Weale, S., 'Government system "fails to address conflicts of interest" at
academy schools', *The Guardian*, 17 Sept. 2014.
Weale, S., 'Free schools policy under fire as another closure announced', *The
Guardian*, 25 Apr. 2018.
Weber, B., 'A new index of house rents for Great Britain 1874-1913', *Scottish
Journal of Political Economy*, 2 (1955), 104–132.
Weber, M., and B. Elbers et al. (translators), 'Bureaucracy', in Waters, T.
and D. Waters, eds., *Weber's rationalism and modern society: New transla-
tions on politics, bureaucracy, and social stratification* (New York, 1921/
2015), 75–127.
Weihe, G., 'Towards a process perspective on public-private partnerships',
in Hodge, G., C. Greve, and A. Boardman, eds., *International handbook
on public-private partnerships* (Cheltenham, 2010), 510–525.
Weiser, B., and V. Wang, 'He was Governor Cuomo's closest aide. Now
he's going to prison for 6 years', *New York Times*, 20 Sep. 2018.
Weitzman, M. L., 'Gamma discounting', *American Economic Review*, 91
(2001), 260–271.
Weitzman, M. L., 'A review of William Nordhaus' *The climate casino: Risk,
uncertainty, and economics for a warming world*', *Review of Environmental
Economics and Policy*, 9 (2015), 145–156.
West, D. M., *Billionaires: Reflections on the upper crust* (Washington DC,
2014).
White, E. N., K. A. Snowden, and P. V. M. Fishback, eds., *Housing and
mortgage markets in historical perspective* (Chicago, IL, 2012).
White, J. R., *The Prussian army, 1640–1871* (Lanham, MD, 1996).
Whitehouse, E., 'Paying for pensions: An international comparison of
administrative charges in funded retirement-income systems', FSA
(London, 2000).
Whitfield, D., 'PPP wealth machine: UK and global trends in trading
project ownership', European Services Strategy Unit (London, Dec.
2012).
Whitfield, D., 'PPP profiteering and offshoring: New evidence', European
Services Strategy Unit Research Report no. 10 (London, Oct. 2017).
Whyte, D., ed., *How corrupt is Britain?* (London, 2015).
Wighton, D., 'Greensill risks long-term damage to private sector role in
government', *The Times*, 4 Apr. 2021.
Wikipedia, 'International Finance Corporation' (2018).

Wikipedia, 'High Speed 1' (2018).

Wikipedia, 'Partnerships UK' (2018).

Wikipedia, 'United Kingdom parliamentary expenses scandal' (2020).

Wikipedia, '2010 cash for influence scandal' (2021).

Wikipedia, 'Dot-com bubble' (2021).

Wikipedia, 'Hinchinbrooke hospital' (2017).

Wikipedia, 'New College of the Humanities at Northeastern' (2021).

Wikipedia, 'Trump University' (2021).

Wilks, S., 'The corporate elite and the rise of the new corporate state in Britain', in Brummer, K. and H. Pehle, eds., *Analysen nationaler und supranational der politik: Festschrift für Roland Sturm* (Opladen, Germany, 2013), 193–201.

Wilks, S., *The political power of the business corporation* (Cheltenham, 2013).

Wilks, S., 'The revolving door and the corporate colonisation of UK politics', High Pay Unit (London, 2015).

Williams, J., *Principles of the law of real property intended as a first book for the use of students in conveyancing*, 9th edn. (London, 1871).

Williamson, J., 'A short history of the Washington Consensus', in Serra, N. and J. Stiglitz, eds., *The Washington Consensus reconsidered: Towards a new global governance* (Oxford, 2008), 14–30.

Williamson, O., 'Opportunism and its critics' *Managerial and Decision Economics*, 14 (1993), 97–107.

Williamson, O. E., S. G. Winter, and R. H. Coase, *The nature of the firm: Origins, evolution, and development* (New York, 1991).

Willis, J. W., 'A short history of rent control laws', *Cornell Law Review*, 36 (1950), 54–94.

Wohl, A. S., *The eternal slum: Housing and social policy in Victorian London* (London, 1977).

Wolff, E. N., *A century of wealth in America* (Cambridge, MA, 2017).

Wolman, W., and A. Colamsoca, eds., *The great 401(k) hoax* (Cambridge, MA, 2003).

Woolcock, N., 'Academies accused of fiddling taxpayer', *The Times*, 10 Sept. 2018.

Woolf, L., *Growing: An autobiography of the years 1904–1911* (London, 1961).

Woolhandler, S., et al., 'Costs of health care administration in the United States and Canada', *New England Journal of Medicine*, 349 (2003), 768–775.

World Bank, *Averting the old age crisis: Policies to protect the old and promote growth* (Oxford, 1994).

World Bank, *World development report 1997: The state in a changing world* (New York, 1997).

World Bank, 'Helping countries combat corruption: The role of the World Bank' (Washington DC, Sep. 1997).

References

World Bank, 'Economic growth in the 1990s: Learning from a decade of reform' (Washington DC, 2005).

World Bank, 'Turn down the heat: Why a 4°C warmer world must be avoided' (Washington DC, 2012).

World Bank, 'Sources of financing for public-private partnership investments in 2015' (Washington DC, 2015).

World Bank, 'Private participation in infrastructure database' (2018), in https://ppi.worldbank.org/.

World Bank Group, 'State and trends of carbon pricing 2020' (Washington DC, 9 May 2020).

Wright, R., 'Private buyers sought for metronet', *Financial Times*, 11 Sep. 2007.

Zaloom, C., *Indebted: How families make college work at any cost* (Princeton, NJ, 2019).

Zelizer, V. A. R., *Pricing the priceless child: The changing social value of children* (Princeton, NJ, 1994).

Zhang, X., 'Financial viability analysis and capital structure optimization in privatized public infrastructure projects', *Journal of Construction Engineering and Management*, 131 (2005), 656–668.

Zucman, G., *The hidden wealth of nations: The scourge of tax havens* (Chicago, IL, 2015).

Index